From the Authors of the Bestselling
HOW TO READ THE BIBLE FOR ALL ITS WORTH

OVER 150,000 copies sold

How to Read the Old Testament
Book by Book *A Guided Tour*

Gordon D. Fee
Douglas Stuart

ZONDERVAN ACADEMIC

Also by Gordon D. Fee and Douglas Stuart

How to Read the Bible for All Its Worth

Also by Gordon D. Fee and Mark L. Strauss

How to Choose a Translation for All Its Worth

ZONDERVAN ACADEMIC

How to Read the Old Testament Book by Book
Copyright © 2002, 2023 by Gordon D. Fee and Douglas Stuart

The content of this book is also published in *How to Read the Bible Book by Book*.

Requests for information should be addressed to:
Zondervan, 3900 *Sparks Dr. SE, Grand Rapids, Michigan 49546*

Zondervan titles may be purchased in bulk for educational, business, fundraising, or sales promotional use. For information, please email SpecialMarkets@Zondervan.com.

ISBN 978-0-310-15601-7 (softcover)
ISBN 978-0-310-15600-0 (audio)
ISBN 978-0-310-15602-4 (ebook)

Cover design: Rob Monacelli
Cover photo: ©Pixel-Shot / Shutterstock
Interior design: Nancy Wilson

For Walker, Maia, and Emma
Joshua, Julia, Cherisa, Nathan, and Benjamin
Zachary and Jackson
Maricel and Annalise
and
Meriwether and Honour
and Mcaela
that they may learn to read the Story well
and love Him whose Story it is
(Psalm 71:14 – 18; Psalm 103:17)

ABBREVIATIONS

OLD TESTAMENT

Gen	Genesis	Song	Song of Songs
Exod	Exodus	Isa	Isaiah
Lev	Leviticus	Jer	Jeremiah
Num	Numbers	Lam	Lamentations
Deut	Deuteronomy	Ezek	Ezekiel
Josh	Joshua	Dan	Daniel
Judg	Judges	Hos	Hosea
Ruth	Ruth	Joel	Joel
1–2 Sam	1–2 Samuel	Amos	Amos
1–2 Kgs	1–2 Kings	Obad	Obadiah
1–2 Chr	1–2 Chronicles	Jonah	Jonah
Ezra	Ezra	Mic	Micah
Neh	Nehemiah	Nah	Nahum
Esth	Esther	Hab	Habakkuk
Job	Job	Zeph	Zephaniah
Ps/Pss	Psalms	Hag	Haggai
Prov	Proverbs	Zech	Zechariah
Eccl	Ecclesiastes	Mal	Malachi

NEW TESTAMENT

Matt	Matthew	1–2 Thess	1–2 Thessalonians
Mark	Mark	1–2 Tim	1–2 Timothy
Luke	Luke	Titus	Titus
John	John	Phlm	Philemon
Acts	Acts	Heb	Hebrews
Rom	Romans	Jas	James
1–2 Cor	1–2 Corinthians	1–2 Pet	1–2 Peter
Gal	Galatians	1–2–3 John	1–2–3 John
Eph	Ephesians	Jude	Jude
Phil	Philippians	Rev	Revelation
Col	Colossians		

A.D.	*anno Domini* (in the year of [our] Lord)	f(f).	and the following one(s)
		i.e.	*id est,* that is
B.C.	before Christ	lit.	literally
ca.	*circa,* about, approximately	NT	New Testament
cf.	*confer,* compare	OT	Old Testament
ch(s).	chapter(s)	p(p).	page(s)
e.g.	*exempli gratia,* for example	par.	parallel (textual parallels)
esp.	especially	v(v).	verse(s)
et al.	*et alii,* and others	*x*	number of times a form occurs
etc.	*et cetera,* and the rest		

Contents

Preface

This book is intended to be a companion to *How to Read the Bible for All Its Worth*. That book was designed to help people become better readers of Scripture by taking into account the various kinds of literature that make up the Christian Bible. Through an understanding of how the various types "work," how they differ from one another, and how they raise different kinds of hermeneutical questions, we hoped that one might learn to read the Bible in a more informed way.

The success of that first book has given us the courage to try another. The aim is still the same: to help people become better *readers* of Scripture. What we hope to do here is to go a step beyond the first book: Assuming the principles of the first book, here we try to help you read—and understand—each of the biblical books on its own but especially to help you see how each one fits with the others to form the great narrative of Scripture.

But this book has undergone its own form of evolution. Some years ago we were asked to write a Bible survey textbook of the kind that many students have been exposed to over the years. For a variety of reasons, but mostly because we could never get our hearts into it, that project simply did not work out. To be sure, we hope this book will still serve the purposes of survey courses, but we have intentionally tried to write something quite different. These differences, as we perceive them, are several.

First, our goal is not simply to dispense knowledge about the various books of the Bible—the kind of knowledge that allows one to pass Bible knowledge exams without ever reading the Bible! Such books and exams usually deal with a lot of data but very often with little sense of how the various books of the Bible function as entities on their own or of how each fits into *God's story*. Our present concern is almost altogether with the latter. And in any case, the concern is with your becoming a better *reader* of Scripture; if you begin to learn some other things about each book along the way, all the better.

Second, we want to show how the separate entities—each biblical book—fit together as a whole to tell God's story. So much is this a concern that our book is introduced with a brief overview of the biblical story—what those who study narratives call the *metanarrative* of Scripture. This is the big picture, the primary story, of which all the others form a part so as to shape the whole.

Third, in coming to the various biblical books, one by one, we follow a generally consistent format that isolates questions of introduction at the beginning as "Orienting Data for ..." These kinds of issues (authorship, date, recipients, occasion, and the like) take up much of the space in most surveys. For these (sometimes important) matters there are several surveys, introductions, and Bible dictionaries for both the Old and New Testaments that you may consult. But these matters are often debatable and therefore consume a lot of time that is not always immediately relevant to the reading of the biblical text in its larger setting. Thus, we simply offer some options, or note the traditional view, or settle on one as the perspective from which this guide is written.

But a further word is needed about the matter of authorship, especially for the Old Testament books, since authors in that period did not normally attach their names to what they wrote (with the exception of letters—and there are none of these as books in the Old Testament). When individuals speak about themselves within a given book (e.g., Moses, Nehemiah, Qohelet ["Teacher" in Ecclesiastes]), we may learn something about probable or possible authorship that we wouldn't otherwise know. But for the most part, modern concerns about matters of date and authorship were not given the same attention in ancient Israel; this is made obvious by their absence from most of these books. Many books (e.g., nearly all the historical and poetical books) are entirely anonymous. And even though the source of the content of some books is given—by way of an editorial title at the beginning—and assumptions can often be made that the source also functioned as author, the concern over the book's actual author is not prominent in the book itself. As to dating, just four books—Ezekiel, Daniel, Zechariah, and Haggai—date any of their material, and of those only Haggai does so consistently. Thus we have chosen to minimize authorship in this *reading* guide, leaving it entirely alone when the biblical book itself is anonymous (one can say "unknown" only so many times!). Our interest is in your reading the biblical document in its final canonical form, not in debating the issues of dates, sources, and authorship.

Most of our energy, therefore, has gone into the three major sections of each chapter. The first, "Overview of ...," is designed to get you into the book by giving you a sense of what the whole is about. In some ways it is a brief elaboration of the "Content" sentence(s) in the "Orienting" section. The second, "Specific Advice for Reading ...," tends to elaborate the "Emphases" from the "Orienting" section. Here we offer a way of reading the text, some key themes to keep in mind as you do, or some crucial background material—all of which are designed to help you as you read the text for yourself. The final section, "A Walk through ...," then takes you by the hand, as it were, and walks you through the book, showing how its various parts work together to form the whole. Sometimes this takes more of an outline form; at other times, because we have purposely tried to keep our chapters brief, you will walk with giant steps. The books of Psalms and Proverbs were understandably the most difficult to fit into this pattern; yet even here we have tried to help you see how the collections are put together.

Above all, we have tried to write a book about the books of the Bible that will not be a substitute for reading the Bible itself. Rather, we hope it may create a desire in you to read each of the biblical books for yourself, while helping you make a fair amount of sense out of what you are reading.

NOTE WELL: The key to using this book is for you to read the first three sections of each chapter ("Orienting Data," "Overview," "Specific Advice"), and then *to read the biblical text* in conjunction with the section titled "A Walk through ..." If you read "A Walk through" on its own, it will become just more data for you to assimilate. Our intent is for you first to have some important preliminary data in hand, then truly to walk with you through your reading of the biblical book. This will, of course, be far more difficult for some of the longer books, just as it was for us to condense so much material into the brief parameters we allowed ourselves. But even here, while you may be reading over a more extended time period, we hope you will find this a helpful guide. A glossary is provided for those who need some guidance through the maze of technical terms that biblical scholars tend to use without forethought (see p. 267). We have also supplied a suggested chronological listing of the books for those who wish to read them in that order (see the appendix at the back of the book, p. 273).

We have tried to write in such a way that you will be able to follow what is said, no matter which English translation you are using, provided it is a contemporary one (see ch. 2 of *How to Read the Bible for*

All Its Worth). For the New Testament, Professor Fee regularly had Today's New International Version (TNIV) in front of him as he wrote; for the Old Testament, the New International Version (1984 edition) was used. Typically, when Bible verses are cited in this book, they are taken either from the NIV or from the New Testament edition of the TNIV.

A couple of words about presuppositions. First, while we have not assumed that the reader will already have read *How to Read the Bible for All Its Worth,* we do refer to it from time to time (as *How to 1,* with page numbers always referring to the third edition [2003] so that we don't have to repeat some presuppositional things from that book (for example, sources of the Gospels). In the case of Acts and Revelation, which received individual chapters in *How to 1,* that material is reset for this book, but one will still be helped by reading those chapters as well.

Second, the authors unapologetically stand within the evangelical tradition of the church. This means, among other things, that we believe that the Holy Spirit has inspired the biblical writers (and collectors) in their task—even though most often we speak of each document in terms of what the (inspired) human author is doing.

At the same time, in most cases we have tried to be apprised of and make use of the most recent biblical scholarship—although any scholar who might venture to look at this work may well wonder whether we have consulted her or his latest work. Along with our own reading of the text, we herewith gratefully acknowledge that we have incorporated suggestions—and even language—from others too many to mention by name. Those who might recognize some of their ideas in what we have written may, we hope, take pleasure in such recognition; we trust they will also be generous to us when we have chosen to go our own way rather than to be beholden to any other scholarly endeavor.

The authors with gratitude also acknowledge the following: Regent College, whose generous sabbatical policy made it possible for Professor Fee to work on the book during spring term 1998 and winter term 2001; colleagues and friends who have read selected chapters and offered many helpful comments: Iain Provan, V. Philips Long, Rikk Watts, John Stek, Bruce Waltke, and Wendy Wilcox Glidden. Professor Fee's wife, Maudine, has taken great interest in this project by reading every word and making scores of insightful suggestions that have made it a better book. And during the month of March 2001, when Professor

Fee was recuperating from surgery, she joined him in reading the entire manuscript and the entire Bible aloud—resulting in scores of changes to the book, as our ears often heard better than our eyes saw. We cannot recommend strongly enough the value of the oral reading of the Bible!

We dedicated *How to 1* to our parents, three of whom have now passed on to be with their Lord. We dedicate this present endeavor to our grandchildren—as of this writing, twelve for the Fees, the oldest of whom are now teenagers, and three for the Stuarts. Thus, in some measure, this book is our own reflection on Psalm 71:14–18.

The Biblical Story:
An Overview

When the authors were boys growing up in Christian homes, one of the ways we—and our friends—were exposed to the Bible was through the daily reading of a biblical text from the Promise Box, which dutifully found its way onto our kitchen tables. Furthermore, most believers of our generation—and of several preceding ones—had learned a kind of devotional reading of the Bible that emphasized reading it only in parts and pieces, looking for a "word for the day."

While the thought behind these approaches to Scripture was salutary enough (constant exposure to the sure promises of God's Word), they also had their downside, teaching people to read texts in a way that disconnected them from the grand story of the Bible.

The concern of this book is to help you read the Bible as a whole, and even when the "whole" is narrowed to "whole books," it is important for you always to be aware of how each book fits into the larger story (on this matter, see *How to 1*, pp. 91–92). But in order to do this, you need first to have a sense of what the grand story is all about. That is what this introduction proposes to do.

First, let's be clear: The Bible is not merely some divine guidebook, nor is it a mine of propositions to be believed or a long list of commands to be obeyed. True, one does receive plenty of guidance from it, and it does indeed contain plenty of true propositions and divine directives. But the Bible is infinitely more than that.

It is no accident that the Bible comes to us primarily by way of narrative—but not just any narrative. Here we have the grandest narrative of all—God's own story. That is, it does not purport to be just one more story of humankind's search for God. No, this is *God's* story, the account of *his* search for us, a story essentially told in four chapters: Creation, Fall, Redemption, Consummation. In this story, God is the divine protagonist, Satan the antagonist, God's people the agonists (although too often also the antagonists), with redemption and reconciliation as the plot resolution.

CREATION

Since this is *God's story,* it does not begin, as do all other such stories, with a hidden God, whom people are seeking and to whom Jesus ultimately leads them. On the contrary, the biblical narrative begins with God as Creator of all that is. It tells us that "in the beginning God …": that God is *before* all things, that he is the *cause* of all things, that he is therefore *above* all things, and that he is the *goal* of all things. He stands at the origin of all things as the sole cause of the whole universe, in all of its vastness and intricacies. And all creation—all history itself—has the eternal God, through Christ, as its final purpose and consummation.

We are further told that humanity is the crowning glory of the Creator's work—beings made in God's own likeness, with whom he could commune, and in whom he could delight; beings who would know the sheer pleasure of his presence, love, and favor. Created in God's *image,* humankind thus uniquely enjoyed the *vision* of God and lived in *fellowship* with God. We were nonetheless *created* beings and were thus intended to be dependent on the Creator for life and existence in the world. This part of the story is narrated in Genesis 1–2, but it is repeated or echoed in scores of ways throughout the whole narrative.

FALL

The second chapter in the biblical story is a long and tragic one. It begins in Genesis 3, and the dark thread runs through the whole story almost to the very end (Rev 22:11, 15). This "chapter" tells us that man and woman coveted more godlikeness and that in one awful moment in the history of our planet they chose godlikeness over against mere creatureliness, with its dependent status. They chose *in*dependence from the Creator. But we were not intended to live so, and the result was a fall—a colossal and tragic fall. (To be sure, this is not a popular part of the story today, but its rejection is part of the Fall itself and the beginning of all false theologies.)

Made to enjoy God and to be dependent on him, and to find our meaning ultimately in our very creatureliness, we now came under God's wrath and thus came to experience the terrible consequences of our rebellion. The calamity of our fallenness is threefold:

First, we lost our *vision* of God with regard to his nature and character. Guilty and hostile ourselves, we projected that guilt and hostility onto God. God is to blame: "Why have *you* made me thus?" "Why are *you* so cruel?" are the plaintive cries that run throughout the history of our race. We thus became idolaters, now creating gods in our own image; every grotesque expression of our fallenness was reconstructed into a god. Paul puts it this way: "Although they claimed to be wise, they became fools and exchanged the glory of the immortal God for images made to look like mortal human beings and birds and animals and reptiles... They exchanged the truth about God for a lie, and worshiped and served created things rather than the Creator—who is forever praised" (Rom 1:22, 24–25).

In exchanging the truth about God for a lie, we saw God as full of caprice, contradictions, hostility, lust, and retribution (all projections of our fallen selves). But God is *not* like our grotesque idolatries. Indeed, if he is hidden, Paul says, it is because we had become slaves to the god of this world, who has blinded our minds, so that we are ever seeking but never able to find him (see 2 Cor 4:4).

Second, the Fall also caused us to distort—and blur—the *divine image* in ourselves, rolling it in the dust, as it were. Instead of being loving, generous, self-giving, thoughtful, merciful—as God is—we became miserly, selfish, unloving, unforgiving, spiteful. Created to image, and thus represent, God in all that we are and do, we learned rather to bear the image of the Evil One, God's implacable enemy.

The third consequence of the Fall was our loss of the *divine presence* and with that our relationship—fellowship—with God. In place of communion with the Creator, having purpose in his creation, we became rebels, lost and cast adrift, creatures who broke God's laws, abused his creation, and suffered the awful consequences of fallenness in our brokenness, alienation, loneliness, and pain.

Under the tyranny of our sin—indeed, we are enslaved to it, Paul says, and guilty—we found ourselves unwilling and unable to come to the living God for life and restoration. And in turn we passed on our brokenness in the form of every kind of broken relationship with one another (this is writ large in Genesis 4–11).

The Bible tells us that we are fallen, that there is an awful distance between ourselves and God, and that we are like sheep going astray (Isa 53:6; 1 Pet 2:25) or like a rebellious, know-it-all son, living in a far country among the hogs, wanting to eat their food (Luke 15:11–32). In our better moments, we also know that this is the truth not only about the murderer or rapist or child abuser, but also about ourselves—the selfish, the greedy, the proud. It is no wonder people think God is hostile to us; in our better moments we know we deserve his wrath for the kind of endless stinkers we really are.

REDEMPTION

The Bible also tells us that the holy and just God, whose moral perfections burn against sin and creaturely rebellion, is in fact also a God full of mercy and love—and faithfulness. The reality is that God pitied—and loved—these creatures of his, whose rebellion and rejection of their dependent status had caused them to fall so low and thus to experience the pain, guilt, and alienation of their sinfulness.

But how to get through to us, to rescue us from ourselves with all of our wrong views about God and the despair of our tragic fallenness; how to get us to see that God is *for* us, not *against* us (see Rom 8:31); how to get the rebel not just to run up a white flag of surrender but willingly to change sides and thereby once again to discover joy and meaningfulness—that's what chapter 3 of the story is all about.

And it's the longest chapter, a chapter that tells how God set about redeeming and restoring these fallen creatures of his so that he might restore to us the lost vision of God, renew in us the divine image, and reestablish our relationship with him. But also woven throughout this chapter is that other thread—the one of our continuing resistance.

Thus we are told that God came to a man, Abraham, and made a covenant with him—to bless him and, through him, the nations (Genesis 12–50)—and with his offspring, Israel, who had become a slave people (Exodus). Through the first of his prophets, Moses, God (now known by his name *Yahweh*) freed them from their slavery and made a covenant with them at Mount Sinai—that he who had rescued them would be their Savior and Protector forever, that he would be uniquely present with them among all the peoples of the world. But they would also have to keep covenant with him, by letting themselves be reshaped into his likeness. Thus he gave them the Law as his gift to them, both to reveal what he is like and to protect them from one another while they were being reshaped (Leviticus–Deuteronomy).

But the story tells us they rebelled over and over again and looked on his gift of law as a form of taking away their freedom. As shepherds who were being brought into an agricultural land (Joshua), they were not sure their God—a God of shepherds, as they supposed—would also help the crops to grow, so they turned to the agricultural fertility gods (Baal and Ashtoreth) of the peoples who surrounded them.

So they experienced several rounds of oppression and rescue (Judges), even while some of them were truly taking on God's character (Ruth). Finally, God sent them another great prophet (Samuel), who anointed for them their ideal king (David), with whom God made another covenant, specifying that one of his offspring would rule over his people forever (1–2 Samuel). But alas, it goes bad again (1–2 Kings; 1–2 Chronicles), and God in love sends them prophets (Isaiah–Malachi), singers (Psalms), and sages (Job; Proverbs; Ecclesiastes). In the end their constant unfaithfulness is too much, so God at last judges his people with the curses promised in Leviticus 26 and Deuteronomy 28. Yet even here (see Deut 30) there is promise for the future (see, e.g., Isa 40–55; Jer 30–32; Ezek 36–37) in which there would be a new "son of David" and an outpouring of God's Spirit into people's hearts so that they would come to life and be transformed into God's likeness. This final blessing would also include people from all the nations ("the Gentiles").

Finally, just before the last scene, with its final curtain and epilogue, we are told of the greatest event of all—that the great, final "son of David" is none other than God himself, the Creator of all the cosmic greatness and grandeur, come to be present on the human scene in our own likeness. Born as the child of a peasant girl, within the fold of an oppressed people, Jesus the Son of God lived and taught among them. And finally with a horrible death, followed by a death-defeating resurrection, he grappled with and defeated the "gods"—all the powers that have stood against us—and himself bore the full weight of the guilt and punishment of the creatures' rebellion.

Here is the heart of the story: A loving, redeeming God in his incarnation restored our lost *vision* of God (took off the wraps, as it were, so that we could plainly see what God is truly like), by his crucifixion and resurrection made possible our being restored to the *image* of God (see Rom 8:29; 2 Cor 3:18), and through the gift of the Spirit became *present* with us in constant fellowship. Marvelous—well nigh incredible—that revelation, that redemption.

The genius of the biblical story is what it tells us about God himself: a God who sacrifices himself in death out of love for his enemies; a God who would rather experience the death we deserved than to be apart from the people he created for his pleasure; a God who himself bore our likeness, experienced our creatureliness, and carried our sins so that he might provide pardon and reconciliation; a God who would not let us go, but who would pursue us—all of us, even the worst of us—so that he might restore us into joyful fellowship with himself; a God who in Christ Jesus has so forever identified with his beloved creatures that he came to be known and praised as "the God and Father of our Lord Jesus Christ" (1 Pet 1:3).

This is *God's* story, the story of his unfathomable love and grace, mercy and forgiveness—and that is how it also becomes *our* story. The story tells us that we deserve nothing but get everything; that we deserve hell but get heaven; that we deserve to be wiped out, obliterated, but we get his tender embrace; that we deserve rejection and judgment but get to become his children, to bear his likeness, to call him Father. This is the story of the Bible, *God's story,* which at the same time is also our own. Indeed, he even let his human creatures have a part in writing it!

CONSUMMATION

Because the story has not yet ended, the final chapter is still being written—even though we know from what has been written how the final chapter turns out. What God has already set in motion, we are told, through the incarnation, death, and resurrection of Jesus Christ and the gift of the Holy Spirit is finally going to be fully realized.

Thus the one thing that makes this story so different from all other such stories is that ours is filled with hope. There is an End—a glorious conclusion to the present story. It is Jesus, standing at the tomb of his friend Lazarus, telling Lazarus's sister Martha that Jesus himself was her hope for life now and for the life to come: "I am the resurrection and the life," he told her, "anyone who believes in me will live, even though they die"—because Jesus is the *resurrection.* And because he is also the *life,* he went on: "and whoever lives and believes in me will never die" (John 11:25–26). And then he proceeded to validate what he had said by raising Lazarus from the grave.

Jesus himself became the final verification of those words by his own resurrection from the dead. The wicked and the religious killed him. They could not tolerate his presence among them, because he stood in utter contradiction to all their petty forms of religion and authority, based on their own fallenness—and he then had the gall to tell them that he was the *only* way to the Father (see John 14:6). So they killed him. But since he himself *was* Life—and the author of life for all others—the grave couldn't hold him. And his resurrection not only validated his own claims and vindicated his own life on our planet, it also spelled the beginning of the end for death itself and became the guarantee of those who are his—both now and forever.

This is what the final episode (the Revelation) is all about—God's final wrap-up of the story, when his justice brings an end to the great Antagonist and all who continue to bear his image (see Rev 20) and when God in love restores the creation (Eden) as a new heaven and a new earth (see Rev 21–22).

This, then, is the metanarrative, the grand story, of which the various books of the Bible are a part. While we have regularly tried to point out how each book fits in, as you read the various books, you will want to think for yourself how they fit into the larger story. We hope you will also ask yourself how you fit into it as well.

The Narrative of Israel
(Including the Law)
in the Biblical Story

We should begin by noting that the arrangement of the Old Testament books in the Hebrew Bible is a bit different from that in our English Bibles. Ours comes to us by way of the second-century B.C. Greek translation known as *the Septuagint.* The Hebrew Bible is divided into three parts: *the Law* (the Pentateuch, or "five books of Moses"), *the Prophets* (the Former Prophets, including Joshua through Kings [minus Ruth], and the Latter Prophets, including Isaiah, Jeremiah, Ezekiel, and the Book of the Twelve [the so-called Minor Prophets]), and *the Writings* (the Psalms [including Lamentations], the Wisdom books [Job, Proverbs, Ecclesiastes, Song of Songs], Daniel, and the four narrative books of Ruth, Esther, Ezra-Nehemiah, and Chronicles). In this book we will follow the English order, except for Lamentations in the Old Testament, which is placed among the Writings, and Acts in the New Testament, which properly belongs with the Gospel of Luke.

As noted in *How to 1* (p. 22), despite the way many of God's good people handle the Bible, it is, in fact, no mere collection of propositions to be believed and imperatives to be obeyed. Rather, the essential character of the Bible, the whole Bible, is *narrative,* a narrative in which both the propositions and the imperatives are deeply embedded as an essential part. And so the Bible begins with a series of narrative books—which is true even of Leviticus and Deuteronomy, which may appear

19

otherwise because they are composed largely of laws, but which, in fact, cannot be properly understood apart from the narrative structure in which they are placed.

Thus the beginning of the biblical story takes root in the lengthy narrative that tells the story of God's chosen people, Israel. The first of the five books of Moses (Genesis) relates the beginnings of everything (Creation and Fall) and then focuses especially on God's call and covenant with Abraham and his seed, promising both to make them a numerous people and to give them the land of Canaan. After rescuing the people from slavery in Egypt (the exodus), God meets with them at Mount Sinai in the vast Sinai wilderness. Here he makes a second covenant with Israel that takes the form of "the law," which includes the building of a tabernacle (Exodus), the place where God will dwell among his people and where they are to worship him with proper offerings and sacrifices (Leviticus) as a part of the way they uphold their end of the covenant.

As the people prepare to leave Sinai and make their way to the promised land, the number of men twenty years old and older are counted (those who will be Israel's warriors) and placed around the tabernacle in battle formation (Numbers). Thus they are prepared to take their place in the holy war by which they are to gain the land God had promised to their fathers—Abraham, Isaac, and Jacob. Before they embark on this conquest, Moses gives them a review of this history, another overview of the law, and the blessings and curses (promises and threats) of a kind that accompany ancient covenants; in their case, disobedience to God's covenant meant exile, but with a promised, even more glorious restoration in the form of a new exodus (Deuteronomy).

After the story of the initial conquest and occupation of the land (Joshua) come stories of their failures to keep covenant with God, their true King (Judges). In this latter story (including Ruth), we are prepared for the next major turn in the main story line—that God will rule Israel through an earthly king. The books of Samuel thus tell the story of David, with whom God makes another covenant—that one of his sons will never fail to sit on the throne in Israel, as long as they keep covenant with God. As in many ancient kingships, David himself was also understood to embody the people, a key element in many of the psalms and in the final unfolding of the story of Jesus of Nazareth. But alas, the story of Israel repeats itself, as one king after another leads Israel astray to pursue other gods (1–2 Kings). Indeed, within two generations David's kingdom is divided into two parts. The northern kingdom (Israel; sometimes called Ephraim by the psalmists and prophets) falls to the Assyrians in 722 B.C. and for all practical purposes ceases to exist as a distinct entity. The southern kingdom (Judah) falls to the Babylonians in 586 B.C. In this case, the leading people carried into exile in Babylon thus form part of the remnant through whom God will still work out his redemptive plans.

The exile brought untold misery and trauma to God's people, since they lost their promised land and their temple — the primary evidence of God's special presence and of their being his people. Especially through the prophetic ministry of Ezekiel, the exiles were held together. Many, though by no means the majority, were finally restored to their land under the Persians and rebuilt the temple (Ezra 1–6); about a century later, Ezra and Nehemiah led a further return of exiles and were instrumental in bringing about a significant reform (Ezra 7–10; Nehemiah). During this same overall restoration period, the story of Judah is retold from a more positive perspective (1–2 Chronicles), while Esther tells the story of the Jewish exiles throughout the Persian Empire being saved from annihilation.

As you read through the books in this section of the Bible, you will find various threads that hold the larger narrative together: God's *covenants* with his people; God's *faithfulness* to them despite their repeated unfaithfulness to him; God's choice of the *lesser* and the *unfavored* ones (his choosing the "weak to shame the strong" [1 Cor 1:27]); God's *redeeming* his people from slavery to make them his own; God's *dwelling* among them in tabernacle and temple as the gift of his renewed presence on earth (lost in the Fall); God's gift of the *law* in order to reshape them into his own likeness; God's provision of a *sacrificial system* — the "red thread" of blood poured out for the life of another — as his way of offering forgiveness; God's choice of a *king* from Judah who would represent him on earth and thus prepare the way for his own coming in the person of Jesus. These are the matters that make the whole story hold together as one story. Be watching for them as you read.

Genesis

ORIENTING DATA FOR GENESIS

- **Content:** the story of the creation, of human disobedience and its tragic consequences, and of God's choosing Abraham and his offspring—the beginning of the story of redemption

- **Historical coverage:** from creation to the death of Joseph in Egypt (ca. 1600 B.C.?)

- **Emphases:** God as the Creator of all that is; God's creation of human beings in his image; the nature and consequences of human disobedience; the beginning of the divine covenants; God's choice of a people through whom he will bless the nations

OVERVIEW OF GENESIS

For modern readers Genesis might appear to be a strange book, beginning as it does with God and creation, and ending with Joseph in a coffin in Egypt! But that strangeness is evidence that even though it has integrity as a book in its own right (careful structure and organization), it is at the same time intended to set the whole biblical story in motion. Indeed, its opening word (*Bereshith* = "in [the] beginning") both serves as its title and is suggestive as to what the book is about. Thus it tells of the beginning of God's story—creation, human disobedience, and divine redemption—while it also begins the Pentateuch, the story of God's choosing and making a covenant with a people through whom he would bless all peoples (Gen 12:2–3).

The narrative of Genesis itself comes in two basic parts: a "prehistory" (chs. 1–11), the stories of creation, human origins, the fall of humanity, and the relentless progress of evil—all against the backdrop of God's enduring patience and love—and the story of the beginning of redemption through Abraham and his seed (chs. 12–50), with focus on the stories of Abraham (11:27–25:11), Jacob (25:12–37:1), and Joseph (chs. 37–50). These stories are structured in part around a phrase that occurs ten times: "This is the account [genealogy/family history] of," a term which can refer both to "genealogies" proper (as with Shem, Ishmael, and Esau) and to "family stories." You will see that the major stories of Abraham, Jacob, and Joseph in each case come under the family story of the father (Terah, Isaac, and Jacob).

The overall narrative of Genesis thus begins immediately after the prologue (1:1–2:3) with the first human family in the Garden of Eden and works successively from Adam's family through Noah and Shem to Terah and Abraham and finally through Isaac to Jacob (Israel) and thus to Joseph. At the same time, the family lines of the rejected sons (Cain, Ishmael, Esau) are also given so that the "chosen seed" and the "rejected brother" are set off in contrast (the one has a story, the other only a genealogy). Finally, watch for one further framing device that holds the major part of the book together: God's use of Noah to preserve human life during the great deluge (chs. 6–9) and of Joseph to preserve human life during the great drought (chs. 37–50).

SPECIFIC ADVICE FOR READING GENESIS

As you read this first book in the Bible, besides being aware of how the narrative unfolds according to the family stories, also be watching for both the major plot and several subplots that help to shape the larger family story, the story of the people of God.

The *major plot* has to do with God's intervening in the history of human fallenness by choosing ("electing") a man and his family. For even though the families of Abraham, Isaac, and Jacob are the major players, you are never allowed to forget that God is the ultimate Protagonist—as is true in all the biblical narratives. Above all else, it is his story. God speaks and thereby creates the world and a people. It becomes their story (and ours) only as God has brought this family into being and made promises to them and covenanted with them to be their God. So keep looking for the way the major plot unfolds and for how the primary players become part of God's ultimate narrative.

At the same time, keep your eyes open for several subplots that are crucial to the larger story of the Old Testament people of God—and in some cases of the people constituted by the *new* covenant as well. Six of these are worthy of special attention.

The first of these — crucial to the whole biblical story — is the occurrence of the first two covenants between God and his people. The first covenant is with all of humankind through Noah and his sons, promising that God will never again cut off life from the earth (9:8–17). The second covenant is with Abraham, promising two things especially — the gift of "seed" who will become a great nation to bless the nations, and the gift of land (12:2–7; 15:1–21; cf. 17:3–8, where the covenant is ratified by the identifying mark of circumcision). The second covenant is repeated to Isaac (26:3–5) and Jacob (28:13–15) and in turn serves as the basis for the next two Old Testament covenants: the gift of law (Exod 20–24) and the gift of kingship (2 Sam 7).

The second subplot is a bit subtle in Genesis itself, but is important to the later unfolding of the theme of *holy war* (see glossary) in the biblical story. It begins with God's curse on the serpent, that God "will put enmity between you and the woman, and between your offspring [seed] and hers" (3:14–15). The crucial term here is "offspring" (seed), picked up again in 12:7 with regard to the chosen people. This curse anticipates the holy-war motif that is accented in Exodus in particular (between Moses and Pharaoh, thus between God and the gods of Egypt; see Exod 15:1–18), is carried on further in the conquest of Canaan and its gods (which explains the curse of Canaan in Gen 9:25–27), and climaxes in the New Testament (in the story of Jesus Christ, and especially in the Revelation). Although in Genesis this motif does not take the form of holy war as such, you can nonetheless see it especially in the strife between brothers, between the ungodly and godly seed (Cain/Abel; Ishmael/Isaac; Esau/Jacob), where the elder persecutes the younger through whom God has chosen to work (see Gal 4:29).

God's choice of the younger (or weaker, or most unlikely) to bear the righteous seed is a third subplot that begins in Genesis. Here it takes two forms in particular that are then repeated throughout the biblical story. First, God regularly bypasses the firstborn son in carrying out his purposes (a considerable breach of the cultural rules on the part of God): not Cain but Seth, not Ishmael but Isaac, not Esau but Jacob, not Reuben but Judah. Second, the godly seed is frequently born of an otherwise barren woman (Sarah, 18:11–12; Rebekah, 25:21; Rachel, 29:31). As you read through the whole biblical story, you will want to be on the lookout for this recurring motif (see, e.g., 1 Sam 1:1–2:11; Luke 1).

24

Related to this theme is the fact that the chosen ones are not chosen because of their own goodness; indeed, their flaws are faithfully narrated (Abraham in Gen 12:10–20; Isaac in 26:1–11; Jacob throughout [note how dysfunctional the family is in ch. 37!]; Judah in 38:1–30). God does not choose them because of their inherent character; what makes them the godly seed is that in the end they trusted God and his promise that they would be his people — an exceedingly numerous people — and that they would inherit the land to which they first came as aliens.

A fourth subplot emerges later in the story, where Judah takes the leading role among the brothers in the long Joseph narrative (chs. 37–50). He emerges first in chapter 38, where his weaknesses and sinfulness are exposed. But his primary role begins in 43:8–9, where he guarantees the safety of his brother Benjamin, and it climaxes in his willingness to take the place of Benjamin in 44:18–34. All of this anticipates Jacob's blessing in 49:8–12, that the "scepter will not depart from Judah" (pointing to the Davidic kingdom and, beyond that, to Jesus Christ).

A fifth subplot is found in the anticipation of the next "chapter" in the story — slavery in Egypt. Interest in Egypt begins with the genealogy of Ham (10:13–14; *Mizraim* is Hebrew for "Egypt"). The basic family narrative (Abraham to Joseph) begins with a famine that sends Abraham to Egypt (12:10–20) and concludes with another famine that causes Jacob and the entire family to settle in Egypt, whereas Isaac, while on his way toward Egypt during another famine, is expressly told *not* to go there (26:1–5).

Finally, the interest in detailing the origins of Israel's near neighbors, who become thorns in their sides throughout the Old Testament story, forms a sixth subplot. Besides the major players, Egypt and Canaan (10:13–19), note, in turn, Moab and Ammon (19:30–38) and Edom (25:23; 27:39–40; 36:1–43), as well as the lesser role of Ishmael (39:1; cf. Ps 83:6).

A WALK THROUGH GENESIS

☐ 1:1–2:3   *Prologue*

Although written as prose, there is also a clearly poetic dimension to this creational prologue. Part of the poetry is the careful structure of this first "week," where day 1 corresponds to day 4, day 2 to day 5, and day 3 to day 6. Notice how the two sets of days respond to the earth's being "formless and empty" (1:2): Days 1–3 give "form" to the earth (light, sky, dry land), while days 4–6 fill the form with content. Thus:

Day 1 (1:3–5)	Light
Day 2 (1:6–8)	Sky and seas
Day 3 (1:9–13)	Dry land/plant life
Day 4 (1:14–19)	Sun, moon, stars
Day 5 (1:20–23)	Sky and sea animals
Day 6 (1:24–31)	Land animals eat plant life
Day 7 (2:2–3)	God rests from this work

Watch for several emphases as you read, some of which are picked up later in the biblical story—that God speaks everything into existence (cf. Ps 33:6; John 1:1–3); that God blessed what he created, including the material world, calling it all "good"; that human beings, male and female, are created in God's own image and are given regency over the rest of creation; that God rested on the seventh day and set it aside as holy (thus setting the pattern of six days of work and one for rest; cf. Exod 20:8–11, God's great gift of rest to former slaves).

☐ 2:4–4:26 *The Account of Human Beginnings*

This is the first of the six "accounts" that make up the prehistory of Genesis 1–11. It falls into three clearly discernible parts, following present chapter divisions. It begins (2:4–25) with human beings created and placed in Eden, with its centerpiece of the two trees (of life; of the knowledge of good and evil—both reflecting God's own being); included are the warning not to eat from the tree of the knowledge of good and evil, and the creation of Eve from Adam's side, with emphasis on their mutuality and partnership. Note how the story descends rapidly from there. The serpent beguiles them into disobedience (3:1–13), followed by God's cursing the serpent and the land and judging the woman and the man (3:14–19) and, after a momentary alleviation (3:21), by their punishment—the loss of God's presence (3:22–24). It is important to be reminded here that Eden is seen as restored in the final vision of the Revelation (Rev 22:1–5)! The descent is completed with the story of Cain's murder of his brother, Abel, and Cain's further banishment from God's presence (4:1–

18), concluding on the twin notes of the arrogance of Cain's descendants (4:19–24) and of the birth of Seth, with the hopeful note that "at that time people began to call on the name of the LORD" (4:25–26).

☐ 5:1–6:8 *The Account of Adam's Family Line*

This genealogy stands in contrast to Cain's line (compare the difference between the two Lamechs at the end of each). Note two important things about this genealogy: First, it begins (5:3) and ends (5:29) with echoes from the prologue (Seth is in Adam's likeness; Noah will bring comfort from the curse). Second, one man in this lineage, Enoch (5:21–24), continues to experience God's presence. Despite some puzzling details, don't miss the point of 6:1–8: The utter degeneration of the human race leads God to act in judgment (6:6–7); mercifully, however, "Noah found favor in the eyes of the LORD" (6:8).

☐ 6:9–9:29 *The Account of Noah*

This narrative is so well known that you could easily miss its significant features. Note at the beginning how Noah's righteousness echoes Enoch's "walking with God" (6:9). Observe also how the story echoes the original creation story, so that in effect it becomes a "second creation" narrative: The flood returns the world to its state of being "formless and empty" (1:2), but Noah and the animals provide a link with the old while yet starting something new. The covenant with Noah is full of echoes from Genesis 1–2—the reestablishment of the seasonal cycles (8:22; cf. 1:14); the command to multiply (9:1, 7; cf. 1:28); humankind in God's image (9:6; cf. 1:27). Here God is starting over, and thus he makes a covenant never to destroy the whole earth in such a fashion again. Alas, the story ends on a sour note (9:20–23)—a "fall" again, leading to the curse of Ham's seed, Canaan—but it concludes with the blessing of Shem (from whose seed redemption will emerge).

☐ 10:1–11:9 *The Account of Shem, Ham, and Japheth*

Here you find the development of human civilization into the three basic people groups known to the Israelites. Singled out in particular are Mizraim (Hebrew for "Egypt") and Canaan (10:13–20). Capping these accounts is the story of Babel, which leads directly to the Abraham narrative, as the story returns from the scattered nations to one man who will found a new nation through whom all the nations will be blessed.

☐ 11:10–26 *The Account of Shem*

This list of names isn't riveting reading, but it gets you from Noah's son Shem to Abram (Abraham), and thus to the "father" of the chosen people.

☐ 11:27–25:11 *The Account of Terah*

You can hardly miss seeing that Terah's son, Abraham, dominates this family story. Here you can watch how skillfully the narrative is presented. It introduces Abraham's family, who have moved partway to Canaan (11:27–32), with a special note about Sarah's barrenness (11:30). The key moments are in 12:1–9, where God calls Abraham to leave Haran and "go to the land I will show you" (12:1) and promises to make him "into a great nation" and to bless "all peoples on earth" through him (vv. 2–3). After obediently traveling to the land inhabited by Canaanites (vv. 4–5), Abraham traverses the whole land and then is promised, "To your offspring [seed] I will give this land" (vv. 6–7), whereupon "he built an altar there to the LORD and called on the name of the LORD" (vv. 8–9). In the rest of the narrative, you will see these several themes played out in one form or another: The *promised land* will be given to the *promised seed,* who will become *a great nation* and thus a *blessing to the nations* — even though the Canaanites now possess the land and Sarah is barren! — and so Abraham *trusts* and *worships* the God who has promised this.

Thus the first narrative, which is about Abram's failure in Egypt (12:10–20), has to do with God's protecting the *promised seed.* The first Lot cycle (chs. 13–14) focuses on *great nation* and *promised land* while introducing Sodom and Gomorrah, and indicating Abraham's considerable significance in the land. The back-to-back narratives of chapters 15–16 come back to the *promised seed* from a *barren woman,* while the centerpiece narrative of chapter 17 focuses on all the themes together. The next narrative focuses again on the promised seed from a barren woman (18:1–15), which is picked up again in the series of three narratives in chapters 20 and 21 (Abimelech, the birth of Isaac, the expulsion of Ishmael). These narratives bookend the second Lot cycle (18:16–19:38), which begins with the great nation that will be a blessing on the nations (18:18). Here the destruction of Sodom and Gomorrah and the incestuous conception of Moab and Ammon stand in contrast to Abraham's trust in God for the promised land, a theme picked up again in 21:22–34.

Four crucial narratives then conclude the family story of Terah. First comes the testing of Abraham as to whether he would be willing to give up to God his firstborn son (ch. 22). In this crucial narrative, be sure to note

(1) the renewal of the promises (vv. 15 – 18),
(2) Abraham's obedience and implicit trust in God throughout,
(3) God's provision of a sacrifice in place of Isaac.

Taken together, the deaths of Sarah (ch. 23) and of Abraham (25:7 – 11) complete the promised-land motif—a piece of the future promised land is purchased so that their bodies can rest there, waiting for the future to be fulfilled! These enclose the story of Isaac's marriage, which is included in the Abraham series because it continues the promised-seed motif, as does the introduction to the narrative of Abraham's death (25:1 – 6).

Note finally that unwise choices made in moments of shaky faith do not thwart God's purposes (the Pharaoh and Abimelech stories in chs. 12 and 20, and Hagar in ch. 16), while Abraham in his turn "believed the LORD, and [the LORD] credited it to him as righteousness" (15:6, a text that becomes especially important in Paul's letters). Thus Abraham's regular response to God is *worship* and *obedience* (12:7 – 8; 13:4, 18; 14:17 – 20; 22:1 – 19).

☐ 25:12 – 18 *The Account of Ishmael*

This, the briefest of the origin stories, confirms that God fulfilled his promise (16:10) to make Ishmael, not just Isaac, into a great twelve-tribe nation.

☐ 25:19 – 35:29 *The Account of Isaac*

The Isaac story is mainly about Jacob, who represents the chosen lineage. Note how the promises made to Abraham are repeated for both Isaac (26:3 – 5) and Jacob (28:13 – 15). Again, following prayer, the promised seed is born to a barren woman (25:21 – 26). Esau's despising his firstborn right (25:29 – 34) shows his character (cf. Heb 12:16) and by implication that of his descendants, the Edomites—perennial enemies of Israel (see the book of Obadiah). In chapter 26 Isaac repeats Abraham's failure (chs. 12, 20) and, as before, God intervenes to protect the promised seed. In chapters 27 – 28, despite Jacob's cheating Esau out of his father's blessing (and thus living up to his name, "he deceives"), note that God renews the Abrahamic covenant with him (28:10–22). This event also marks the beginning of a change in Jacob's character, evidenced in the events surrounding his reconciliation with Esau (chs. 32–33; note especially the narrative where his name is changed from Jacob to Israel).

In chapters 29–31 you begin to follow the expansion of the nation of Israel. The chosen family now numbers twelve sons whose offspring will form the twelve tribes, a concept reflected later in the tribal districts of the land and later still in Jesus' choosing twelve disciples, and even in the final architecture of the new Jerusalem that comes down out of heaven (Rev 21:12, 14, 21). Unfortunately, Jacob's sons (ch. 34) reflect the character of the younger Jacob, a factor that plays a huge role at the beginning (37:12–36) of the final family story in Genesis (chs. 37–50).

☐ 36:1–37:1 *The Account of Esau*

Esau's lineage, the Edomites, became a great nation as promised but are also another of the neighbors who continually threaten the chosen people and their security in the promised land.

☐ 37:2–50:26 *The Account of Jacob*

The final family story is primarily about Joseph, whom God uses to rescue Israel (and the nations, thus blessing them, 12:2–3) from famine so that the promised seed can be preserved. You will find reading this story to be a different experience from what has gone before, since it is a single cohesive narrative (the longest of its kind in the Bible), with just three interruptions (the story of Judah in ch. 38, the genealogy in 46:8–27, and Jacob's "blessing" in ch. 49). Note how it begins and ends on the same note—his brothers bowing to him (37:5–7; 50:18; cf. 42:6). Look for the various themes that hold the story together: God overturns the brothers' evil against Joseph; he allows Joseph to languish in prison (which came about because of Joseph's refusal to sin) but finally rescues him and elevates him through his divinely given ability to interpret dreams (note the repeated "the LORD was with Joseph," 39:2, 3, 21, 23)—again, God works through a younger, despised son. Note also at the end (ch. 48), Jacob's blessing of Joseph's two sons continues the pattern of God's choosing the younger (the unfavored one).

Finally, you will want to observe the role Judah plays in the narrative. Although his beginnings are anything but salutary (ch. 38), Judah later shows a repentant heart for his past role in the story (44:18–34). And eventually he is blessed as "the lion" through whose lineage will come the Davidic king (49:8–12) and eventually the messianic king himself, Christ Jesus.

Although the narrative ends with Joseph in a coffin in Egypt (50:26), this too anticipates the next part of the narrative, the book of Exodus, where special note is made that the Israelites took the bones of Joseph with them because he had made them swear an oath, "God will surely come to your aid" (Exod 13:19).

Genesis begins the biblical story with God as Creator, human beings as created in God's image but fallen, and God's response through a redemptive creation of a chosen people — and doing so through all kinds of circumstances(good and ill) and despite their faults.

Exodus

ORIENTING DATA FOR EXODUS

■ **Content:** Israel's deliverance from Egypt, her constitution as a people through covenant law, and instructions for and construction of the tabernacle — the place of God's presence

■ **Historical coverage:** from Joseph's death (ca. 1600 B.C.?) to Israel's encampment at Sinai (either 1440 or 1260 B.C.)

■ **Emphases:** God's miraculous rescue of Israel from Egypt through Moses; covenant law given at Mount Sinai; the tabernacle as the place of God's presence and Israel's proper worship; God's revelation of himself and his character; Israel's tendency to complain and rebel against God; God's judgment and mercy toward his people when they rebel

OVERVIEW OF EXODUS

You may find Exodus a bit more difficult than Genesis to read all the way through. The first half (chs. 1–20) is easy enough, since it continues the narrative that began in Genesis 12, but after that you get a series of laws (chs. 21–24), followed by detailed instructions about the materials and furnishings for the tabernacle (chs. 25–31). The narrative then returns for three chapters (chs. 32–34), only to be followed (chs. 35–40) by a repetition of chapters 25–31, as the tabernacle and its furnishings are constructed exactly per instructions. Both the details and repetitious nature of chapters 25–31 and 35–40 can serve to derail you unless you keep them in the context of the big picture, both of Exodus itself and of the larger story found in the Pentateuch as a whole.

The narrative portion begins with Israel's enslavement in Egypt (ch. 1), followed by the birth of Moses, his flight and subsequent call (where Yahweh's name is revealed), and his return to Egypt (chs. 2–4). This is followed by the exodus itself (5:1–15:21), including Israel's forced labor, Yahweh's conflict with Pharaoh in the holy war by way of the ten plagues, the Red Sea miracle, and a hymn celebrating God the Divine Warrior's victory over Pharaoh. The rest of the narrative (15:22–19:25) gets Israel to Sinai in preparation for the giving of the covenant law (chs. 20–23) and its ratification (ch. 24). Part of this narrative is Israel's constant complaining to God, which in chapters 32–34 becomes full-blown idolatrous rebellion, followed by judgment and renewal of the covenant.

The book concludes with a final moment of narrative (40:34–38) in which God's glory (his presence) fills the tabernacle, the last essential act of preparation, thus making the people ready for their pilgrimage to the promised land. Note especially how the two parts of this short scene anticipate the next two books of the Pentateuch: The glory of the Lord filling the tabernacle/Tent of Meeting leads directly into Leviticus, where God speaks to Moses (and thus to the people) from the Tent of Meeting and gives instructions on the uses of the tabernacle (Lev 1:1; "Tent of Meeting" and "tabernacle" are used interchangeably thereafter), and the cloud reappears in the narrative early in Numbers, to give guidance when Israel finally breaks camp and sets out toward the promised land (Num 9:15–23).

The parts of the law enclosed in the Exodus narrative include the Ten Commandments (ch. 20), the Book of the Covenant (chs. 21–23)—various laws dealing mostly with relationships among the people—and the instructions regarding the tabernacle (chs. 25–31), followed by its construction and implementation (35:1–40:33).

SPECIFIC ADVICE FOR READING EXODUS

Any sense of confusion as you read this book may be lessened greatly if you have a sense of the why of its overall structure. Why especially the instructions about and construction of the tabernacle in *this* narrative? Why not wait until Leviticus, where it would seem to fit better? The answer is that Exodus narrates the crucial matters that define Israel as a people in relationship to their God, Yahweh. As you read, therefore, watch especially for the three absolutely defining moments in Israel's history, which cause this narrative with its embedding of portions of the law to make sense: (1) God's miraculous deliverance of his people from slavery, (2) the return of the presence of God as distinguishing his people from all other peoples on the earth, and (3) the gift of the law as the means of establishing his covenant with them.

First, the crucial defining moment, and the one referred to over and again throughout both the Old Testament and the New, is the exodus itself. Israel is repeatedly reminded that "it was because the LORD loved you and kept the oath he swore to your forefathers that he brought you out with a mighty hand and redeemed you from the land of slavery, from the power of Pharaoh" (Deut 7:8); Israel itself repeatedly affirms, "The LORD brought us out of Egypt with a mighty hand and an outstretched arm" (Deut 26:8).

Watch for the ways the narrative highlights this event—that the story of Moses is given solely with his role in the exodus in view; that Israel's desperately hopeless situation is overcome by God's miraculous intervention on their behalf; that this is God's victory above all else, over both Pharaoh and the gods he represents; that God's victory is commemorated with the first of two celebratory hymns in the Pentateuch (15:1–21; cf. Deut 31:30–32:43), emphasizing his unrivaled greatness and his triumph in the holy war. Yahweh here "adopts" Israel as his *firstborn son,* who is to be set free so that "he may worship me" (Exod 4:22–23). Notice finally in this regard how the narrative is interrupted twice, on either side of the actual exodus (12:1–28; 12:43–13:16), in order to give instructions for the Passover (the annual celebration of the exodus) and for the consecration of the firstborn male (as a reminder of God's rescue of them as his firstborn while protecting their own firstborn).

Second, the divine presence, lost in Eden, is now restored as the central feature of Israel's existence. This theme begins with the call of Moses at "the mountain of God" (3:1), where he did not dare "look at God" (3:6). It is picked up again in chapter 19, where the people encamp "in front of the mountain" (19:2) and experience a spectacular theophany (a visible manifestation of God), accompanied by warnings against touching the mountain. The awesome nature of this encounter with the living God is further highlighted by the ascending and descending of Moses "up to God" (19:3, 8, 20) and "down to the people" (19:7, 14, 25).

The pivotal nature of this motif can be seen especially in chapters 25–40 and helps to explain the repetition about the tabernacle on either side of chapters 32–34. For the tabernacle was to assume the role of "the Tent of Meeting" (40:6) and was thus to function as the place where Israel's God would dwell in their midst (after he "left" the mountain, as it were). Thus the debacle in the desert (ch. 32) is followed by Moses' pleading for Yahweh not to abandon them, for "if your *Presence* does not go with us ... what else will distinguish me and your people from all the other people on the face of the earth?" (33:15 – 16, emphasis added; later identified in Isa 63:7 – 14 as the Holy Spirit). Notice, finally, that Exodus concludes with God's glory covering the tabernacle/Tent of Meeting, which means the Israelites are now ready for their journey to the promised land. At the same time, these final chapters (25 – 40) prepare the way especially for the regulations for worship and sacrifice that appear in the next book, Leviticus.

Third, there is the giving of the law with its centerpiece of the Ten Commandments (ch. 20), followed by the Book of the Covenant (chs. 21 – 24). These laws together focus on Israel's relationship with God and with one another, the latter as an expression of their living out God's character in those relationships. This first expression of the law in the narrative of Exodus thus prepares the way for its further elaboration in the final three books of the Pentateuch. On the nature of these laws and how they function in Israel, see *How to 1*, pp. 169 – 75.

It is also important to note here that these laws are patterned after ancient covenants known as "suzerainty treaties," where a conqueror made a treaty with the conquered in which he benefited them with his protection and care as long as they would abide by the treaty stipulations. There are six parts to such covenants:

1. Preamble, which identifies the giver of the covenant ("the LORD your God," 20:2)
2. Prologue, which serves as a reminder of the relationship of the suzerain to the people ("who brought you out of Egypt," 20:2)
3. Stipulations, which are various laws/obligations on the part of the people (20:3 – 23:19; 25:1 – 31:18)
4. Document clause, which provides for periodic reading and relearning of the covenant
5. Sanctions, which describe the blessings and curses as incentives for obedience
6. List of witnesses to the covenant

You will note that only the first three of these six covenant ingredients are found in Exodus. It is only the first portion of the full covenant that continues on in Leviticus and Numbers and finally concludes at the end of Deuteronomy. Nevertheless, already in Exodus the key elements of the covenant are evident — (1) the revelation of who God is and what he wants from his people, and (2) the enumeration of obedience as the path of covenant loyalty and thus of maintaining its blessings.

A WALK THROUGH EXODUS

☐ 1:1 – 2:25   *The Setting: Growth and Oppression of Israel in Egypt*

Here you find the two primary narratives that comprise the setting for the exodus: (1) the multiplication and subjection of the Israelites under Pharaoh, including infanticide in a vain attempt to control their population (ch. 1); (2) enter Moses, an Israelite who grows up as a privileged Egyptian but sides with his own people (2:1 – 15). Years later, as an escaped elderly outlaw settled in Sinai (vv. 16 – 22), he is a most unlikely candidate for the role of deliverer of Israel (vv. 23 – 25), picking up a central motif from Genesis.

☐ 3:1 – 6:27   *The Call and Commission of Moses*

Watch for several important features in this narrative: God's revelation of himself to the unsuspecting Moses, including the disclosure of his name (Yahweh, "the one who causes to exist"; translated in small capitals [LORD] in most English versions); God's repeated announcement that he has seen the misery of his people in Egypt and intends to deliver them by his mighty power; Moses' fourfold "thanks but no thanks" response to the call; and his first encounter with Pharaoh, which leads to increased oppression and Israel's rejection of Moses. The startling episode in 4:24 – 26 reminds us that Moses as an Israelite father had not even circumcised his own son, so poorly was he prepared for this task.

☐ 6:28 – 15:21   *The Miraculous Deliverance from Bondage*

This narrative is in four parts, each blending into the next. Watch for them as you read. First is the confrontation with Pharaoh (6:28 – 11:10), which begins with Aaron's staff becoming a serpent and swallowing those of the Egyptian sorcerers (perhaps echoing the curse of the serpent in Eden), followed by nine plagues and the announcement of the tenth; each of these strikes at the heart of Egyptian idolatry and arrogance.

The second part (12:1–30) is a careful weaving together of the institution of the Passover and the actual narrative of the tenth plague. The reason for the instruction here is that the Passover meal is to be an annual celebration in which the momentous event of deliverance is recounted. Notice also the foreshadowing of redemption through the shedding of blood, which in the New Testament happens when God's "firstborn" sheds his blood (Col 1:15–20), as he assumes the role of the lamb and thus lives out this narrative in reverse.

Part 3 is the account of the exodus itself (12:31–14:31). Note especially how reminders of the first two parts are carefully woven into this narrative: It begins with additional Passover regulations and the law of the firstborn; the actual crossing of the Red Sea involves one final confrontation with Pharaoh—and ends with the demise of his whole army. Here also you are introduced to the *grumbling* motif (14:10–12; cf. 5:21) that will become the main theme of the next section of narrative.

Part 4 is the celebratory song of Moses, Israel, and Miriam (15:1–21). Note that it begins as a celebration of the triumph of God the Warrior over Pharaoh and his gods (vv. 1–12) and concludes by anticipating the same victory in the conquest of Canaan (vv. 13–16) and Yahweh's future settled presence on Zion (vv. 17–18; cf. Ps 68). It may be helpful to note how often this aspect of God's victory continued to be celebrated in Israel's hymns (Neh 9:9–11; Pss 66:5–7; 78:12–13; 106:8–12; 114:3, 5; 136:10–15).

☐ 15:22–18:27 *The Journey to Mount Sinai*

The first thing you meet after Israel's great deliverance is a series of three episodes in the desert in which the people grumble against Moses and thus test God (15:22–17:7); these episodes foreshadow many such moments throughout the rest of the story. This is followed by their first encounter with opposition along the way (17:8–16), which also anticipates future encounters of this kind, as well as the future leadership of Joshua. The story of Moses as he takes Jethro's advice about shared leadership, especially for judging (ch. 18), not only prepares for the later organization of the tribes but also for many of the laws in the Book of the Covenant (21:1–23:19; e.g., 21:6, 22; 22:8–9).

☐ 19:1–24:11 *The Covenant at Sinai*

The prelude (ch. 19) is especially significant to the narrative. Note how it begins (vv. 3–6). Here God combines his deliverance of Israel "on eagles' wings" (v. 4) with the call to obedience and his adoption of them as his own treasured possession (much of the language in these verses is picked up by New Testament writers with reference to the church). The rest takes the form of a great theophany, with the reminder of the awful distance between the holy and living God and his people.

Note also that God speaks the Ten Commandments (the "Ten Words," 20:1–17) directly to the people (20:18–21)—a sign of their primacy. Here fundamental responsibilities to both God and neighbor are addressed in proper order (first "vertical," then "horizontal"). When the people plead for indirect communication with God, the first order of business is to repeat the injunction against idolatry (20:22–26).

The Book of the Covenant (chs. 21–23) gives specifics as to what the Ten Words mean in practice. Note that they primarily cover various aspects of societal living—treatment of slaves/servants (standing first in order and in stark contrast to their conditions in Egypt), compensations and penalties for injuries, property law, rape, fairness in dealings with others, and worship. They conclude with a promise of divine guidance and the eventual conquest of Canaan, predicated on the people's obedience to the covenant (23:20–33). The covenant is ratified by Israel's consent, the sprinkling of blood, and a theophanic meal for Israel's elders in the presence of God (24:1–11).

☐ 24:12–31:18 *Instructions regarding the Tabernacle*

As you read these instructions, keep in mind the reason for their many and very precise details—that the tabernacle will be the place of God's presence among them. This not only is said expressly (25:8, 22; cf. Lev 16:2), but it also accounts for the order of the instructions. The ark, where Yahweh dwells between the cherubim (25:22; cf. Lev 16:2), stands in first place, followed by the table on which will sit "the bread of the Presence" (25:30). All the rest of the furnishings, including the bronze altar and the priests' attire, are predicated on the primary reality that Yahweh has chosen to dwell here on earth in the midst of his people. Note, for example, that the reason for the priests' attire is "to give him/them dignity and honor" (28:2, 40). And when you come to Leviticus, you will see that the reason for the bronze altar is for sacrifices, so that the priests may approach Yahweh on behalf of the people. Note how this section ends with a renewal of the Sabbath commandment, which is related especially to Yahweh's "rest" (repeated here because this is God's gift to former slaves who worked all day, every day of the week).

☐ 32:1–34:35 *Rebellion, Covenant Breaking, Covenant Renewal*

Note the contrast: While Moses is atop Sinai receiving instructions for the place of Yahweh's dwelling among them, his brother is below, leading the people in constructing and worshiping idols (32:1–26)—although note that they are allegedly worshiping Yahweh (v.5). Punishment (32:27–29) is followed by Moses' intercession for the people, thus securing God's promise that his own Presence will accompany them and thus distinguish them from all other peoples (32:30–33:23). This is the significance of including here the brief narratives about the Tent of Meeting (33:7–11) and the (foretaste) vision of God's glory (33:18–23). In chapter 34, the covenant is renewed (vv. 1–28; a brief condensation of the Book of the Covenant [chs. 21–23] is included) in the context of another significant theophany. The language of Yahweh's self-revelation in verses 4–7 is one of the more important moments in the biblical story and is appealed to throughout the rest of the Old Testament. The concluding narrative—having to do with Moses emerging from the Tent of Meeting with a face that radiates God's glory (34:29–35; cf. 2 Cor 3)—anticipates the glory that will descend on the tabernacle when it is finished (40:34–38).

☐ 35:1–39:43 *The Construction of the Tabernacle and Its Furnishings*

This lengthy repetition of the matters from chapters 25–31 serves further to highlight the significance of the tabernacle as the place of Yahweh's presence. Note that the order changes slightly so that the tabernacle will be in place before the symbol of the Presence (namely, the ark) is constructed. But it begins with the Sabbath command (35:1–3). Even something as important as the construction of the tabernacle must not supersede the gift of Sabbath.

☐ 40:1–38   *The Tabernacle Is Set Up and the Glory Descends*

Note how this final event in Exodus follows the preceding pattern: Instructions on setting up the tabernacle (vv. 1–16), followed by the implementation (vv. 17–33). All of this so that the glory of Yahweh—the same glory that had so impressed the Israelites when it was seen on Mount Sinai—might fill the tabernacle (v. 34; cf. 1 Kgs 8:10–11), taking the form of a pillar of cloud by day and fire by night (v. 38), a constant visible reminder of God's presence with his people.

Exodus plays an especially important role in the rest of the biblical story, since it tells the basic story of God's saving his people from bondage and of his giving them the law so that they will become the people of his presence. Exodus also serves as a pattern for the promised "second exodus" in Isaiah (esp. chs. 40–66) and thus for Jesus' own "departure" (exodus) that would be accomplished in Jerusalem (Luke 9:30, spoken in the presence of Moses[!] and Elijah).

Leviticus

ORIENTING DATA FOR LEVITICUS

- **Content:** various laws having to do with holiness before God and with love of neighbor, including sacrifices, ritual cleanness, and social obligations, as well as laws for the Levites regarding their priestly duties.

- **Emphases:** getting it right with regard to worship, for both people and priests; institution of the priesthood under Aaron; laws protecting ritual cleanness, including atonement for sins (the Day of Atonement); laws regulating sexual relations, family life, punishments for major crimes, festivals, and special years (sabbaths and jubilees)

OVERVIEW OF LEVITICUS

The title of this book (by way of Latin from the Greek *levitikon*) means "pertaining to the Levites," which not only aptly describes its basic contents but also gives a clue as to why it is so often unappealing to contemporary readers—not to mention that it has so little narrative (chs. 8–10; 24:10–23 are the exceptions). But with a little help, you can come to a basic understanding of both its contents and its place in the narrative of the Pentateuch—even if the nature of, and reason for, some of the laws themselves may escape you (for this you may wish to consult a good commentary; e.g., Gordon J. Wenham, *The Book of Leviticus* [see *How to 1,* p. 268]).

It is important to note that Leviticus picks up precisely where Exodus left off—with the Lord speaking to Moses "from the Tent of Meeting" and saying, "Speak to the Israelites and say ..." From that point on, the movement from one section to another is signaled by the phrase, "The Lord said to Moses" (4:1; 5:14; 6:1, 8; and so forth). It will be no surprise, then, to discover that the first main part of the book (chs. 1–16,

41

commonly known as the Levitical Code) has primarily to do with regulations for the people and the priests related directly to the tabernacle,
which appeared toward the end of Exodus (chs. 25–31; 35–40).

This code outlines easily. It begins with offerings by the people
(1:1–6:7), followed by instructions for the priests (6:8–7:38). These
are followed (logically) by the institution of the Aaronic priesthood
(chs. 8–9) and the judgment on two of Aaron's sons who thought they
could do it their own way (10:1–7), with further instructions for the
priests (10:8–20). The next section (chs. 11–15) then begins with a
new rubric, "The LORD said to Moses *and Aaron*" (11:1, emphasis
added; see also 13:1; 14:33; 15:1, but nowhere else in Leviticus). Here
you find laws that deal especially with ritual cleanness (purity)—with
a view to avoiding what happened to Aaron's two sons. Here also
appears for the first time the very important injunction, "Be holy,
because I am holy" (11:44, 45). This is followed, appropriately, by the
institution of the Day of Atonement (ch. 16).

What follows (chs. 17–25) is commonly known as the Holiness
Code, which is governed by the repeated charge to "be holy, because I
am holy" (beginning in 19:2 and throughout). But now a significant part
of being holy is to "love your neighbor as yourself" (19:18). Thus the
section is a collection of various laws dealing with one's relationship
both to God and to others. At the end are requirements for the sabbath
and jubilee years (ch. 25), while the book concludes with covenant
blessings and curses (ch. 26) that provide a formal conclusion to the
covenant structure that began in Exodus 20. The book itself concludes
with an appendix on vows and tithes (Lev 27).

SPECIFIC ADVICE FOR READING LEVITICUS

In order to get the most out of your reading, you need to remind
yourself of two things: (1) These laws are part of God's covenant with
Israel, and therefore they are not just religious rites but have to do with
relationships, and (2) Leviticus is *part of the larger narrative* of the
Pentateuch and must be understood in light of what has preceded and
what follows.

To pick up the second point first: Just as the legal portions of Exodus
make good sense when you see their place in the larger narrative, so
you need to see Leviticus as a longer expression of the same before the
narrative resumes in Numbers. Crucial here is the fact that Israel is still

camped at the foot of Sinai—a wilderness area—where they will spend a full year being molded into a people before God will lead them toward the conquest of Canaan. Here they will need double protection—from diseases of various kinds and from one another! Therefore, in order for these individuals who grew up in slavery to be formed into God's people, there is great need for them to get two sets of relationships in order, namely, with God and with one another. Note, then, that Leviticus continues with the same ordering of things found in the Ten Commandments (first vertical, then horizontal).

The covenantal aspect of these various laws is their most important feature. Recall the parts of the covenant noted in our Exodus chapter (p. 37). God has sovereignly delivered these people from slavery and has brought them to Sinai; here he has promised to make them his own "treasured possession" out of all the nations on earth (Exod 19:5), who will also therefore be for him "a kingdom of priests and a holy nation" (v. 6). That is, their role as a "kingdom" is to serve as God's priests for the world, and to do so they must bear his likeness ("be holy, because I am holy"). Thus, God covenants with them on his part to bless them (Lev 26:1–13); what he requires on their part is that, even though they are his treasured possession, they maintain a holy awe and obedience toward him. So note in this regard how often, especially in chapters 18–26, the requirement is punctuated with the words, "I am the LORD [Yahweh]" or "I am the LORD your God."

Thus the first set of laws in Leviticus has to do with their "getting it right" when they come to God with various sacrifices. You will note that they are not told what the sacrifices mean (which they already knew), but how to do them properly—although we can infer some things about their meaning from these descriptions. The covenantal nature of these sacrifices appears in three ways: First, the sacrifice constitutes a *gift* on the part of the worshipers to their covenant Lord; second, some of the sacrifices imply *fellowship* on the part of the worshiper with God; third, sacrifice sometimes functions as a way of healing a break in the relationship—a form of *atonement*.

So also with the laws of purity. Here the concern again is that the people have a proper sense of what it means for God to be present among them (see 15:31). At issue here is who may be in the camp, where God himself dwells at the center, and who must remain outside (because they are unclean). Included is the separating out of certain animals and insects that are clean or unclean. At the heart of all of this is the fact that "God is holy" and therefore his people also must be holy.

But holiness does not deal simply with rites and being clean. God's holiness is especially seen in his loving compassion that made the Israelites his people. Therefore, the laws—particularly in the Holiness Code—demand that God's people bear God's likeness in this regard. Since the Israelites are thrown together (in a very orderly way, of course!) in this very tight camp where God dwells in the midst of them, they must display his character in their dealings with one another. Thus, even though this code also contains further "relationship with God" laws, it is especially concerned with how people in community treat one another. And it includes treating them justly and mercifully, which is why the collection ends with the sabbath and jubilee years, so that the land also may "rest," and a time to "proclaim liberty to all" may occur on the sabbath of the sabbath years (25:10).

If you look for these covenantal moments as you read these laws, you may find it to be a far more interesting experience than you might have expected.

A WALK THROUGH LEVITICUS

☐ **1:1 – 7:38 *Instructions for the Five Offerings***

You need to know that Israel's offerings (sacrifices) were regularly crucial elements in symbolic meals. A portion of the sacrifice was burnt on the altar as God's part, but the rest was eaten by the worshipers and priests as a fellowship meal—a meal at God's house, in God's presence (see Deut 14:22 – 29), with God as the host (see Ps 23:5 – 6; cf. "the *Lord's* table" in 1 Cor 10:21). This is especially important in your reading these laws about offerings, since what is described is not their function or meaning but only their proper preparation. Not all were sacrifices for sins. Some offerings were for fellowship and had different covenantal functions altogether.

Note that only the burnt offering (ch. 1) was dedicated entirely to God and thus burned entirely as an atonement for sin. Again, the principle was this: If you are to live, something must die in your place (see Exod 12:1 – 30). Leviticus 2 describes the grain offering (various options for oil and flour ingredients within a balanced meal). Chapter 3 addresses the fellowship offering (sometimes translated "peace offering"), which was an animal offering with the general purpose of keeping one in fellowship with God. The sin (also "purification") offering (4:1 – 5:13) provided atonement for accidental sin, since "transgression" is not limited to intentional disobedience. Finally, the guilt (sometimes "reparation") offering in 5:14 – 6:7 provided a means for making amends for the transgression. The rest of the section (6:8 – 7:38) reviews the role of the priests in supervising the five offerings, as well as prescribing their share of the sacrificed animal.

☐ 8:1 – 10:20   *Priesthood Begins*

Since priests specially represented God to the people and the people to God, Aaron and his sons were ordained to their assignments (chs. 8 – 9), and Aaron's first official sacrifices are listed. Note that his sons failed to follow clear rules and so died, showing the importance God placed on proper worship, further emphasized in various commands from Moses (ch. 10).

☐ 11:1 – 16:34   *On Cleanness and Uncleanness*

You need to know that *clean* here means acceptable to God in worship. *Unclean* means unacceptable to God and banned from the tabernacle, or sometimes (in the case of skin diseases) from the encampment itself. This mixture of food, health, sanitation, and ritual laws is thus aimed at helping the covenant people to show that they belong to God and reflect his purity (holiness, 11:44 – 45). The laws seem to be partly a matter of simple hygiene and partly symbolic obedience, but always in light of the divine presence (15:31).

Thus certain animals, for reasons not given, are unclean (ch. 11). Childbirth (ch. 12) and some diseases (ch. 13) require ritual cleansing (ch. 14) before one is restored to purity. The Israelites were to regard any bodily discharges as unclean (ch. 15, perhaps because in general these are unsanitary). The Day of Atonement (ch. 16) was a special solemn day of forgiveness that not only cleansed the people of their sin but also purified the tabernacle itself and kept it a holy place for worship.

☐ 17:1 – 25:55   *The Holiness Code*

Notice that the first part (17:1 – 20:27) concentrates on personal and social holiness in daily life. It begins with prohibitions regarding non-regulated sacrifices and drinking blood (17:1 – 16), aimed especially at countering Canaanite practices (idolatry and drinking blood in an attempt to capture its life force; cf. Acts 15:20, 29; 21:25), followed by rules for sexual behavior (Lev 18) and for neighborliness, which means truly caring for others, not just for those who live near you (ch. 19). Here occurs for the first time the second love command, "love your neighbor as yourself" (19:18), picked up by Jesus (Mk 12:28–34 and par.) and his followers (e.g., Rom 13:8–10). Note how the punishments for serious crimes in Leviticus 20 respond directly to the prohibitions in chapter 18.

With chapter 21, note the shift back to holiness in matters of religious observance—rules for priests (ch. 21); for the proper offering and eating of sacrifices (ch. 22); for observing the religious festivals, both weekly (sabbath) and annual (ch. 23); and for lamp oil and offering bread at the tabernacle (24:1–9).

Finally in 24:10–23 you come to another narrative—about punishment for blasphemy (cursing God)—that is used to introduce prescriptions for various crimes. At the end of Leviticus are laws concerning the seventh (sabbath) and fiftieth (jubilee) years, which provided liberation for those indebted or enslaved (ch. 25), and a sabbath for the land as well.

☐ 26:1–46 *Covenant Sanctions*

These sanctions (blessings and curses as incentives to keep the covenant) both conclude the Sinaitic covenant and anticipate the conclusion of the covenant in Deuteronomy 27–28.

☐ 27:1–34 *Redemption Laws*

This appendix deals with the cost of redeeming persons who have been promised to God and of redeeming tithes (material goods belonging to God).

Leviticus is the part of God's story where the Israelites are given instructions on how to be holy, on how to be truly acceptable to God and in good relationship with one another—which they could not achieve without his special provision.

Numbers

ORIENTING DATA FOR NUMBERS

- **Content:** the Israelites' long stay in the desert as they journey from Mount Sinai to the plains of Moab, with supplemental covenant laws

- **Historical coverage:** forty years, a period within which the generation that left Egypt died off

- **Emphases:** preparation for military conquest of the promised land; God's covenant loyalty toward Israel with regard to the land; Israel's repeated failure to keep covenant with God; God's leadership of his people and affirmation of Moses' leadership; preparations for entering and worshiping in the promised land; conquest and settlement of the land east of the Jordan River

OVERVIEW OF NUMBERS

If Leviticus tends to be an unappealing book to contemporary readers, then Numbers must be one of the most difficult in terms of "what in the world is going on?" The problem for us is that it is such a mixture of things—narrative, additional laws, census lists, oracles from a pagan prophet, the well-known Aaronic blessing—and it is not easy to see how it all fits together.

Numbers primarily records the pilgrimage of Israel through the desert from the foot of Mount Sinai to its encampment in the plains of Moab (on the east bank of the Jordan River), poised for conquest. But it is the second generation that ends up on the east bank—because the exodus generation refused to enter by way of the more direct southern route (at Kadesh) and so were judged by God as unworthy to enter at all. The basic travel narratives are found in 9:15–14:45 (from Sinai to Kadesh, including the refusal to enter and the declaration of God's judgment) and 20:1–22:1 (from Kadesh to the plains of Moab along the Jordan).

There are four other major sections of narrative that have slightly different functions: (1) 7:1–9:14 records the preparations for the journey; (2) chapters 16–17 speak to the issue of Moses' and Aaron's God-given (and recognized) leadership; (3) the Balaam cycle (22:2–24:25) and the seduction at Shittim with the Baal of Peor (ch. 25) anticipate both the fulfillment of God's giving them the land and their own capacity nonetheless to be seduced by Canaanite idolatry; (4) chapters 31–36 narrate events on the east bank as they prepare for conquest.

Interspersed among these narratives, but at the same time adding meaning to them, are two census lists (chs. 1–2; 26–27), plus a genealogy/account of Aaron's family and of the Levites (chs. 3–4), as well as several collections of laws (chs. 5–6; 15; 18–19; 28–30), most of them picking up items from the Levitical Code (Lev 1–16; 21–22).

This, then, is what Numbers is all about: the journey to the edge of the promised land and further laws pertaining to proper worship. The question is, Can one make sense of its arrangement as narrative?

SPECIFIC ADVICE FOR READING NUMBERS

In order to appreciate how the narrative of Numbers works (both the journey and the various surrounding matters), you need to recall several items from Genesis and Exodus.

First, the primary driving force behind everything is God's promise/covenant with Abraham that his seed would inherit the land of Canaan. This is what keeps the narrative going in all of its parts. And God will bring about the fulfillment of that covenant promise, even in the face of Israel's reluctance and disobedience.

Second, the conquest of the land involves the second stage of the holy war. The first stage — against Pharaoh in Exodus — even though led by Moses, was carried out by God the Divine Warrior through miraculous intervention. In this second stage, God intends his own people to be involved. He rescued them from slavery in order to make them his own people and place them in the land, but they must take ownership of the actual conquest of the land. This accounts for the two census lists, which count the men who can fight and put the tribes in battle formation around the tabernacle. The list at the beginning (from which Numbers derives its name) prepares the first generation for conquest by way of Kadesh; the second prepares the second generation for conquest by way of the Transjordan. This motif also accounts for the various narratives at the end, including the succession of Joshua (27:12–23) and the various matters in chapters 31–36 that anticipate the conquest.

Third, recall that in Genesis 12:7, immediately following the promise of the land, Abraham built an altar to the Lord. As you now read the various law portions interspersed within this narrative, you will find that they focus primarily on the Israelites' relationship with their God. Thus both the central role of the tabernacle and the priestly matters in Numbers continue to focus on two previous concerns in the Pentateuch to this point: the *presence* of God in the midst of his people—both his being with them and his guiding their journey—and the proper *worship* of God once they are settled in the land.

Finally, God's people themselves do not come off well in Numbers. You can hardly miss the relentless nature of their complaints and disobedience. In fact, apart from the future blessing that God speaks through a pagan prophet, there is hardly a good word about them in the entire narrative. The same complaints against God and his chosen leader Moses that began in Exodus 15:22–17:7—and then some—are repeated here (Num 11–12; 14; 16–17; 20:1–13; 21:4–9). This is simply not fun reading. In the New Testament, the Israelites' disobedience serves as warning for us (1 Cor 10:1–13; cf. Heb 3:7–13); in the Old Testament, even though their sins are expressly remembered, so also is God's "great compassion" on them (Neh 9:16–21; cf. Pss 78:14–39; 106:24–33, 44–46; see also the invitation and warning in Ps 95).

Thus, even though the narrative has some abrupt shifts of focus, Numbers carries on the burden of the Pentateuch in grand style. You are not allowed to forget that, despite Israel's waffling, this is *God's story* above all, and God will keep his part of the covenant with Abraham regarding his seed inheriting the land. At issue is whether Israel will keep covenant with God—and Numbers reminds you over and again that the divine provision for them to do so is always ready at hand.

A WALK THROUGH NUMBERS

☐ 1:1–2:34 *The Census at Sinai*

This introduction to Numbers is in two parts: (1) the census and (2) the arrangement of the tribes around the Tent of Meeting (the place of God's presence). Note that the census is for those "twenty years old or more who were able to serve in the army" (1:3) and that the arrangement of the tribes concludes in each case, "All the men assigned to the camp of ..." These are preparations for their engagement in the holy war; former slaves are being transformed into an army.

☐ 3:1–4:49 *The Account of the Levites*

Observe how this section begins with the narrative theme formula of Genesis ("This is the account of ..."). As you read, recall two things from before: (1) the central role of the Tent of Meeting with its ark of the covenant, the place of God's presence, for the journey to Canaan — and beyond — and (2) in making covenant with Israel at Sinai (where they still are), Yahweh adopted them as a "kingdom of priests and a holy nation" (Exod 19:6). Hence the reason for this material: This is part of what makes them a "kingdom of priests," a nation set apart for God.

☐ 5:1–6:27 *Cleansing the Camp*

Note how this section is structured around the rubric of Leviticus: "The LORD said to Moses" (Num 5:1, 5, 11; 6:1, 22), who in turn is to instruct the people. Remember also their calling to be a "holy nation." Thus the narrative about purifying the camp (5:1–4) is followed by three sets of laws: (1) the restitution of wrongs (5:5–10, they must be in accord with one another); (2) purity/faithfulness in marriage (5:11–31, thus keeping the holy "seed" pure); (3) the Nazirites, lay-people who dedicate themselves to God's service, as special illustrations of Israel's holy calling (6:1–21). The section concludes with the Aaronic blessing (6:22–27), a reaffirmation of God's covenant promise as the Israelites look toward the promised land.

☐ 7:1–9:14 *Final Preparations for Departure*

Notice how 7:1 picks up from Exodus 40:2, so that each part of this section deals with final preparations for their journey. Everything now centers on the tabernacle, the place of sacrifice (worship) and of God's presence. Thus the narrative proceeds from the twelve-day dedication of the altar (Num 7:1–89), through setting up the lamps (8:1–4) and the purification of the Levites (8:5–26), to the celebration of the Passover as they set out (9:1–14; cf. Exod 12).

☐ 9:15–14:45 *From Sinai to Kadesh*

Israel is now ready to go, so observe how this narrative begins: with the reminder from Exodus 40:34–38 of God's presence, symbolized especially by the cloud that would lead them (Num 9:15 – 23), and with the blowing of the trumpets (10:1 – 10). And so they take off in battle formation (10:11 – 28). See also how each day ends: with a call for God the Divine Warrior to lead in battle and to return to Israel (10:35 – 36).

You can hardly miss the emphasis in the rest of the narrative (11:1 – 14:45): Israel complains to God and rejects Moses' leadership. Note how much of this recalls Exodus 15:22 – 18:27 and 32:1 – 34:35, where Israel complains rather than offers praise and gratitude to God and where God gives them what they need but also judges them; Moses' intercession for the people (in Num 14:18, recalling the very words of Exod 34:6 – 7); the seventy elders, who now also anticipate Spirit-empowered prophecy in Israel; God's reaffirmation of Moses' leadership. Note also the crucial roles of Joshua and Caleb (from Ephraim [the northern kingdom] and Judah [the southern kingdom]). Their stories will continue (Num 27:12 – 23; the book of Joshua; Judg 1:1 – 26), as will the roles of the two tribes they represent (1 – 2 Kgs).

☐ **15:1 – 41** *Supplemental Laws*

Since the next generation *will* enter the promised land, this section records God's giving his people laws in anticipation of that time. Note that it includes provisions even for unintentional sins, no matter how the failure occurs. Note also how the death of a Sabbath violator (15:32 – 36) carries forward the theme of covenant obedience both from the beginning of the whole story (Gen 2:1 – 3) and from the beginning of the covenant (Exod 20:8 – 11).

☐ **16:1 – 19:22** *The Crisis over Leadership and Priesthood*

The narrative portion of this section (chs. 16 – 17) has to do with Moses as God's chosen leader and with Aaron as God's chosen high priest. This second matter explains the placement here of the law portion as well (chs. 18 – 19).

☐ **20:1 – 25:17** *From Kadesh to the Plains of Moab*

As you read this next portion of the journey narrative, look for several narrative clues: (1) The deaths of Miriam and Aaron (20:1, 22 – 29) indicate that the forty years are coming to an end and the transition to the next generation is beginning. (2) The refusal of Edom (descendants of Esau, Jacob/Israel's brother) to let Israel pass through their lands marks the beginning of a long history of enmity (see the book of Obadiah). (3) The defeats of the Canaanite king of Arad (21:1–3) and the Amorite kings (21:21–35) mark the beginning of Israel's victories in the holy war and anticipate the book of Joshua; it is of some importance that the first victory (Arad, 21:1–3) eliminates a foe that had defeated them a generation earlier (Num 14:45; cf. Josh 12:14). (4) The Balaam cycle (chs. 22–24) and its sequel — the cultic immorality with the Baal of Peor (Num 25) — both recapitulate the story to this point and anticipate the rest of the Old Testament story. Note especially how the Balaam cycle is told with mockery — and a touch of humor (an ass speaks and Balaam thinks it reasonable to talk back!) and irony, as God uses a pagan prophet(!) to announce God's certain fulfillment of his covenant, even as many in Israel fall prey to cultic prostitution and thus to idolatry.

☐ **26:1–36:13** *In Moab: Preparations for Entry into the Land*

Again, watch for the various narrative clues that give significance to this section and anticipate the actual possession of the land: (1) The second census (ch. 26) reaffirms God's promise that the new generation will indeed enter the promised land, as does the repetition of the stages of the journey in 33:1–49. (2) Various succession and inheritance issues (chs. 27; 32; 34–36) reaffirm God's promise of a long stay in the land, as do (3) the repetition (and enhancement) of the annual cycle of worship festivals (chs. 28–29). (4) The vengeance on the Midianites (ch. 31) anticipates the long story of success and failure in Judges (cf. Num 33:50–56). (5) The sanctity of people and of the land must be preserved (ch. 35), because it is "the land ... where I dwell, for I, the LORD [Yahweh], dwell among the Israelites" (v. 34).

The significant part of Israel's story we find recorded in Numbers had a long history in Israel's memory (Deut 1–4; Neh 9; Pss 78; 105; 106; 135; Acts 7), stressing God's faithfulness to his people despite their many failures, and the story continues to be sung in the Christian church ("Guide Me, O Thou Great Jehovah").

Deuteronomy

ORIENTING DATA FOR DEUTERONOMY

- **Content:** rehearsal of the covenant for a new generation of Israelites just before the conquest

- **Historical coverage:** during the final weeks east of the Jordan

- **Emphases:** the oneness and uniqueness of Yahweh, the God of Israel, over against all other gods; Yahweh's covenant love for Israel in making them his people; Yahweh's universal sovereignty over all peoples; Israel as Yahweh's model for the nations; the significance of the central sanctuary where Yahweh is to be worshiped; Yahweh's concern for justice—that his people reflect his character; the blessings of obedience and the dangers of disobedience

OVERVIEW OF DEUTERONOMY

As with Genesis, two kinds of structure are evident in Deuteronomy at the same time. First, there is a concentric (chiastic) structure to the book, which looks backward at the beginning and forward at the end. Thus:

A   The Outer Frame: A Look Backward (chs. 1–3)
   B   The Inner Frame: The Great Exhortation (chs. 4–11)
      C   The Central Core: The Stipulations of the Covenant (chs. 12–26)
   B* The Inner Frame: The Covenant Ceremony (chs. 27–30)
A* The Outer Frame: A Look Forward (chs. 31–34)

Note how easily you could read each of the two parts of both framing sections as continuous narrative: chapters 1–3 and 31–34; chapters 4–11 and 27–30. The first part of the outer frame (A) repeats the essential narrative of Numbers, up to where Moses is forbidden to enter the land; the second part (A*) picks it up right at that point and concludes with the appointment of Joshua, Moses' song, his blessing, and his death. The inner frame (B), which calls Israel to absolute devotion to God, concludes with the *announcement* that God is setting before them "a blessing and a curse" (11:26); the second part (B*) picks up right at that point by offering the *content* of the curses and blessings.

This insight into how Deuteronomy works also highlights its second structural feature—that Deuteronomy presents this restatement of God's covenant (for the new generation) in the style of an ancient Near Eastern suzerainty treaty-covenant (see "Specific Advice for Reading Exodus," p. 37), with preamble, prologue, stipulations, document clause, sanctions, and witnesses. These last three items both supplement and reiterate the final three elements of the covenant of Exodus 20–Leviticus 27.

Thus, as a restatement of the covenant, Deuteronomy begins with a *preamble* and *historical prologue* (chs. 1–4), which look both to the past and to the future. God has been faithful in the past, rewarding Israel for their faithfulness and likewise punishing them for unfaithfulness. Now they must again commit to being his people. The *stipulations* (chs. 5–26) begin with a restatement of the Ten Commandments, while the laws in chapters 12–26 tend to follow their vertical/horizontal order, having first to do with an individual's relationship with God and then with one another. The *document clauses,* reminders of the terms of the covenant, are found mainly in chapters 27 and 31, joined immediately by a long list of blessings and curses (prose in chs. 28–29 and poetry in 32–33), which serve as the *sanctions* of the covenant. Finally, there are three kinds of *witnesses* to the covenant: "heaven and earth" (4:26; 30:19–20), the song of Moses (31:19; 31:30–32:43), and the words of the law itself (31:26).

On this reading, Moses' death and Joshua's succession to leadership (ch. 34) form a kind of epilogue—not part of the covenant per se, but a narrative that connects Deuteronomy to the book of Joshua that follows.

SPECIFIC ADVICE FOR READING DEUTERONOMY

Deuteronomy has perhaps had more influence on the rest of the biblical story (both Old and New Testaments) than any other book of the Bible. The continuation of Israel's history (Joshua–Kings) is written mostly from its perspective, so that this history portion has come to be called the Deuteronomic History. Deuteronomy likewise had considerable influence on Israel's and Judah's prophets, especially Isaiah and

Jeremiah, and through them deeply influenced the major figures of the New Testament (especially Jesus and Paul).

As you read, you will discover what drives Deuteronomy from beginning to end — an uncompromising monotheism coupled with an equally deep concern for Israel's uncompromising loyalty to Yahweh ("the LORD") their God. This comes out in any number of ways, but its primary moment is in the Shema (6:4–5), which became the distinguishing mark of Judaism and is identified by Jesus as "the first commandment": "Hear, O Israel: The LORD our God, the LORD is one. Love the LORD your God with all your heart and with all your soul and with all your strength." The reason they are to love Yahweh in this way is that he first loved them — when they were slaves and counted for little: "The LORD did not set his affection on you and choose you because you were more numerous than other peoples.... But it was because the LORD loved you and kept the oath he swore to your forefathers that he ... redeemed you from the land of slavery" (7:7–8; cf. 4:37). Thus, everything is predicated on Yahweh's love and faithfulness and his actions that flow out of that love and faithfulness.

This concern in turn accounts for the other distinctive features in the book, three in particular that are closely allied with this first one. Watch for the following:

1. The constant reminder that Israel is about to possess "the land" (a word that occurs more than one hundred times in Deuteronomy). God in his love is about to fulfill the oath he made with Abraham. But the land is currently under the control of the Canaanites.

2. The relentless demand that, when entering the land, Israel not only avoid idolatry but that they completely destroy the places of Canaanite worship as well as the Canaanite peoples. If they do not, Canaanite idolatry will destroy Israel's reason for being. This motif begins in the historical prologue (2:34; 3:6) and continues as a divine demand throughout (7:1–6, 23–26; 12:1–3; 13:6–18; 16:21–17:7; 20:16–18; cf. 31:3). The only hope for Israel to bless the nations (4:6) is for them to obliterate all forms of idolatry and to walk in the ways of the God who redeemed them to be his people (5:32–33).

3. The requirement that they regularly worship at one central sanctuary, "the place the LORD your God will choose as a dwelling for his Name" (12:11). You will recognize this as carrying over the

theme of the presence of God in the tabernacle into their new setting in the promised land. Note how often this theme, which begins in 12:5, is repeated thereafter (12:11, 14, 18, 26; 14:23 – 25; 15:20; 16:2 – 16; 17:8 – 10; 26:2). Yahweh, the one and only God, will dwell among his one people in one place; he is not like the many pagan gods who can be worshiped at many high places throughout the land.

Why are these matters so important? Because the whole biblical story depends on them. At issue is not simply a choice between Yahweh and a Baal — although that too is involved — but syncretism, i.e., thinking that Yahweh can be worshiped in the form of, or alongside, Baal and Ashtoreth (Asherah), the Canaanite fertility gods. Since Yahweh is *one* Lord, not many — as are the pagan gods — he must not be worshiped at the high places where Baal and Ashtoreth were worshiped, and since Yahweh made human beings alone to bear his image (Gen 1:26 – 27) and does not have "form" as such (the second commandment), they must not think that he can be given form in some way by human beings (see especially Deut 4:15 – 20). You will notice how this issue recurs throughout the rest of the story, right through 2 Kings, and continues as a predominant feature in the prophets.

Two final items: God's love for his people in redeeming them and in making them his own, and then in giving them "this good land" (9:6), also lies behind the special nature of the Law Code in Deuteronomy (12:1 – 26:19). Be watching for how the code follows the pattern of the Ten Commandments, beginning with requirements that have to do with loving God (chs. 12 – 13) and continuing with various laws that have to do with sacred days and with loving neighbor (chs. 14 – 26). But note especially how often God's people are required to include "the poor and needy" (see 15:11; 24:14), which in Deuteronomy specifically takes the form of "the alien, the fatherless and the widow," and sometimes includes "the Levite" (26:13). Their common denominator is that they do not own land among a people who will become agrarian in culture. As you read, observe how often these laws are tied either to God's character or to the redemption of Israel.

Finally, don't lose sight of one other important characteristic of Deuteronomy, namely, its forward-looking thrust throughout. This includes not only the immediate generation, which is poised to take possession of the land, but also future generations (4:9, 40). This motif in particular creates tension throughout the book between God's goodness in bringing them into "this good land" and God's awareness that Israel will fail nonetheless. Thus at both the beginning and the end, there are prophecies that the curses will eventually come upon them; their failure to keep covenant will result in loss of the land and in exile (4:25–28; 30:1; see 29:19–28 and 32:15–25), but God's enduring love will result in their being restored to the land through a "second exodus" (4:29–31; 30:2–10; 32:26–27, 36–43). As you read on from here in both the Old Testament and New, you will see how often this theme recurs.

A WALK THROUGH DEUTERONOMY

☐ 1:1–3:29   *Historical Prologue*

You will recognize that most of this prologue is a succinct, carefully designed retelling of the narrative portions of Numbers. Note how the preamble (1:1–5) introduces you to the format of Deuteronomy—a speech of Moses by which God speaks to his people.

The story is recounted in three parts, each with an eye toward the rest of the book: (1) The appointment of leaders, because Moses is not going to enter the land (1:6–18), (2) a reminder of wasted opportunity and rebellion at Kadesh (1:19–46), and (3) a reminder of God's being with them nonetheless and bringing them to where they are now (2:1–3:29).

☐ 4:1–43   *Introduction to the Great Exhortation*

Note how this introduction sets forth the emphases of the rest of the book: God's speaking his covenant directly to the people in the form of the Ten Commandments (vv. 12–14); God's uniqueness, both as to his character and over against idols, which cannot speak or hear (vv. 15–31); God's choice of Israel to be his unique people (vv. 32–38); the prophecy of Israel's eventual failure and restoration (vv. 25–31).

☐ 4:44–11:32   *The Great Exhortation*

Watch now as the themes introduced in 4:1–43 are developed in this eloquent speech. It opens with the Ten Commandments (5:1–21), for this is the code that will be spelled out in chapters 12–26. This is followed by a reminder of Moses' mediatorial role at Horeb/Sinai (5:22–33), but even here the emphasis is on God and his longing for the Israelites' obedience. Then comes the primary commandment of all, namely, that they should love Yahweh their God totally (6:1 – 25), with emphasis on (1) Yahweh's being the only God there is, (2) his redeeming them so as to make them his people, and (3) his gracious gift of the bountiful land. Next comes the Israelites' need to destroy the pagan peoples who now inhabit their promised land so that Israel will not succumb to syncretistic idolatry (7:1 – 26), followed by Moses' urging them not to forget God in the midst of their plenty (8:1 – 20), accompanied by the reminder that the gift of the bountiful land had nothing to do with their own righteousness (9:1 – 6). Indeed, Israel has a history of stubbornness (9:7 – 29). The final section (10:1 – 11:32) anticipates what comes next, reminding the people of the central role of the ark of the covenant and urging that they fear and obey God. The choice is theirs with regard to whether it will be blessing or curse (11:26 – 32).

□ 12:1 – 26:19   *The Deuteronomic Code*

This second giving of the law (*deutero-nomos* = "second law") is the heart of the book of Deuteronomy. Toward the end it is called "this Book of the Law" (28:61; 29:21; 30:10; 31:26), a term picked up five times in Joshua to refer to Deuteronomy (as the covenant-renewal ceremony at Mount Ebal in Josh 8:30 – 35, with its references to Deut 11:29 – 30 and 27:12 – 13, makes clear).

Laws Governing Worship (12:1 – 16:17). Note how the specific law code of Deuteronomy begins: with the future replacement of the tabernacle by a central sanctuary as the place where God will choose to put his Name (12:4 – 32, eventually Jerusalem). This is surrounded by reminders to destroy the idolatrous high places (12:1 – 3) and to avoid every vestige of idolatry (13:1 – 14:2). These are followed by the clean and unclean statutes (14:3 – 21; cf. Lev 11), in this case limited to what the people eat, since this also set Israel apart from surrounding nations. These laws lead to regulations about the tithe of the field's produce and the firstborn of the animals, which are to be eaten at the central sanctuary and shared with the Levites (Deut 14:22 – 29; 15:19 – 23). These latter two laws surround statutes related to caring for the poor (15:1 – 18), which were to be constant reminders of their own deliverance from slavery. Worship includes the annual cycle of feasts, whose regulations also include reminders of the Israelites' redemption and of their need to care for the poor (16:1 – 17).

Laws Governing Leadership (16:18 – 18:22). Note that most of the next series of laws pick up the theme of "leadership after Moses" from the prologue (1:9 – 18). In turn these laws deal with judges (16:18 – 20, 17:8 – 13, which surround another prohibition of idolatry in 16:21 – 17:7), kings (17:14 – 20), priests and Levites (18:1 – 8), and prophets (18:14 – 22), the latter two also surrounding yet another prohibition of idolatrous practices in 18:9 – 13. Note especially the emphasis on social justice on the part of the leaders, who are thus pivotal for the two crucial matters of the people's obedience to God, namely, detesting idolatry and promoting social justice (cf. Isaiah; Hosea; Amos; Micah).

Laws Governing Community Life (19:1 – 25:19). Be sure to notice here that most of the rest of the code deals with matters from the second half of the Ten Commandments and focuses especially on personal and community relationships. Note also how various themes keep reappearing. For example, the laws governing war (20:1 – 20) show special care for men and their families (vv. 5 – 10) and even for trees (vv. 19 – 20), while at the same time repeating the command to destroy idolatrous nations (vv. 10 – 18). Be sure to observe the recurrent concern about social justice, especially caring for the poor and needy.

Conclusion (26:1 – 19). Observe how the specific laws of Deuteronomy end, with reminders of the Israelites' need always to put their God first (firstfruits and tithes, vv. 1 – 15) and with a final injunction to obedience.

☐ **27:1 – 30:20** *The Covenant Ceremony*

As Deuteronomy now returns to the inner frame, recall what was said above (and in Exodus) about suzerainty treaties. Here in sequence you find the *document clause* (27:1 – 8), a picture of how Israel is to preserve the laws for the future, and its *sanctions* in the form of curses and blessings (27:9 – 28:68). The final part of the covenant ceremony contains a concluding charge from Moses, which anticipates Israel's future rebellion and exile, as well as God's restoring them once again to the land (chs. 29 – 30).

☐ **31:1 – 34:12** *The Look Forward*

The conclusion of the outer frame of Deuteronomy is full of anticipations about the future. The larger section (chs. 32 – 33, where you find the poetic expression of covenant sanctions) offers the song of Moses — a prophetic word about future rebellion and restoration — and Moses' blessing of the twelve tribes (cf. Joseph in Gen 49). These are enclosed within the two essential transitional matters: (1) the succession of Joshua, including another prediction of future rebellion (Deut 31), and (2) the death of Moses, with a concluding eulogy (ch. 34). Note Yahweh's charge to Joshua, "Be strong and courageous" (31:23), which is then how the book of Joshua begins (Josh 1:6, 7, 9, 18).

Deuteronomy brings the Pentateuch to a conclusion with its constant reminders of God's love and faithfulness despite his people's constant rebellion, but the final word is one of hope that God will ultimately prevail with his people.

Joshua

ORIENTING DATA FOR JOSHUA

- **Content:** the partial conquest, distribution, and settlement of the promised land

- **Historical coverage:** from the beginning of the conquest to the death of Joshua

- **Emphases:** the engagement of the holy war, as God through his people repeatedly defeats the idolatrous Canaanites; the gift of the land to God's people, thus fulfilling his covenant promise to the patriarchs; Israel's need for continuing covenant faithfulness to the one true God

OVERVIEW OF JOSHUA

Following the five books of Moses, the book of Joshua begins the second large section of the Hebrew Bible known as the Former Prophets (Joshua—2 Kings, apart from Ruth). Later scholarship has called the same group of books the Deuteronomic History. Both designations are full of insight. This section of the Old Testament is intended to be prophetic, in the sense that it records Israel's history with the purpose of instructing and explaining from the divine perspective how and why things went the way they did; they are Deuteronomic in that they tell the story from the very decided point of view of Deuteronomy. Thus, for example, Joshua's farewell speech in chapter 23 repeats language from Moses' farewell exhortation in Deuteronomy 7, but now from the perspective after the conquest; at the same time Joshua calls for obedience to "the Book of the Law of Moses" (Josh 8:31), a term that occurs only in Deuteronomy in the Pentateuch—and will appear again at the end of the Former Prophets in 2 Kings (2 Kgs 14:6; 22:8, 11; cf. 23:2).

Joshua itself tells the story of how a second generation of former slaves succeeded in invading and possessing Canaan, thus inheriting the land that God had promised to Abraham and his seed hundreds of years earlier (Gen 12 and 15). The story is told in four parts:

Chapters 1:1 – 5:12 focus on Israel's *entrance* into the land (with several echoes of the account of Israel's exit from the land of Egypt). After some crucial preparatory matters, the Jordan River is crossed. Accounts of circumcision and the celebration of the Passover (recall Exod 12) bring closure to this part of the story.

Chapters 5:13 – 12:24 tell the story of the (partial) *conquest* of the land. Featured here are the divine overthrow of Jericho (ch. 6) and the defeat at Ai (ch. 7), which are told in detail and serve as the paradigm for what follows — that this is God's holy war, not theirs, and everything is predicated on obedience and loyalty to the covenant with Yahweh. Hence the covenant renewal ceremony (8:30 – 35) immediately follows the taking of Ai (8:1 – 29). Following the Gibeonite deception (ch. 9), which serves as grounds for victory in the south (ch. 10), the rest of the conquest is briefly summarized (chs. 11 – 12).

Chapters 13 – 21 narrate the *distribution* of the land, setting out the administrative organization of Yahweh's earthly kingdom. After repeating the settlement of the eastern tribes (ch. 13; cf. Num 32), the focus is on the tribes that will play the leading roles in the history that follows (Judah, Ephraim; Josh 14 – 17); Benjamin (from whom the first king comes) leads the summation of the rest of the tribes (ch. 18 – 19). It concludes with provision for those who kill unintentionally (ch. 20) and for the Levites, who otherwise do not inherit land (ch. 21).

Chapters 22 – 24 are concerned primarily with Israel's continued loyalty to Yahweh and thus conclude with the *renewing of the covenant* at Shechem (cf. 8:30 – 35).

SPECIFIC ADVICE FOR READING JOSHUA

You will notice that the story in Joshua is told from the perspective of a later time, as the narrator repeatedly mentions certain kinds of memorials that "are there to this day" (4:9; 5:9; 7:26; 8:28 – 29; 10:27), as are many of the Canaanite peoples (13:13; 15:63; 16:10). The former serve as reminders of God's faithfulness in the past, the latter as reminders of what had not been done.

Both the structure of the book and God's opening words to Joshua (1:2 – 9) reveal the three major concerns. First, there is the engagement in the holy war. Notice how the emphasis is always on God's initiative and participation ("I will be with you," 1:5). Thus the opening battle (Jericho) is God's alone; after that, the Israelites are themselves militarily involved, but always with God fighting for them (8:1; 10:14; 23:10); as David would put it later, "the battle is the LORD's" (1 Sam 17:47). This is God's holy war, not just to give Israel the land, but especially to rid the land of idolatry (false gods)—all of this so that Yahweh will dwell as King among a people who are to reflect his likeness and follow his ways. In this regard be watching also for the several instances when the author speaks of the gift of "rest" following the holy war (Josh 1:13, 15; 14:15; 21:44; 22:4; 23:1), a theme picked up negatively in Psalm 95:11 regarding the wilderness generation and then in Hebrews 4:1–11 as warning and assurance.

Second, even though chapters 13–21 are not a good read as such, they are profoundly important to the story, for here at last is the fulfilling of God's promise to Abraham and to his seed that they would one day inherit this very land. It was to be their special territory precisely so that here God could develop a people who, by honoring and serving Yahweh, would bless the nations.

Third, and most important, everything has to do with the Israelites' covenant loyalty to the one God. This is the key element in the opening address to Joshua ("Do not let this Book of the Law depart from your mouth; meditate on it day and night, so that you may be careful to do everything written in it," 1:8). This is the central factor in the defeat at Ai (7:11, 15). It also accounts for the early insertion of the covenant renewal at Mount Ebal (8:30–35) and for the final covenant renewal at Shechem with which the narrative concludes (24:1–27).

You will readily see how much all of this picks up and carries on the concerns of Deuteronomy: God's war against false gods; God's promise of the land; and the concern for loyalty to the one true God against all forms of idolatry.

Two further things might help you to read Joshua well. First, read with helpful maps in hand (such as those found in Marten Woudstra's commentary on Joshua [see *How to 1*, p. 269]). This will give you a good sense of the geography mentioned throughout.

Second, it may help you to know that, at the time of Israel's invasion, Canaan was not occupied by a superpower, as it had been earlier by the Egyptians and Hittites. Thus, Israel did not have to face that kind of powerful opposition. Rather, the land was organized in the form of city-states, so that each major city and its surrounding villages had its own king, each of whom was politically independent. Such an arrangement meant that the Israelites, though a small people themselves, could fight each state or small grouping of states (9:1–2; 10:5–27; 11:1–9) separately and thus gradually possess much of the land.

A WALK THROUGH JOSHUA

☐ **1:1–18** *Introduction*

This chapter introduces all the main themes: God as the protagonist of the story; the call of Joshua and recognition of his role as true successor to Moses; that Joshua would lead the people to inherit the land God had promised to their ancestors; and the central concern for covenant loyalty. Note Yahweh's repeated exhortation to Joshua to "be strong and courageous" (vv. 6, 7, 9), repeated at the end of the chapter by the people (v. 18) and by Joshua to the army at the beginning of the southern campaign (10:25). Note also the beginning of the theme of "rest" (1:13, 15).

☐ **2:1–5:12** *Preparation for and Entrance into the Promised Land*

Look for the ways the several narratives of these chapters describe the preparation of the people for the conquest of the land. The first is military (ch. 2): sending spies to Jericho, who, protected by Rahab, learn of the dread their previous victories (Num 21:21–35) have aroused in the people. The second is the miraculous crossing of the Jordan (Josh 3–4), which echoes the previous crossing of the Red Sea during the exodus. The final two are spiritual: the renewal of the rite of circumcision and the celebration of the Passover. Israel can only possess the land as a circumcised people (recall Gen 17:9–14), with the "reproach of Egypt" removed (Josh 5:9), and Passover can now be celebrated again (after a hiatus of 39 years; see Exod 12:25 and Num 9:1–14) as the gift of manna ceases (Josh 5:10–12).

Take note also of the significant role that Gilgal will play in the rest of the conquest (5:9; 9:6; ch. 10); later it becomes one of Israel's sacred sites (1 Sam 7:16; 11:14) and eventually a place of syncretistic idolatry (Hos 4:15; 9:15; 12:11; Amos 4:4; 5:5).

☐ **5:13–8:35** *Jericho and Ai*

Note especially how the conquest begins—with Joshua's encounter with "the commander of the LORD's army" (Josh 5:13–15). Already on the scene to take charge of the conquest, he is Joshua's (and Israel's) assurance that Yahweh's heavenly army is committed to the conquest—a conquest of which Joshua and his army are the earthly contingent. This item is full of echoes of—and significant contrasts with—Moses' encounter with Yahweh in the burning bush (Exod 3:1–4:17).

Observe how closely linked the two stories of Jericho and Ai are, both in the present narrative and beyond (Josh 9:3; 10:1). Together they disclose the conditions under which Israel can conquer and then retain possession of the land. Don't miss the important features of the well-known account of the fall of Jericho—that it is God's victory altogether; that, except for the trumpets, the role of Israel's army is quite nonmilitary; that it is the firstfruits of victory, and therefore everything in the city belongs to God (the city itself is burned as a thing "devoted ... to the LORD," 6:21; its precious stones and metals will go into the Lord's house); and that Rahab and her family are spared because she had confessed that the future belongs to Yahweh (2:8–13).

The first part of the Ai story (ch. 7) picks up the theme of the "devoted things" from chapter 6, focusing on Israel's defeat because of one man's covenant disobedience (7:11, 15; cf. 22:18–20). Note the significance of Achan, a man from Judah whose story may be read against the background of the account of Rahab the harlot (Achan and his family lose all inheritance in the land, while Rahab the foreigner and her family gain inheritance).

The second part of the Ai story (ch. 8) then narrates how God enabled Israel through a shrewd military stratagem to defeat and destroy Ai. These two decisive victories at the point of entry, one miraculous and one through human instrumentality—and told in detail as they are—suggest to the reader how to understand the rest of the stories that are not told in detail. So at this point the narrator includes the covenant renewal at Mount Ebal (8:30–35; see Deut 27:4–8).

□ 9:1–10:43   *The Gibeonite Ruse and Its Consequences*

The first account after the covenant-renewal ceremony is another breach of the covenant, this time by Joshua himself, who "did not inquire of the LORD" (9:14); note that the Gibeonites are Hivites (9:7; 11:19), who are one of the seven Canaanite people groups who are to be utterly destroyed (9:1; cf. Deut 7:1–2). Nonetheless, their deception leads directly to the defeat of the five "kings of the Amorites," who intend to subdue Gibeon but are then defeated (Josh 10:1–28). This in turn leads to the narrative of the conquest of the southern city-states (vv. 29–43); note that the army immediately heads for the cities of the kings who have been killed.

☐ 11:1–12:24   *The Northern Conquest and Summary of Defeated Kings*

Here as before, the defeat of the southern kings leads in turn to the defeat of many in the north (ch. 11). Then chapter 12 summarizes all the kings and their city-states that were destroyed.

☐ 13:1–21:45   *The Distribution of the Land*

Although this part of Joshua is not exciting reading, you need to be aware of its importance for the rest of the biblical story. For here is the actual fulfillment of the gift of the land made to Abraham and his seed. But observe especially the importance given to certain parts of the narrative— both by placement and by the amount of space devoted to them.

The account begins with a reminder of what still needs to be done (13:1–7), which becomes important for reading both Judges and 2 Samuel 5 and 8, where David finally succeeds in subduing these peoples. After repeating the allotment given to Gad, Reuben, and half of Manasseh (13:8–32; cf. Num 32), the focus is first of all on Caleb and the tribe of Judah (chs. 14–15) and then on the two tribes of Joseph (Ephraim and half of Manasseh, Josh 16–17). Note that a clear break (18:1–2), highlighted by the appearance of the Tent of Meeting at Shiloh, separates these allotments from the rest that follow (18:3–19:48); observe further that these latter begin with Benjamin, which includes Jerusalem (18:28), even though it has not yet been conquered. The distribution narrative itself concludes with Joshua's allotment (19:49–51) so that Caleb and Joshua bookend this narrative (see comments on Num 9:15–14:45, p.53).

Appended to the distribution narrative are two other very important land matters: provision for unintentional killing (ch. 20) and for the Levites (ch. 21). Note how these repeat Numbers 35, but in reverse order and by condensing the one and expanding the other.

☐ 22:1–24:33   *Epilogue*

The three chapters that conclude Joshua have loyalty to God and the covenant as their common denominator. The near outbreak of war over an altar built by the eastern tribes had to do with fear that they had broken faith with the God of Israel (22:16). The two farewell addresses by Joshua have covenant loyalty as their singular theme. Observe how much these speeches reemphasize the concerns of Deuteronomy.

The book concludes on the encouraging note that not only Joshua and Eleazar are buried in the promised land, but that the bones of Joseph, first buried in Egypt (Gen 50:26; cf. Exod 13:19), are also reinterred at Shechem, in the tribal lands of Joseph's son Ephraim. And so God keeps covenant with his people! Unfortunately, the next chapter in the story (Judges) tells of Israel repeatedly breaking covenant with God.

Joshua contributes to God's story of redemption by bringing closure to the covenant promise of the land made in Genesis (and throughout the Pentateuch), thus setting the stage for the next phases of the story.

Judges

ORIENTING DATA FOR JUDGES

- **Content:** the cyclical narrative of the time of the judges, with emphasis on Israel's repeated lack of covenant loyalty

- **Historical coverage:** from the death of Joshua to the beginning of the monarchy

- **Emphases:** the tenuous results of the conquest; God's constant rescue of his people, despite their habitual failure to keep covenant with him; the desperate conditions and overall downward spiral during this period; the need for a good king

OVERVIEW OF JUDGES

The book of Judges, which tells the story of Israel between Joshua and the beginning of the kingship (1 Samuel), is a carefully composed narrative in three essential parts:

1:1–3:6	Introduction: An "overture" setting forth the main themes
3:7–16:31	Main Narrative Cycle: A series of "variations" on the themes
17:1–21:25	Epilogue: A "coda" illustrating the primary theme

As you read, be looking for the ways these various parts interplay with each other so that the whole narrative presents a vivid picture of the times, concluding with the repeated refrain that much of this is related to Israel's not having a king.

The introduction is in two parts. Part 1 (1:1–2:5), which picks up and enhances some of the conquest narrative from Joshua, has two emphases, both found in the conclusion (2:1–5)—(1) that God did not break covenant with Israel, but that they broke covenant with him by not driving out the Canaanites (1:21, 27–36), and (2) that God will no longer come to their aid in this cause; instead, the Canaanites "will be thorns in your sides and their gods will be a snare to you" (2:3). Thus this part gives the basic reason for what follows.

Part 2 (2:6–3:6) rehearses in summary form how the narrative will unfold. Here the basic Deuteronomic cycle is introduced:

1. Israel does evil in the eyes of Yahweh by serving the Canaanite Baals (2:11–13).
2. They experience Yahweh's anger in the form of failure in battle and oppression by their enemies (vv. 14–15).
3. The people cry out in their distress, and God rescues them by sending a judge-deliverer (vv. 16, 18).
4. When the judge dies, the cycle begins all over again (vv. 17, 19–23).

You will notice that the epilogue is also in two parts, giving in gruesome detail case studies of Israel's syncretism and failure to keep covenant with their God.

Between these two framing sections lies the main narrative itself, in which the cycle is repeated again and again, but with the emphasis on the stories of deliverance. Common to these stories is that God stands behind all deliverance, even though the deliverers themselves are seldom shining examples of devotion to Yahweh!

This central series appears to be carefully constructed, presenting twelve "judges" corresponding to the number of Israelite tribes. It begins with Othniel, whose story is told only in summary and as a pattern for the rest. This is followed by the exploits of five judges (Ehud, Deborah/Barak, Gideon/Abimelech, Jephthah, and Samson), interspersed with what amounts to a list of other such judge-deliverers (Shamgar, Tola, Jair, Ibzan, Elon, Abdon). This series is framed by accounts of two loners (Ehud, a Benjamite; Samson, a Danite). In the inner frame of stories (Deborah/Barak, Jephthah) deliverance is dependent on a woman and an outcast/outlaw. At the center is the account of Gideon and his son Abimelech (whose name means "father of the king"), and here surface the two central issues in the narrative: Who is the true God? Who is Israel's king? The narratives of Samuel and Kings pick it up from there.

SPECIFIC ADVICE FOR READING JUDGES

So that you keep focused as you read Judges, you need to know three things in advance. First, the word traditionally translated "judges" (*shophetim*) does not in this book refer primarily to judicial officials (although the word does carry that sense; see, e.g., Exod 18:13). Rather they were military leaders and clan chieftains whom God used to deliver Israel from enemies who threatened parts of Israel over a long period of time. Hence the NIV compromises by translating the noun in the traditional way, but uses "lead/led" for the verb.

Second, even though such terms as "led Israel" and "the Israelites" regularly appear, you should not imagine that each (or any) of these judges was the leader of all Israel in the same sense that Moses and Joshua were. In fact, as the stories unfold, you will recognize that part of the concern of the narrator is that precisely the opposite is true—that one or several tribes are oppressed and call on other tribes for help, which sometimes comes and sometimes doesn't, often resulting in intertribal strife. The irony of the narrative is that only at the end, in a case of intertribal disciplinary warfare, are all twelve tribes "united," as it were. Note, for example, the stinging words in Deborah's song about Reuben (5:15–16), who in a time of crisis and after "much searching of heart" stayed home "to hear the whistling for the flocks."

Third, and related to this, is the matter of overall chronology. You will note that chronological language is frequently employed ("after the time of ..." and "the land had peace for ... years") and that the overall scheme reflects the history of the times, beginning with sporadic oppression (Moab in the east) and concluding with Philistine oppression, which is where the Samuel narrative picks up. Even so, you should not think of all of this as happening in chronological order. Peace in one place does not mean peace in another. And the parenthetical note in 20:27–28 sets that story very early on in the period (the priest at Bethel is Aaron's grandson). The point is that the narrator is not as interested in a time line as such, as in the overall picture of the times he is portraying.

But the one chronological matter that is crucial to his narrative is the gradual but unrelenting deterioration of things in Israel down to the time of Samuel. This is portrayed first of all by the structure itself, with its concluding stories in chapters 17–21. It is also reflected in the portrayal of the six major judges. The portrayals of Othniel, Ehud, and Deborah are basically positive, despite some subterfuge on the part of Ehud and Jael (4:18–21). But beginning with Gideon, things begin to tilt. The Gideon story begins well, but turns out badly in the form of an idolatrous ephod (8:24–27) and a murderous son, Abimelech (ch. 9). The Jephthah and Samson stories paint a picture of God's Spirit using less than exemplary leaders. Another way this theme is carried through is the use of "in the eyes of." Watch how each of the cycle stories begins: "Again the Israelites did evil in the eyes of the LORD." At the end we are told what this means: "In those days there was no king in Israel; all the people did what was right in their own eyes" (17:6; 21:25 [NRSV]). The hinge point of this theme is an idiom that is usually expressed differently in English translation, where Samson rebelliously desires a young Philistine as his wife because (literally) "she is right in my eyes" (14:3, 7).

Yet despite all this, God's care for his people holds the story together. This is especially discernible in the repeated notice that "the Spirit of the LORD [Yahweh]"—mentioned in the opening Othniel story but absent in the Ehud and Deborah episodes—does come upon Gideon (6:34), Jephthah (11:29), and Samson (13:25; 14:6, 19; 15:14). Even so, what is noticeably absent from Judges is any mention of, or even any sense of, the presence of the Lord in the midst of his people. The Tent of Meeting that Joshua set up at Shiloh (Josh 18:1) reappears there in 1 Samuel 2:22. In Judges we are told that the idolatry of the tribe of Dan continues "all the time the house of God was in Shiloh" (18:31), but Israel never consults with Yahweh there to hear from him. Israel is a people who have lost their way and their primary identity, and only God in mercy can bring order to this chaos.

A WALK THROUGH JUDGES

☐ 1:1–2:5 *The Basic Problem: Failure to Destroy the Canaanites*

Watch for the narrator's purposes to unfold. After a review of some victories in the south, led by Judah (1:1–18), he notes Israel's failure to dislodge all the Canaanites (1:19–21). The same thing happens again in the north—victory at Bethel (1:22–26), but mostly failure (1:27–36). This failure is then denounced as an act of disobedience (2:1–5), so God will now leave Canaanites in the land as thorns in Israel's sides. And this means that the Canaanite gods "will be a snare" to them (2:3).

☐ 2:6–3:6 *The Pattern Established*

In 2:6–19 you encounter the Deuteronomic cycle, which sets the pattern for the rest of the book: The people stop serving Yahweh; he abandons them to their enemies; they suffer subjugation; they pray for help; God's Spirit comes on a person who leads them to defeat their enemies; they then become complacent and repeat the cycle. Note that the rest of this introduction (2:20–3:6) picks up the theme from 2:1–5, but now indicating that God himself has left the hostile nations within and on the outskirts of the promised land to trouble the Israelites.

☐ 3:7–11 *Othniel (from Judah/against the Arameans)*

Note that in this initial judge episode, the cycle (2:6–19) is fully represented: Israel abandons God (v. 7), incurring his anger and their subjugation to the Arameans (v. 8); this results eventually in prayers for help that cause God to send a deliverer (v. 9). The "Spirit of the LORD" then gives Othniel the wisdom to lead, so that "the land had peace" (v. 11).

☐ 3:12–31 *Ehud (from Benjamin/against the Moabites) and Shamgar*

"Once again the Israelites did evil in the eyes of the LORD," which leads to their subjugation to a (very fat) Moabite king. Note how his obesity and Ehud's being left-handed are the intrigue on which the story turns. Although this is basically the story of a loner, Ehud nonetheless prepares the way for an Israelite victory (vv. 26–30). The Spirit is not mentioned here, but "the LORD" is nonetheless responsible for the victory (3:28). The appended report about Shamgar (3:31) introduces the Philistines, who later become Israel's worst foreign foe.

☐ 4:1–5:31 *Deborah (from Ephraim/against Northern Canaanites)*

The intrigue of this story is its focus on two women, Deborah and Jael, who overshadow the actual "deliverer," Barak. Note that Deborah initiates the action in the name of the Lord, and that Barak's refusal to go to battle without her leads to the prophecy that the Lord will hand over Sisera to a woman—but the woman turns out not to be Deborah but Jael! Deborah's song (see 5:7, also sung by Barak, 5:1) retells the story with some added detail, while it praises God and shames the tribes that did not help.

☐ 6:1 – 10:5 Gideon (from Benjamin/against the Midianites and Amalekites) and Tola and Jair

Notice how in this case the narrator fills out the various parts of the cycle in more detail than before. As always it begins with, "Again the Israelites did evil in the eyes of the LORD" (6:1). The oppression is from hordes of easterners, led by Midian and Amalek, and is particularly desperate (6:2 – 6) so that Israel cries out to God, who again reminds them that they have broken covenant with him (6:7 – 10). But the greatest elaboration is with the deliverer and the tale of victory. As you read, watch for signs of the book's downward-spiral motif within the narrative itself.

Gideon is portrayed as fearful and diffident (6:11 – 19), obedient but doubting (6:20 – 40). He starts well — by tearing down the altar of Baal (6:24 – 32) and "leading" a decisive, God-orchestrated victory over Midian (ch. 7). But then a quite different Gideon pursues Zebah and Zalmunna (8:1 – 18); nonetheless, even though his zeal represents something of a personal vendetta over the death of his brothers (8:19 – 21), he is still pictured as carrying on the holy war. But he ends up making an ephod that becomes idolatrous, and his son Abimelech is thoroughly degenerate.

Key to this episode is the demand of the Israelites that Gideon rule over them (8:22), which he rejects — a rejection that includes his sons — in favor of the rule of Yahweh (v. 23). Note how the story hits a low point with Gideon's son, Abimelech, who makes himself a king after killing all but one of his seventy brothers. But also note the irony: An unnamed woman kills him with a dropped millstone (9:50 – 53). Israel is thus delivered from one of her own! The notices about Tola (10:1 – 2) and Jair (vv. 3 – 5), who represent Issachar (and Ephraim) and Gilead (eastern Manasseh), conclude the Gideon cycle and prepare the way for Jephthah. By so briefly mentioning Tola and Jair, the narrator reminds you that his stories are purposely selective rather than exhaustive accounts of all that transpired.

☐ 10:6 – 12:14 Jephthah (from Eastern Manasseh/against the Ammonites) and Ibzan, Elon, and Abdon

The downward spiral continues. Jephthah is something of a successful outlaw (11:3 – 6) at the time his fellow Gileadites appeal to him for help against the Ammonites. He is pictured as rash and self-centered, a man for whom a vow is more important than a daughter. He is successful in battle because the Spirit of the Lord was upon him (11:29), but he is also responsible for the deaths of thousands of Israelites (12:1–6). The accounts of Ibzan, Elon, and Abdon (12:8–15) are apparently the author's brief reminders that God continued to work through judges in various locales.

☐ 13:1–16:31   *Samson (from Dan/against the Philistines)*

This final cycle story is the most tragic—and ambiguous—of all. Samson in his own person represents all that is wrong in Israel during the period of the judges: born of a barren woman, dedicated to be Yahweh's special servant from birth (ch. 13), unbeatable when the Spirit of Yahweh is with him—but he breaks his vows (see comments on Num 5:1–6:27, p. 52) by getting honey from a dead (Philistine) lion, by marrying a foreigner (Judg 14), and by dallying with a prostitute (ch. 16). Note how all of these mirror Israel's own story of prostitution with the Baals and Ashtoreths. Nonetheless the Spirit of God continues to come on him to defeat small groups of Philistines. Blind and imprisoned, Samson is enabled by God to kill a temple full of Philistines, as he himself dies in the process (16:23–30). This narrative also sets the stage for the long struggle with the Philistines that marks the Saul and David stories that are to come, but more immediately it serves as a transition from the sins of Israel as a people to the sins of individuals narrated in chapters 17–21.

☐ 17:1–21:25   *Two Stories Illustrating Israel's Degeneracy*

Note how this conclusion is carefully crafted around the phrase, "In those days Israel had no king; everyone did as [they] saw fit [what was right in their own eyes]" (17:6; 21:25; cf. 18:1; 19:1). With these words the narrator gives you the perspective from which the whole story has been told: Israel is in disarray; it has no central leadership—and no accepted central sanctuary, as had been commanded in Deuteronomy.

Thus, the first episode (ch. 17) in the first story illustrates Israel's syncretism (Micah's mother consecrates her silver to Yahweh for her son to make an idol), while the second (ch. 18) illustrates both the Danite context out of which Samson came and the unsettled conditions in Israel due to the failure of conquest with which the book began. Both episodes illustrate the failure of true worship in Israel.

The gruesome nature of the second story (chs. 19–21) illustrates both the depth of Israel's remembered moral decay (see Hos 9:9–10) and the reality that she teeters regularly on the brink of intertribal war. Israel needs God's appointed king.

The tragic pattern in Judges points to the next phase of God's great story of redemption, which will begin to move forward considerably through the stories of Ruth and of her great-grandson David.

Ruth

ORIENTING DATA FOR RUTH

- **Content:** a story of loyalty to Yahweh during the period of the judges, in which Naomi's fortunes mirror Israel's during this period (while also providing the lineage of King David)

- **Historical coverage:** a few years around 1100 B.C.

- **Emphases:** life in a village that remains loyal to Yahweh during the time of the judges; the welcoming of a foreign woman under Yahweh's wings; God's superintending care that provides Israel with its great king

OVERVIEW OF RUTH

What a relief to find Ruth after Judges! Indeed, here in bold relief is another story from the same period, about one good man and two good women, not to mention a whole community, who are portrayed as faithful to the covenant. Although the book of Ruth (along with Esther) appears among the Writings in the Hebrew canon, in the Greek Bible—used by the Christian tradition—Ruth was placed between Judges and 1 Samuel, almost certainly because of the way it begins ("In the days when the judges ruled") and ends ("Obed [was] the father of Jesse, and Jesse the father of David"). You will see how perceptive that move was.

The book of Ruth is sometimes treated as a love story—and in some ways it is indeed a love story, but not a romance. Yahweh's love for Israel here finds expression in Ruth's and Boaz's loving concern for Naomi, and in Boaz's for Naomi and Ruth. Although the heart of the story features the actions of Ruth and Boaz, the central figure throughout is Naomi, as the prologue (1:1–5) and epilogue (4:13–17) make clear. The narrative plot deals with Naomi's moving from "emptiness" in a foreign land to "fullness" back home in Bethlehem in Judah, from a form of barrenness (widowhood with no male heir) to full inheritance through

Boaz's assuming the responsibilities of kinsman-redeemer and, through his marriage to Ruth, providing her with a male heir—and what an heir he turned out to be!

The story is told in four scenes, each employing an opening thematic sentence and each, except for the last, containing a closing sentence that sets up the reader for the next scene. In turn the scenes depict Naomi's emptiness (1:6–22), her awakened hope (ch. 2), the progress toward fulfillment (ch. 3), and fullness realized in the birth of an heir (ch. 4).

And how does fullness come? Through Ruth, a young Moabite widow, and Boaz, the established, wealthy, upstanding man of Judah—extremes on the sociological scale—who both act toward the needy one (Naomi) in the way that is open to them and without considering their own benefit, and both risking all to do so. Indeed, the role played by their two foils (Orpah and the other kinsman) highlights the risk factor for each.

SPECIFIC ADVICE FOR READING RUTH

In telling this story as he does, the narrator probably intends the reader to see here a comparison with Israel as a whole during the time of the judges (1:1). In a time of famine, the family of Elimelech seeks life away from Yahweh's promised land in the land of Moab, only to find death and emptiness. By returning home—to Bethlehem, the "house of bread" with its abundant harvest—the one whose name means "sweet" but calls herself "bitter" (1:20) starts on a journey from hope to fulfillment, to having a "son" who will serve as her ultimate kinsman-redeemer. And in so doing, she sets in motion events that will lead to Israel's receiving their foremost king. You can hardly miss the final blessing of Naomi by the women of Bethlehem in 4:14: "May he become famous throughout Israel!" Indeed!

In this regard it is important that you also watch how both the town of Bethlehem in general and the three main characters in particular are portrayed as loyal to Yahweh and the covenant, and thus experience the covenant blessings (see esp. Deut 28:3–6) during "the days when the judges ruled" (1:1). This comes out in a variety of ways: Ruth's determination to follow Yahweh because of her relationship with Naomi (1:16–18); the greetings of Boaz and the harvesters, reflecting God's presence and blessing (2:4); Boaz's welcoming of Ruth, who has chosen to take refuge under the wings of Yahweh (2:12); Boaz's own generosity and largeheartedness (2:8–9, 14–18); and Naomi's "blessing" of Boaz (2:20).

But this theme is especially evident in the way the narrator weaves into the story indications of their obedience to the covenant law — gleanings left for an alien; the kinsman-redeemer; inheritance through the covenant marriage-inheritance laws. The narrator assumes his readers will recognize all these covenantal factors. These are not people who need to be portrayed as consulting the law for guidance on what to do; rather they are simply demonstrating their covenant loyalty to Yahweh by the way they live and treat people. The author seems concerned in the end to show that David's forebears were themselves faithful Yahwists in a time when much of Israel was not.

Note finally how Ruth herself becomes an example of the blessing of Abraham working out in practice (Gen 12:3, "all peoples on earth will be blessed through you"). She is an alien from a hated foreign nation (Deut 23:3). Yet she chooses to follow Israel's God and thus becomes part of his people (Ruth 1:16–17); as such she herself loves Naomi (4:15) by showing Yahweh's kindness (2:11–12) to one who has experienced exile and bitterness (1:19–21). In turn she is blessed by Boaz as one who has chosen to come under Yahweh's care and blessing (2:12); and at the end Yahweh thus "enabled her to conceive" (4:13). Though a foreigner without the covenant history enjoyed by the other Israelites, she nonetheless shows covenant love and loyalty in a way that most Israelites did not at this time in history. She, a non-Israelite, is used as an example to Yahweh's own "firstborn" (see Exod 4:22). Thus she is one of four Gentile women included in Matthew's genealogy (Matt 1:5b; cf. vv. 3, 5a, 6), which in his Gospel anticipates the gospel as good news for "all nations" (Matt 28:19).

A WALK THROUGH RUTH

☐ **1:1–5 *Prologue***

Note how the narrator sets up the whole story with this prologue. Because of famine, Elimelech and Naomi and sons leave Yahweh's land for Moab; Naomi ends up in exile in a foreign land, destitute, without husband or sons.

☐ **1:6–22 *Scene 1: Naomi and Ruth —***
                 Grief, Loyalty, and Conversion

With the opening sentence (v. 6), the narrator sets the stage for this first scene: Naomi's determination to go back to Bethlehem. You will recognize that the heart of this opening scene is Ruth's determination to remain loyal to her mother-in-law and thus to convert and become a true Yahwist herself. Note how the final sentence (v. 22) sets the stage for the next scene.

☐ **2:1 – 23   Scene 2: Ruth, Boaz, and Naomi — Surprising Kindness**

Watch for the buildup of anticipation as this chapter unfolds. You are introduced to Boaz (v. 1) and to Ruth's initiative (v. 2), who "as it turned out" [!] gleans in Boaz's fields (v. 3). Then it is Boaz's turn to show kindness (vv. 4–17): He blesses Ruth in Yahweh's name for her kindness to Naomi (v. 12), she works and eats with the harvesters under his protection (vv. 9, 14), and her gleanings become greater by design (vv. 15–16). Notice also how toward the end Naomi blesses Boaz (vv. 19–20) for his kindness to Ruth, and through Ruth to herself. With a final sentence (v. 23) the narrator moves on to the end of harvest to set you up for what happens next.

☐ **3:1 – 18   Scene 3: Naomi, Ruth, and Boaz —
Ruth Petitions Marriage**

Naomi now takes the lead — on the obvious, and correct, assumption of Boaz's goodness — while Ruth carries out the plan (vv. 1–9). Her action in verse 9 invites Boaz to become Naomi's kinsman-redeemer and thus to take Ruth as his wife. Boaz accepts, but the law requires that he offer her first to one who is more qualified (vv. 10–12). Note how carefully the author portrays Boaz as a man of moral nobility, just as he did with Ruth in the former scene. Again, the last sentence (v. 18) sets up the final scene.

☐ **4:1 – 22   Scene 4: Boaz, Ruth, and Naomi ... and David —
Marriage and a Son**

Following ancient custom in Israelite towns, the matter is decided between Boaz and his kin in the presence of the town elders at the town gate. Boaz risks, as Ruth had risked earlier. So Boaz marries Ruth; Naomi has an heir — "bitter" becomes "sweet" again (see comment on p. 79) — and eventually Israel gets her premier king.

The book of Ruth tells the story of God's faithfulness to his people in a specific case, as a Moabite woman becomes part of his story of redemption.

1 and 2 Samuel

ORIENTING DATA FOR 1 AND 2 SAMUEL

- **Content:** the transition from the last judge, Samuel, to the first king, Saul; the rise and reign of David

- **Historical coverage:** from Samuel's birth (ca. 1100 B.C.) to the end of David's kingship (970 B.C.)

- **Emphases:** the beginning of kingship in Israel; the concern over kingship and covenant loyalty; the ark of the covenant as representing God's presence; the choice of Jerusalem as "the City of David"; the Davidic covenant with its messianic overtones; David's adultery and its consequences

OVERVIEW OF 1 AND 2 SAMUEL

The books of Samuel and Kings together form a continuous history of the Israelite monarchy from the time of Samuel to its demise in 587/6 B.C. It is important as you read them to remember that in the Hebrew Bible they belong to the Former Prophets. Like the books of the Latter Prophets, these books present God's perspective on the history of his people; although they concentrate on Israel's kings, prophets play an important role as well.

The book of Samuel tells the story from the beginnings of kingship to the declining years of David's reign. The story centers on three key people: *Samuel,* the last of the judges and the prophet who anoints the first two kings; *Saul,* Israel's first king; and *David,* Israel's most important king. The book itself is in four basic parts, related to these three men.

Part 1 is about Samuel alone (1 Sam 1–7). Essential here are the birth, call, and early career of Samuel (1:1–4:1a) and the loss and return of the ark of the covenant (4:1b–7:1), followed eventually by a great victory over the Philistines (7:2–14).

In part 2 (1 Sam 8–15), Samuel and Saul overlap. Two matters are essential here: (1) Yahweh's affirmations of and warnings about the monarchy (chs. 8–12; cf. Deut 17:14–20) and (2) the beginning of Saul's reign and Yahweh's rejection of him as king (1 Sam 13–15).

In part 3 (1 Sam 16–31), Saul and David overlap. Its essential story is told at the beginning and the end: the anointing of David to replace Saul as king (16:1–13) and the death of Saul and his heir apparent, Jonathan (ch. 31). Thus it is all about David's rise and Saul's decline, as well as Saul's constant pursuit of David in order to kill the upstart rival to his dynasty.

Part 4 (2 Samuel) concentrates on David—although concern over Saul continues (chs. 1–4; 9; 21)—while Nathan (chs. 7, 12) and Gad (ch. 24) now don the prophetic mantle of Samuel. Chapters 1–9 set out the basic story of David's reign, the most significant part of which is the covenant in chapter 7 that establishes David's dynasty "forever" (vv. 15–16). Chapters 10–20 narrate David's sin with Bathsheba that becomes a catalyst to expose the internal weaknesses in David's family and the tenuous nature of the united kingdom. Chapters 21–24 are a kind of reflective appendix to the story of David.

SPECIFIC ADVICE FOR READING 1 AND 2 SAMUEL

The book of Samuel is full of many intriguing and riveting individual stories. But this very fact, which makes reading Samuel so interesting, can also cause you to miss some significant things with regard to the bigger picture of the story of Israel. To read Samuel well, you need to be aware of a few of these, especially some Deuteronomic themes that pervade the whole.

The history itself takes place roughly over the eleventh century B.C., a time when no superpower is a major player in Palestine (see "Specific Advice for Reading Joshua," p. 65). Thus the time was ripe for a strong local power to arise and subdue the others, which was precisely what David did (see 2 Sam 8). The major obstacle to such a program came not from the Canaanites but from the Philistines, whom you first meet in the book of Judges (Shamgar, Samson). They were sea peoples who had settled on the Mediterranean coast and held sway over the coastal area (and often further inland) from their five major cities (Gaza, Ashdod, Ashkelon, Gath, and Ekron). It is their influence that pushes the Israelite tribes toward the unification and protection afforded by the monarchy, and it is their presence that lies behind so much of the story of the book of Samuel, until David defeats them "in the course of time" (2 Sam 8:1).

The book of Samuel, therefore, is especially the story of transitions—from the periodic, partial rule of judges to an institutionalized, hereditary monarchy; from a king who looks like the typical Near Eastern king (warned about by Samuel as a prophet, 1 Sam 8:10–18) to one who is loyal to Yahweh; from no central place where God's Name dwells to a new center in Jerusalem. All of this is marvelously told—with wit, irony, suspense, wordplays—but above all with an eye to what God is doing with and among his people, even as he gives them a king.

One of the central (Deuteronomic) concerns of the book, evident in the structure itself, is the true worship of God at the place of his dwelling (his presence). This theme begins with a prophecy against the house of Eli because they "scorn my sacrifice and offering that I prescribed for my dwelling" (1 Sam 2:29). Then chapters 4–7 focus on the ark of the covenant, whose capture meant "the glory has departed from Israel" (4:22). Later, a central feature of David's reign is his bringing the ark to Jerusalem (2 Sam 6), where he desires to build a temple for it, but is forbidden (ch. 7). And the book ends with David's building an altar on the threshing floor of Araunah (24:18–25), which the intended reader would know is the precise place where the temple will eventually stand.

Linked to this is another theme that is a central feature of the narrative, namely, the tension between monarchy and covenant loyalty. You will see how this is set up near the beginning—in the contrasting sentiments between Samuel and the people in 1 Samuel 8–12. As the story proceeds, you are regularly reminded that even divinely appointed kings can, and do, act like other kings (as warned about in Deut 17:14–20). Yet David's essential loyalty to Yahweh lies at the heart of the story, and God covenants with him that his dynasty will endure forever (2 Sam 7)—a covenant that becomes a central feature in much of the rest of God's story.

Note how this tension lies at the heart of the contrasting stories of Saul and David (1 Sam 16–31). At issue in the end for our narrator is not *whether* Israel has a king, but *what kind of king* they will have. Key to this is whether the king will both be *faithful* to Yahweh and display Yahweh's *character,* since whatever else is true about Israel's king, he is to be the earthly representative of Yahweh's own kingship over Israel. Thus, even though Saul is anointed by Samuel and appears to begin well, there are deep flaws in his character, many of which are already subtly present at the beginning. At the end he is rejected because he thinks like any other king—that he is above the law and can act autonomously. Moreover, the prophetic tradition in Israel, represented by Samuel and Nathan, serves as a constant reminder that kings were *not* autonomous. Israel may indeed have rejected theocracy (the direct rule by God) for monarchy (1 Sam 8), but the role of her king was to mediate Yahweh's rule in Israel and thus to *lead God's people in obedience* to Yahweh.

A similar ambivalence pervades the story of David's reign as well (2 Sam 5–20). The fact that David's *kingly* exploits are merely summarized in 2 Samuel 8 while the story of his *sin* and the evil it let loose in the kingdom is narrated in considerable detail (chs. 10–20) should get our attention! Thus the narrator reminds us in various ways of David's genuine loyalty to Yahweh, not least by his placing the two great poems of David's devotion and praise to the Lord (22:1–23:7) as the centerpiece of his summarizing appendix (chs. 21–24). Yet this picture of "the man of faith" (21:15–17; 23:13–17) is set in the context of "the man of weakness" (24:1–17)—but who, when confronted with his sin, repents by means of prayer and sacrifice.

You will also want to watch for two parts of a subplot from Genesis (see "Specific Advice for Reading Genesis, p. 26) that mark this story as well: (1) the barren-woman motif that begins the story of Samuel (echoed in a variety of ways in Luke 1) and (2) God's choice of the "lesser" to fulfill his covenant purposes (David the shepherd boy).

There is one other important matter to keep in mind as you read, which leads to how this narrative fits into the metanarrative of the biblical story. In the ancient Near East the king was considered both the embodiment of his people (that is, he stood in for them at all times as their representative) and the representative of the deity for the people (cf. Ps 2:7, where the Davidic king is called "God's Son"). This is why Samuel and Kings tell the story of Israel almost exclusively as the story of their kings—and why the king speaks for the people in the Psalter. But this also explains why kingship was such a frightening prospect in Israel. At the same time, however, the role of David in the biblical story is affirmed, for in the end it is David's greater Son who comes as the true *embodiment* of Israel while also, as the true Son of God, *representing* God to Israel. This is why Jesus' kingship plays such an important role in the New Testament telling of his story.

A WALK THROUGH 1 AND 2 SAMUEL

The Story of Samuel (1 Samuel 1–7)

The narrator intends for you to admire Samuel, who serves as Israel's last judge and next great prophet after Moses. He is also the one who will anoint Israel's first two kings.

☐ 1 Samuel 1:1–4:1a   The Birth and Call of Samuel

Note the decisive role that Hannah plays in this story: a barren woman praying for a son (1:1–20), dedicating him to God (1:21–28), and rejoicing in the Lord (2:1–11). Note also how her prayer anticipates at least two motifs of the story — (1) God blesses the weak, not the strong, and (2) God will give strength to his king. Samuel's origins are then set in contrast to the wickedness of Eli's sons (2:12–36), followed by Samuel's call (3:1–18) and a concluding summary of his ministry (3:19–4:1a). Note how Eli's acceptance of Yahweh's rejection of him as priest (3:18) serves as a foil for Saul's later refusal to accept Yahweh's rejection of him as king.

☐ 1 Samuel 4:1b–7:17   The Loss and Return of the Ark

Note how this section is dominated by the loss and return of the glory of God, associated with the ark, where God "is enthroned between the cherubim" (4:4). The ark is not a talisman for Israel to use at a whim (4:1b–22), but neither are the Philistines to think that they have conquered Israel's God (ch. 5), so it is returned partway toward its final resting place (6:1–7:1). Some twenty years later, Samuel calls for national repentance, which results in God's aid in defeating the Philistines (7:2–13, echoes of Judges). Note how the concluding section summarizes Samuel's ministry, even though there is more to say about him (cf. the role of 1 Sam 15:34–35 in the Saul narrative).

The Story of Samuel and Saul (1 Samuel 8–15)

Here watch for the tension between kingship in Israel and covenant loyalty; Samuel warns of this three times, and the first king then comes to represent covenant disloyalty.

☐ 1 Samuel 8:1–12:25   Saul Anointed King

You might want to read this section in light of Deuteronomy 16:18–17:20. Note how it starts (8:1–3) with echoes from Deuteronomy

16:18 – 20 (judges who pervert justice and show partiality). The rest of this section is bookended by two warnings about the potential evils of monarchy, including statements about the people's rejection of Yahweh's kingship (8:4 – 22 and 11:14 – 12:25). These frame the narratives about Saul's becoming king — first, his anointing by Samuel (9:1 – 10:8), which emphasizes Saul's humble beginnings, and second, his being presented to the people and their confirmation of him (10:9 – 11:13), emphasizing his continuity with the prophetic tradition, his timid nature, and his military success (the holy war).

☐ **I Samuel 13:1 – 15:35** *The Failure of Saul's Kingship*

Here Saul's entire reign (13:1) is reduced to three incidents that occurred well into his reign. Two framing narratives demonstrate his covenant disloyalty — offering his own sacrifice (13:2 – 15) and violating the covenantal holy-war rules (15:1 – 35; cf. Achan's sin in Josh 7). The central narrative (13:16 – 14:48) demonstrates his weakness of character and personal failure in engaging the holy war. Each of these is symptomatic of his general disobedience and provides evidence of his lack of true faith in Yahweh. Thus Yahweh rejects him as Israel's king (encapsulated in 15:22 – 23). Note how, despite the fact that Saul lives on until chapter 31, his reign comes to its effective end at 15:35, where he is rejected (though mourned) by Samuel and by Yahweh.

The Story of Saul and David (I Samuel 16–31)

As you read this part of the story, look for the interweaving of David's rise to power, even though a fugitive, and Saul's decline. You need to be aware that the author's interest at the beginning is not so much with the chronology of events as with their significance for the story as a whole.

☐ **I Samuel 16:1 – 17:58** *The Rise of David*

Notice how the opening story of David's anointing as future king (16:1 – 13) concludes on the twin notes that the Spirit of Yahweh came on David (v. 13) but had departed from Saul (v. 14). The first two scenes (16:14 – 23; 17:1 – 58) set up the program: David's initial positive relationship with Saul; David's first exploit — a shepherd boy who trusts Yahweh ("the battle is the LORD's [Yahweh's]," 17:47) slays the Philistine champion Goliath (thus success in the holy war).

☐ I Samuel 18:1–31:13 *The Decline and Death of Saul*

This section begins with a story illustrating its central theme: Saul's jealousy of David and his attempts to kill him (ch. 18). Note how the rest of the section is dominated by Saul's pursuit of David, while David in turn has two opportunities to kill Saul, but will not lift his hand against "the LORD's anointed" (chs. 24 and 26, which encircle his being saved from his own anger by Abigail).

Interwoven into this theme are (1) other accounts of Saul's downward spiral, in the end consulting a medium (ch. 28) and finishing in shame (ch. 31); (2) accounts of David's existence as the fugitive head of a band of guerrillas; (3) evidence of David's obedience to Yahweh and consideration of his character (e.g., his largeheartedness toward Saul and Jonathan)—note especially how Abigail's speech in 25:26–31 not only saves David from vengeful wrongdoing but in effect allows the narrator to express his theme for these chapters; and (4) David's frequent, temporary stays in enemy territory, where God protected him from harm and covenant disloyalty under conditions that could have produced either result.

The Story of David (2 Samuel)

You will observe that the first part of the story is dominated by the theme of David's covenant loyalty, which leads to the Davidic covenant, yet one particular moment of covenant disloyalty sets up much of what goes wrong with the rest of the story (1 and 2 Kings).

☐ 2 Samuel 1:1–4:12 *The Story of David as King of Judah*

This section presents the aftermath of Saul's death; note how it emphasizes David's *non*role in the civil war that followed. Thus he laments over Saul and Jonathan (ch. 1). Following the account of his becoming king of Judah (ch. 2), he is notably exonerated in all the tragedies that follow (chs. 3–4). Keep your eyes open for the rift between north and south, which is picked up again in chapters 19–20 and becomes final in 1 and 2 Kings.

☐ 2 Samuel 5:1–9:13 *The Story of David as King over All Israel*

Following David's assuming the kingship over all Israel (5:1–5) is a sequence of four narratives (5:6–7:29) that are especially crucial: (1) David's conquest of Jerusalem, (2) the conquest of the Philistines,

(3) bringing the ark to Jerusalem, and, above all, (4) God's covenant with David that "your house and your kingdom will endure forever before me" (7:1–16), to which David responds in an outpouring of praise and gratitude (7:18–29).

The importance of the preceding narratives is highlighted by the brevity of chapter 8, which serves to bring the conquest to a conclusion (see Joshua). Here you find David's many years as king condensed into two brief summaries. And because our narrator is ultimately concerned not with David's kingly exploits but with his character, he concludes with another narrative of David's kindness to the house of Saul (ch. 9), where the "lame" enter the palace—despite the saying in 5:8! But note how this scene sits in contrast to the unfortunate story that follows.

☐ 2 Samuel 10:1–20:26   *David's Sin and Its Consequences*

Note how the account of David's sin against Bathsheba and Uriah is told in detail. It is set up in chapter 10, recounted in chapter 11, and condemned in chapter 12. And watch for the irony in chapter 11—the faithful foreigner Uriah honors an unfaithful Israelite king; the foreigner retains sexual purity during war, while the Israelite king dallies with his wife; the king, who has not gone into battle himself, sends the faithful soldier to his death in battle. The king is portrayed throughout as one who is accountable to God for his actions (note how crucial ch. 12 is to the Israelite view of kingship), but in contrast to Saul, David repents—and is then filled with remorse over the dying child, the result of his sin.

This event sets in motion the rest of the story (chs. 13–20) in two ways. First, watch how illicit sexuality, murder, and intrigue are multiplied in David's family, as Nathan's prediction (12:10–12) is fulfilled. In turn there is rape, fratricide, treachery, rebellion, seizure of David's concubines, and civil war, and the fissures between north and south portrayed in 19:8b–20:26 anticipate the unbridgeable chasm related in 1 Kings 12. And second, observe how this whole series of events is related to the question later raised by Bathsheba in 1 Kings 1:20: "Who will sit on the throne of my lord the king after him?"

☐ 2 Samuel 21:1–24:25   *Final Reflections on David and His Reign*

Notice how the narrator also summarizes David, as he did Samuel and Saul, before David's story is actually over (cf. 1 Sam 7:15–17;

15:34–35). But in this case it is a purposeful arrangement (in a concentric, nonchronological pattern) of two narratives, two accounts of David's mighty warriors, and two poems. The two poems (2 Sam 22:1–51 [a version of Ps 18] and 23:1–7) review, first, God's mighty acts for and through David and, second, God's covenant promise of an enduring throne. Note especially how both poems ascribe glory to God at every point. If David is "the lamp of Israel" (21:17), *God* is in fact David's lamp (22:29).

The inner frame for these affirmations comprises two accounts of David's mighty warriors (21:15–22; 23:8–39), reminding you of God's role both in battle and in times of David's humanity and vulnerability. Significantly, the famine and plague stories (3 years/3 days) that frame the whole (21:1–14; 24:1–25) end with obedience and sacrifice. Again watch for the irony: Following the two poems and the list of David's mighty men, 2 Samuel concludes with the story of David counting his fighting men, in violation of holy-war law, to begin preparations for further conquests, and to establish his own importance (24:1–17). At the same time, the sacrifice on the site of the future temple (24:18–25) prepares the way for 1 and 2 Kings.

The book of Samuel takes God's story into the monarchy, especially by means of the story of King David, a man of faith even while a man of weakness. God's covenant with David is the basis for Jewish messianism, fulfilled finally in the ultimate Son of David, Jesus of Nazareth.

1 and 2 Kings

ORIENTING DATA FOR 1 AND 2 KINGS

- **Content:** starting with the reign of Solomon, the story of the decline and eventual dissolution of the monarchy in Israel and the expulsion of God's people from the land

- **Historical coverage:** from the death of David (970 B.C.) to the sixth-century exile of Judah (586)

- **Emphases:** the evaluation of the monarchy on the basis of covenant loyalty; the fateful national consequences of disloyalty to Yahweh, resulting finally in expulsion from the land; the schism and civil wars between north and south; the rise of superpowers that, under the direction of God, subjugated Israel and Judah; the role of prophets who speak for God in Israel's national life

OVERVIEW OF 1 AND 2 KINGS

As with Samuel, the book of Kings was divided to fit on two scrolls. The title tells the story of its content, but it is also important to remember that in the Hebrew Bible, Kings concludes the Former Prophets, as a description of God's verdict of judgment on Israel's history. And you will hardly be able to miss the important role of the prophets in this book.

Kings covers the story of the monarchy from Solomon through its subsequent division into two kingdoms, to its demise in the north (Israel) and the exile of the final king in the south (Judah). This pretty well describes its "parts" also: 1 Kings 1–11 give an abbreviated account of Solomon's reign. Four things are important to the narrator: (1) how Solomon came to the throne, (2) his renown for wisdom, (3) the building of the temple and his palace, and (4) his demise and the reasons for it. The events surrounding the schism are narrated in 1 Kings 12–14.

Crucial here is the reign of Jeroboam I, who, with echoes of Aaron and the golden calf, declares his golden calves in Dan and Bethel to be "your gods ... who brought you up out of Egypt" (12:28; Exod 32:4). This is then followed by alternating accounts of the northern and southern kings as their reigns overlap (1 Kgs 15–2 Kgs 17), where each northern king in turn is judged by God for "walking in the ways of Jeroboam and in his sin" (e.g., 1 Kgs 15:26, 34). Here the narrative is dominated by prophetic activity in the north, especially of Elijah and Elisha (1 Kgs 17–2 Kgs 13), until the capture and destruction of Samaria, the northern capital.

The rest of the book (2 Kgs 18–25) tells the story of another 150 years of Judah's kings, until the fall of Jerusalem in 587/6 B.C. Over half of this last section concentrates on two notably good kings (Hezekiah, chs. 18–20; Josiah, chs. 22–23) and includes the prophetic activity of Isaiah (chs. 19–20).

SPECIFIC ADVICE FOR READING 1 AND 2 KINGS

Whereas all history is written from a point of view, not all historians reveal their point of view as clearly as this narrator does (note his own summary of the history after the fall of Samaria, 2 Kgs 17:7–23). The Deuteronomic perspective on Israel's history that began with Joshua is especially pronounced in this telling of the story, both by its clear echoes of Deuteronomic themes and by the way the story is structured. Therefore, it is not surprising—since all the northern kings and the majority of those in the south evidenced disloyalty—that the story has distinct echoes of Judges with its spiral downward, as the promised curses of Deuteronomy 28:15–68 come to their inevitable fulfillment.

The key to everything is whether a given king has been loyal to the covenant with Yahweh. In Kings this is expressed in Deuteronomic terms—his attitude toward the central sanctuary (the temple in Jerusalem) and whether or not he advocated syncretism (e.g., Jeroboam's golden calves; see 2 Kgs 17:41) or rival gods altogether, especially Canaanite Baal worship (note how these distinctions are assumed in 1 Kgs 16:31–32 and 2 Kgs 10:28–29). This "program" is set up by the narrative of Solomon, whose long and prosperous reign is finally reduced to two matters. His one significant deed is the *building of the temple* in Jerusalem, which is filled with the glory of God (God's presence, 1 Kgs 8:10–11), precisely as with the tabernacle in Exodus 40:34–35. But he is finally judged for *going the way of all kings* (see Deut 17:16–17; 1 Sam 8:11–18) and for *promoting idolatry* through his many foreign wives (1 Kgs 11:1–13). These two items sit side by side in 1 Kings 8 and 9—in Solomon's prayer and Yahweh's response. The former emphasizes the significance of the temple for Israel's loyalty to Yahweh; the latter repeats the Deuteronomic blessings and curses, especially outlining the nature of the latter: "I will cut Israel off *from the land* I have given them" (9:7, emphasis added), "because they have forsaken the LORD [Yahweh] their God ... and have embraced other gods" (v. 9). For our narrator, this foretells the story he will proceed to unfold.

This view of things is also accented by several structural matters. First, all the kings are placed within the story by means of a common regnal formula:

1. when a king came to reign (in Israel or Judah) in relation to another king
2. how long he reigned and in what capital
3. (for Judean kings) the name of his mother
4. his religious policy: for the northern kings this consistently takes the form of following in "the sins of Jeroboam son of Nebat"; for Judah the issue was whether the king followed Yahweh and whether or not he removed "the high places"
5. often the source for further information about the king
6. at the end, information about his death/burial and who succeeded him

Items 4 and 5 are especially telling. Item 4 is the only basis on which a given king is judged—no matter how long he ruled or what his other exploits or accomplishments might have been; item 5, therefore, tells the reader where the other kinds of materials might be found, e.g., in "the book of the annals of the kings of ..."

The second structural matter may be especially trying for those who might want a different kind of history. Many of the kings have almost nothing said about them beyond the regnal formula itself. And what is narrated about those who get more press, apart from accounts of civil war, has almost altogether to do with their loyalty or disloyalty to Yahweh. This results in purposeful disproportions of major kinds: the overlapping reigns of Jeroboam II of Israel (forty-one years in Samaria) and Azariah (Uzziah) of Judah (fifty-two years in Jerusalem) are merely skimmed in seven verses each (2 Kgs 14:23–29; 15:1–7), while the twenty-two-year reign of Ahab and twenty-nine-year reign of Hezekiah cover several chapters each.

Third, this also accounts for the disproportionate space given to the prophets Elijah and Elisha. They become God's agents in the holy war, but now over against the northern kings themselves and the foreign-born Baalist Jezebel. Through them God demonstrates that he is still Lord over all the earth (creation, nature; the nations; Israel). And thus the Deuteronomic cycle brings the story to its crashing end in the north; eventually the same thing happened in the south in terms of promised exile.

Finally, note that in contrast to the book of Samuel this story is even-tually told in the context of major superpowers that have arisen — Assyria, then Babylon and Egypt. They become the instruments of God's judgment that drive his people from the land, but they do so because Yahweh is the God of the nations and has brought them into power for this very purpose (Deut 28:49–52).

A WALK THROUGH 1 AND 2 KINGS

☐ 1 Kings 1:1–2:46 *Solomon Becomes King*

This opening section tells of Solomon's succeeding David (1:1–53) and David's charge to him (2:1–12), which is then followed by Solo-mon's consolidating his position by disposing of Adonijah and his co-conspirators Joab and Abiathar (2:13–46). Note the question about succession that is being answered (1:20): How did it happen that David was succeeded by Solomon, who was not first in line? (1:6; 2:22; cf. the narratives of Gen 12–50). The answer lies with an oath made to Bath-sheba. Note also how the section concludes in 1 Kgs 2:46 ("The king-dom was now firmly established in Solomon's hands"), which sets up what follows.

☐ 1 Kings 3:1–11:43 *The Reign of Solomon*

You need to be alert to two important things about this narrative: (1) The narrator signals that (a) with the reign of Solomon, the promise to Abraham of vast population increase has been fulfilled (4:20; see Gen 22:17; 32:12) and (b) with the construction of the temple, the exodus is now completed, as Yahweh gets his permanent dwelling place in

Jerusalem (1 Kgs 6:1). Thus, (2) the centerpiece of this section is the temple narrative (5:1 – 9:9), which is told in some detail while the many long years of Solomon's reign are merely summarized on either side of it. Indeed, a careful reading makes it clear that Solomon's relationship to the temple is the one thing that "saves" him, as it were.

Otherwise the narrator shows considerable ambivalence toward Solomon. As you read, note, for example, how much of 3:1 – 4:34 and 9:10 – 11:43 fulfill Samuel's prophecy (1 Sam 8:11 – 18). The narrator recognizes that Solomon's wisdom and splendor are a gift from God, and at the heart of it all is the fact that Solomon is David's son (1 Kgs 3:3, 7, 14; 8:15 – 26; 9:4 – 5). Yet he also knows that the seeds of future decline and schism are being sown (heavy taxation and slave labor, 4:27 – 28; 5:13 – 18; cf. 12:4; note the contrast with Joash's repairing the temple, 2 Kgs 12:4 – 16 [freewill offerings and paid workers!]). God's judgment on Solomon sets the tone for the rest of the story ("You have not kept my covenant and my decrees, which I commanded you," 1 Kgs 11:11, 33). Thus despite all of Solomon's greatness, wisdom, and splendor and the construction of the temple, and despite the fact that God appeared to him twice (11:9; cf. 3:5 – 15; 9:2 – 9), in the end he abandoned God in order to worship idols (11:1 – 10) and thereby split the nation, incurring God's wrath (11:11 – 40).

☐ I Kings 12:1 – 16:20 *The Kingdom Divides (931 – 885 B.C.)*

Chapters 12 – 14 describe the nation's dissolution into politically unstable and religiously rebellious Israel (ten northern tribes) and the somewhat more orthodox and stable Judah (sometimes plus Benjamin, 12:20 – 23). Note four emphases: (1) the dominant role of prophets, who both reveal God's plans and call the northern kings to account (12:22 – 24; 13:1 – 4; 14:1 – 18; 16:1 – 4; cf. 11:29 – 39); (2) civil war that pits north against south with foreign alliances (15:6 – 7, 16 – 22); (3) God's commitment to Judah for the sake of David (14:8; 15:4 – 5, 11; note especially the echo of 2 Sam 21:17 that David is the "lamp of Israel"; cf. 2 Kgs 8:19); (4) "succession" in the north is by treachery and power politics (1 Kgs 16:9 – 13), not by the will of God.

The story of Jeroboam I is especially important to the rest of the narrative. Watch how the narrator tells Jeroboam's story in two parts: His beginning echoes similarities to Moses (chosen by God, he comes out of Egypt to deliver a people laboring under a "heavy yoke"; 12:1 – 4; cf.

Exod 6:6–7), but in the end he resembles Aaron (Exod 32), making golden calves and repeating Aaron's words verbatim: "Here are your gods, O Israel, who brought you up out of Egypt" (1 Kgs 12:28). This repetition of the rebellion at Sinai marks all the rest of the kings of Israel, who walked in the ways of Jeroboam (e.g., 15:26, 34). But note carefully that this is a form of syncretism (Yahweh in the form of an Egyptian deity), not Baalism, as 2 Kings 10:28–29 and 17:41 make clear.

□ I Kings 16:21–2 Kings 10:36 *The Divided Kingdom: The Omri Dynasty (885–841 B.C.)*

With Omri comes another dynasty that neither descended from David nor worshiped at Jerusalem. Omri's son Ahab outstrips even Jeroboam in his sin, marrying a Baal worshiper and thus adding Baal worship to that of the golden calves. Note how this brings on the holy war, as the prophet Elijah contests for Yahweh against the prophets of Baal. Note also that for all his sins, it is when Ahab seizes the vineyard of Naboth by treachery and murder (thus breaking the covenant law in several ways; cf. Deut 19:14) that God's judgment comes on him and Jezebel (1 Kgs 21:17–24). And even though Ahab himself dies in accord with the prophetic judgment (22:37–38), we wait until 2 Kings 9–10 before the rest of the prophecy is fulfilled against Jezebel and against Ahab's house. Thus judgment is held in suspense while Elisha succeeds Elijah and performs Elijah-like miracles, and Ahab is succeeded by two sons. The execution is carried out by an ardent (but bloody) Yahwist, Jehu, who destroys Baal worship, but not the golden calves at Dan and Bethel. Be aware also in this section that outside pressure is still coming only from neighboring local kingdoms (Aram/Damascus), but all of that will change in the next section, as the superpower Assyria looms on the horizon (2 Kgs 15:19).

Note finally how this part of the story concentrates on affairs in Israel; the Judean exceptions are brief summaries of Jehoshaphat (1 Kgs 22:41–50, a "good" king) and of Jehoram and Ahaziah (2 Kgs 8:16–29), evil kings who walked in the ways of the kings of Israel. The intrigue of their stories is that Jehoram marries into the house of Omri; Athaliah, a daughter of Ahab and Jezebel, turns out to be like her mother and nearly succeeds in wiping out the Davidic dynasty (2 Kgs 11).

□ 2 Kings 11:1–17:41   *The Divided Kingdom: Jehu to the Fall of Samaria (841–722 B.C.)*

From here on the story begins to shift back again to the kings of Judah. Note how Israel's kings are merely summarized, as one story of covenant unfaithfulness follows another, until Samaria is conquered and Israel is annexed to the Assyrian Empire. Notice how the author's summary in 17:7–23 tells the story in the way he has expected you to read it. The Assyrian resettlement of the land (vv. 24–41) sets in motion the many difficulties that will be faced in Ezra and Nehemiah—including northerners of mixed ethnicity, whom you will meet again as the Samaritans in the New Testament Gospels.

Three kings of Judah are featured in this section, highlighting concerns you've met earlier in the narrative. The story of Joash (chs. 11–12) is important for two reasons: (1) He represents God's commitment to keep "a lamp for David" (8:19); having been protected by his aunt, he is proclaimed king while the usurper Athaliah of Samaria cries "treason" but is killed (11:14–16). (2) He repairs the temple—and does so with the freewill offerings of the people (12:4–5)!

Amaziah (14:1–22), another "good" king, continues his father Joash's policies, but he is noted mostly for continuing the civil war with the north. And obviously everything is not well in Jerusalem, as both his father and he are assassinated by unnamed officials.

Ahaz (ch. 16), unlike David his father, "did not do what was right in the eyes of the LORD his God." He is remembered primarily for bringing Judah under Assyrian influence and, in contrast to Joash, who repaired the temple, for reconfiguring the temple on the basis of foreign influence.

□ 2 Kings 18:1–25:30   *Judah's Final Years: The Babylonian Exile (722–560 B.C.)*

In contrast to the story of Israel, where the narrative concentrates on the gross evil of the worst of the kings (as judged by Deuteronomic criteria), the story of Judah tends to concentrate on the good kings. Note how this is especially so in this final episode, where only two kings, Hezekiah (chs. 18–20) and Josiah (chs. 22–23), do what is right in the eyes of Yahweh. And again they are judged on the basis of covenant loyalty (18:5–6; 22:11; 23:1–3). In the case of Hezekiah, his loyalty to Yahweh is the reason for his escaping Assyrian conquest, but some of his actions actually forecast the Babylonian exile (20:12–21). And despite Josiah's reforms and devotion to Yahweh, the die has been cast by the idolatrous reign of Manasseh (23:24–27), so the story from there heads inexorably toward exile. Kings ends with Judah in exile, but the release of Jehoiachin presents the reader with a ray of hope regarding "the lamp of David," even at the end.

———————————————

The book of Kings is ultimately answering the question, "In light of God's covenant with Abraham [the land] and with David [an everlasting throne], how did all of this happen to us?" The answer: God has not failed his people; his people, led by their kings, have failed their God. The covenants, after all, have the contingency of Israel's faithfulness written into them. But the covenant also promises return from exile for those who return to Yahweh (Deut 30:1–10).

1 and 2 Chronicles

ORIENTING DATA FOR 1 AND 2 CHRONICLES

- **Content:** a postexilic, positive history of Judah's kings, with emphasis on the temple and its worship

- **Historical coverage:** an opening genealogy goes back to Adam; the narrative itself covers the kingdom of Judah from David (ca. 1000 B.C.) to the decree of Cyrus (539/8)

- **Emphases:** the continuity of the people of Judah (and others) through the exile and beyond; David's and Solomon's covenant loyalty as models for the time of restoration; the central role of the temple and worship for the restoration; true worship as a matter of the heart and full of joy and song; divine blessing and rest for obedience, and retribution for disobedience

OVERVIEW OF 1 AND 2 CHRONICLES

The book of Chronicles is the final book in the Hebrew Bible, taking its place at the end of the Writings. Its present place and division into two books come from the Greek Bible, where it was (perceptively) placed after Kings and followed by Ezra-Nehemiah. Using Samuel and Kings as his basic narrative, the Chronicler adds other materials—genealogies, lists, psalms, speeches—to present the continuous story of Israel (especially Judah) from Adam to the decree of Cyrus, which brought the exile to its official end.

The story itself is in three parts. It begins with the infamous *genealogies* (1 Chr 1–9), which is what has made it one of the more neglected books in the Old Testament. What is crucial here is that the Chronicler takes the line of descent all the way back to Adam, while concentrating finally on Judah and the Levites (which is where his narrative interests lie).

Part 2 (1 Chr 10–2 Chr 9) tells the story of the *united monarchy* under David and Solomon, a section that is longer by some pages than the whole rest of the story from Rehoboam to the end of the exile. Concentrating only on the positive dimensions of their lives, the author also deliberately overlaps their stories. Thus 1 Chronicles 10–21 tells the story of David alone, 1 Chronicles 22–29 introduces Solomon into David's story, whom David prepares for the construction of the temple, and 2 Chronicles 1–9 then picks up the story of Solomon alone, who constructs the temple. The temple and correct worship is the obvious focus of this section. More than half of David's story is concerned with preparations (1 Chr 22–26; 28–29) and over two-thirds of Solomon's with its construction and dedication (2 Chr 2–7).

These same concerns carry over to part 3 (2 Chr 10–36), which relates the story of Judah (only) during the period of the *divided monarchy*. But here you will note a further pattern as well: Success in battle and material prosperity are related directly to obedience to Yahweh, while failure is due to unfaithfulness or lack of trust. The story includes the exile, ending with the edict of Cyrus, king of Persia, who in fulfillment of the prophecy of Jeremiah was "appointed" by Yahweh "to build a temple for him at Jerusalem," and thus he invites the people to go up (2 Chr 36:22–23).

SPECIFIC ADVICE FOR READING I AND 2 CHRONICLES

To read Chronicles well, it will help you to have a sense of the times in which the Chronicler wrote. His era was that of the restoration, a period that began limply at the end of the sixth century B.C. with the repeatedly postponed, yet finally completed, temple project (see "Specific Advice for Reading Haggai," p. 253; "Zechariah," pp. 257–58; Ezra 1–6, p. 111), which picked up real steam only with the systematic reforms of Ezra and Nehemiah in the middle of the fifth century. The Chronicler most likely wrote somewhere within this period—a time of identity crisis in the Persian province of Judah. The restoration thus far had been a far cry from the glorious "second exodus" envisioned by Isaiah (e.g., Isa 35:1–10; 40:1–11; 44:1–5). Cyrus had technically inaugurated the new era, which included the initial token rebuilding of Jerusalem and the temple (Isa 44:28–45:5, 13). But in fact only a relative handful of Jews had returned to their "promised land," and the second temple was neither of the grandeur of Solomon's (Hag 2:3) nor had it yet attained its promised glory (Hag 2:6–9)—while Jerusalem itself lay in general decay with few inhabitants (Neh 1; 11). So a time of general spiritual malaise had settled in, including, increasingly, a great deal of intermarriage (Ezra 9–10, a sure way to lose national identity).

Into this context stepped Haggai and Zechariah to urge on the work of a priest (Jeshua) and a governor (Zerubbabel). A generation later it was a priest (Ezra) and a governor (Nehemiah) who themselves stepped in with their reform movement—and with greater results. Into the same overall context also steps the Chronicler, with a brilliant retelling of the story of Judah intended to give the present generation a sense of continuity with its great past and to focus on the temple and its worship as the place where that continuity could now be maintained.

As you read, you will note that several emphases stand out: The Chronicler is interested altogether in the Davidic dynasty, and in the northern kingdom only as she is in allegiance with Judah. About Judah his interest focuses on two concerns: the Davidic dynasty (David and Solomon) and the temple in Jerusalem. About the temple his interest focuses altogether on the nature and purity of the worship (over 60 percent of the story). Combine these emphases with the fact that the book ends with Cyrus's edict that the temple be rebuilt, and you can see where our author thinks the hope for the future lies, namely, in getting it right this time around with regard to the temple.

But getting it right for the Chronicler is not a matter of mere ritual. Be watching for his repeated emphasis on devoting "your heart and soul to seeking the LORD [Yahweh] your God" (1 Chr 22:19; cf. 29:17; 2 Chr 6:38; 7:10; 15:12), plus an accent on singing "joyful songs" (1 Chr 15:16), which is where the emphasis on the Levites comes out. The book abounds with the language of praise, thanksgiving, and joy in God's goodness and love. Note especially the thrice-repeated "He is good; his love endures forever"—(1) when the ark is brought into Jerusalem and then (2) into the temple, and (3) when the temple is consecrated (1 Chr 16:34; 2 Chr 5:13; 7:3). The presence of God (from the exodus) is thus renewed in Israel.

The Chronicler's focus on the southern kingdom, however, is not over against the north as such; rather he tells the story of the north only in terms of its failure to worship at the place of God's choosing, namely, the temple in Jerusalem. For example, the Chronicler regularly uses the expression "all Israel," by which he means north and south together in allegiance to temple worship in Jerusalem. In this regard you will see how his two main themes (the authenticity of the Davidic dynasty and the temple in Jerusalem) merge in Abijah's speech in 2 Chronicles 13:4–12 as the real point of condemnation against Jeroboam and his successors. And watch further for Hezekiah's invitation—and acceptance by some—to the north (now no longer functioning as a nation) to join once more in the worship in Jerusalem, after he had purified the temple (2 Chr 30:1–31:1).

It is also in this regard that you should understand the Chronicler's presentation of David and Solomon. What may appear to some as a kind of whitewash job on their lives is best understood as his concentrating only on those dimensions of their stories that serve as ideals both for the people as a whole (when they no longer have a king) and for the appropriate emphases as they live for the future (proper worship at the temple). The Chronicler knows that his readers are well aware of the faults of these kings (see Neh 13:26). His interest is in how their positive accomplishments can inspire hope for a new day.

This is also how you should understand the emphases in the narrative of the divided kingdom—that God blesses those who obey and punishes those who do not. Although life is not quite that simple, the Chronicler knows that this is a biblical pattern established from the beginning. And so he retells the story to encourage such loyalty in a new generation who live in and around Jerusalem (1 Chr 9).

Finally, you should also note the Chronicler's interest in the role of "the nations." In the midst of his readers' present sense of insignificance, he reminds them that not only are the nations ultimately under the control of Yahweh (e.g., Shishak king of Egypt, 2 Chr 12:5–9; Cyrus king of Persia, 2 Chr 36:22–23), but by placing Psalm 105 in the midst of the narrative of David (1 Chr 16:8–36), he emphasizes that God's goodness to Israel will be the source of making Yahweh known among the nations (recall the blessing of Abraham, Gen 12:3).

A WALK THROUGH 1 AND 2 CHRONICLES

☐ 1 Chronicles 1–9 *The Genealogies*

There are several important things for you to notice as you look through these genealogies. First, the fact that the Chronicler begins his narrative this way says something about what he wants the postexilic community to understand—that they have continuity with a divinely ordained past that ultimately goes back to the creation of the world.

Second, note that both the focus and the larger amount of space are devoted to the tribes of Judah, Benjamin, and Levi. These are the surviving tribes of the southern kingdom who also represent in turn the Davidic dynasty, Jerusalem, and proper worship in the temple; they also led the original return from Babylon (Ezra 1:5). Thus the first set of genealogies (1:1–4:23) go through to the sons of Israel (2:1–2) only then to concentrate primarily on Judah (2:3–4:23), with the Davidic dynasty as its centerpiece (3:1–16) and including the royal line after the exile (3:17–24)—the time of our author.

Notice how the genealogies of the remaining tribes (4:24–7:40) then have the Levites as their centerpiece (ch. 6), with special emphasis on the temple musicians (vv. 31–47). Finally, the genealogy of Benjamin is expanded in chapter 8 (see 7:6–12).

Chapter 9 is not a genealogy but a list of Babylonian exiles who had returned, with special emphasis on the Levites who ministered in the temple. Note that in 9:35–44, the last part of the Benjamite genealogy (8:29–38) is repeated in order to introduce Saul at the beginning of the narrative proper.

□ **1 Chronicles 10–21** *The United Monarchy: The Story of David*

Watch for the Chronicler's concerns as they emerge in this section, noting his arrangement and emphases. He begins (ch. 10) with the death of the failed king (Saul) in order to introduce the great king (David) by way of contrast. Then in chapters 11–12, he selects and arranges various materials from 2 Samuel (5:1–3, 6–10; 23:8–39) and other sources to emphasize that "all Israel" came together to make David king (1 Chr 11:1, 4, 10; 12:38).

The next section (chs. 13–16) tells the story of bringing "the ark of the covenant of the LORD [Yahweh]" (15:25) into Jerusalem. Note (1) how it continues the theme of "all Israel" (13:1–4); thereafter the author considerably expands 2 Samuel 6 by breaking apart its two phases (1 Chr 13:1–14; 15:1–16:6) so that, in contrast to Uzzah's death, he can focus especially on the role of the Levites with their joyful songs (15:2–24); (2) how it climaxes with a marvelous collage of portions of three psalms (1 Chr 16:8–36 = Pss 105:1–15; 96:1–13; 106:1, 47–48), extolling God's greatness in all the earth and over the nations, and especially his goodness toward his people; and (3) how the psalm ends with a cry to God to "deliver us from the nations" (1 Chr 16:35–36), to which all the people said, "Amen" and "Praise the LORD" (thus reflecting the author's own situation).

This is followed by the Davidic covenant (ch. 17), with its emphasis now on Solomon as the one who will build "God's house," which is followed in turn (chs. 18–21) by a collage from 2 Samuel 8–21 of David's wars. You'll want to especially note two points here: (1) The significance of this section is to explain why David himself could not build the temple—he was a man of war (1 Chr 22:8), while his son Solomon (whose name means "peace") is a "man of peace and rest" (v. 9), and (2) it concludes with the only negative story about David (21:1–22:1), necessary to relate because Araunah's threshing floor, which David refuses as a gift but instead purchases, is to be the site of the temple (22:1).

□ **I Chronicles 22–29** *The United Monarchy:*
David and Solomon

The material in this section serves for what is essential to the transition between David and Solomon. Note how the Chronicler's concerns are highlighted by the structure itself. The larger central section (chs. 23–27) deals with David's preparations of the Levites for worship in the temple. These are framed by three speeches of David (chs. 22; 28; 29), which get at the heart of the author's concerns. The first one (22:5–16) is addressed to Solomon himself and repeats the essence of the Davidic covenant (17:10b–14), focusing especially on his calling to build the temple; the second (28:2–10) repeats the essence of this to all the officials of Israel; while the third (29:1–5) calls for them to follow David's own example of generous giving toward the project. It then ends with a Davidic blessing and thanksgiving (vv. 10–19). Thus the overall intent is (1) to designate Solomon as the divinely appointed builder of the temple and (2) to secure the support of "all Israel" for his kingship and for the erection of the temple. So the section concludes with Solomon's being acknowledged as king by all Israel (vv. 21–25) and with David's death (vv. 26–30).

□ **2 Chronicles I–9** *The United Monarchy:*
The Story of Solomon

Note two things in particular as you read this section. First, all of the ambiguity toward Solomon found in 2 Kings has been removed, since he serves for our author as exhibit A of devotion to Yahweh at the one essential point—faithfulness to the temple as the place of true worship. Therefore, second, the bulk of this section is its centerpiece (2 Chr 2–7)—the preparations for and the building and dedication of the temple. Two additions to the 1 Kings narrative reflect the Chronicler's concerns: (1) The twice-repeated theme from David's psalm (1 Chr 16:34) in 2 Chronicles 5:13 and 7:3—when the ark of God's presence rests in the temple that is dedicated to him—emphasizes *God's goodness* to his people; (2) the best known passage from this book—the addition to God's response to Solomon's prayer (7:13–16)—seems especially included for the sake of the author's own readers.

☐ 2 Chronicles 10–36 *The Divided Monarchy: The Davidic Dynasty*

The rest of the story is about the kings who succeed Solomon. Besides continuing all the themes of the narrative to this point ("all Israel"; the Davidic dynasty; the central place of the temple), here the Chronicler also puts special emphasis on God's direct intervention for blessing and judgment on the basis either of the kings' "seeking" or "humbling themselves before" Yahweh or of their "abandoning" or "forsaking" Yahweh.

Chapters 10–12. Three things to note in the Chronicler's account of Rehoboam: (1) The divided kingdom is Yahweh's doing (11:2–4); (2) nonetheless it is immediately followed by the theme of all Israel coming to Jerusalem to sacrifice (11:5–17); and (3) the new theme of judgment for abandoning Yahweh begins with Rehoboam and Israel's leaders (12:2–5).

Chapter 13. Note how the author uses a speech by Abijah to Jeroboam and Israel (13:4–12) to set forth his own emphases: Yahweh has given the kingship to David and his descendants forever (v. 5), and true worship occurs only in Jerusalem at the temple (vv. 10–12). Thereafter the northern tribes are included when they join Judah in Jerusalem (15:9–15) or are invited to do so (29:1–31:1). Note also that it was when the people cried out to Yahweh that "God routed Jeroboam" (13:14–15).

Chapters 14–16. In this longer account of Asa, watch for two emphases: (1) that Asa "called to the LORD his God" (14:11), to which God responds by striking down the Cushites (v. 12), and (2) that in response to a prophetic word, Asa institutes a reform with respect to the temple and proper worship (ch. 15). But note also that his long reign ends on something of a sour note due to failure to rely on Yahweh (16:1–9, 11–12) and oppression of some of the people (16:10).

Chapters 17–20. In the still longer account of Jehoshaphat, note that he is praised because in his early years he "walked in the ways that his father David had followed" (17:3–6), which found expression in the Levites' instructing the people through the law (17:7–9; 19:4–11). The centerpiece of his narrative is the defeat of Moab and Ammon (20:1–30), which is punctuated by a speech at the temple (vv. 4–19) and thanksgiving, song, and praise by the troops (vv. 20–26). But this narrative is sandwiched by an unholy alliance with Israel (18:1–19:3; 20:31–37), which leads to his downturn at the end.

Chapters 21–24. Next come two evil kings, Jehoram and Ahaziah, who aligned with Ahab (21:1–22:9). Note that Ahaziah "did evil in the eyes of the LORD" (22:4); therefore "God brought about Ahaziah's downfall" (v. 7). Even so, the dynasty continues because of Yahweh's covenant with David (21:7; cf. 23:18). The account of Joash concentrates on two of the themes: the divine rescue of the Davidic dynasty (22:10–23:21) and the repairing of the temple (24:1–16). Note that both of these highlight the ministry of the high priest Jehoiada, after whose death Joash comes under the influence of officials who abandon Yahweh (24:17–27), even to the point of murdering Jehoiada's son. Unfortunately, Joash's son then follows in these later steps.

Chapters 25–28. Joash is followed by two kings (Amaziah and Uzziah) toward whom the Chronicler shows considerable ambiguity. They in turn are followed by one who is praised (Jotham) and one who is condemned (Ahaz). Note how thoroughgoing the theme is here of blessing or judgment based on the kings' loyalty or disloyalty to Yahweh. Observe especially that this series ends with Ahaz's shutting the doors of Yahweh's temple (28:24).

Chapters 29–32. Then comes Hezekiah, whose story concentrates on the temple purification; this is also where you find all the themes noted above in the introductory paragraph on 2 Chronicles 10–36 (p. 105) brought together in this good king.

Chapters 33–36. Finally, after Manasseh, an evil king who repents at the end, and his son Amon, who does not, comes the story of Josiah. Note that the Chronicler again concentrates on a great renewal of the

Passover, calling attention especially to the central role of the priests and Levites (35:1 – 19). With Josiah's death the book moves quickly through the final four kings to the fall of Jerusalem, but given the Chronicler's emphasis, it is no surprise that the final words in the book remind you of Cyrus's decree that the temple be rebuilt (36:23).

By this retelling of the story of God's people, Chronicles reminds us of the central role of worship; for the readers of the New Testament, it also points forward to the one whose own "cleansing" of the temple and death and resurrection replace the temple as the place of God's presence (John 2:19 – 22).

Ezra-Nehemiah

ORIENTING DATA FOR EZRA-NEHEMIAH

- **Content:** rebuilding and reform in postexilic Judah through the latter half of the fifth century B.C.

- **Historical coverage:** from the first return (539/8 B.C.) to the end of the fifth century, but especially from 458 to 430, during the reign of Artaxerxes of Persia

- **Emphases:** successful completion of the second temple despite opposition; successful rebuilding of the walls of Jerusalem despite opposition; the crisis of intermarriage and national identity; concern for covenant renewal and reform, based on the law, among the exiles who had returned to Jerusalem

OVERVIEW OF EZRA-NEHEMIAH

Just as with Samuel, Kings, and Chronicles, the books of Ezra and Nehemiah, which appear in our English Bibles as separate books, originally formed one book in the Hebrew Bible. They were not separated until well into the Christian era. You will do well to read them together, since they do in fact tell one story, not two.

Using the memoirs (journals?) of Ezra and Nehemiah (noticeable for their use of "I"), plus archival letters and lists of various kinds, the author-compiler of this book (conceivably Nehemiah himself) records the story of Jewish reform between 458 and 430 B.C. The reform includes the building of the walls around Jerusalem (thus giving definition again to "the place I have chosen as a dwelling for my Name," Neh 1:9; cf. Deut 12:5, 11), repentance over intermarriage, and a covenant-renewal ceremony with the reading from the Book of the Law as its center point. In so doing, the author provides us with the most important source for the history of Judah in the postexilic period.

By watching for the shift between first-person and third-person narratives, you can easily track the flow of the narrative. It begins (Ezra 1–6) with a historical review of events some seventy years earlier—the building of the second temple (538/7 to 516 B.C.). Based on several archival records, this review emphasizes the Persian kings' role in seeing that the temple was, in fact, completed. At the same time the author inserts by way of digression (4:6–23) a much later opposition to rebuilding the walls, which is the more immediate problem of Ezra-Nehemiah. With this literary stroke he ties the two events together as having the same sorts of difficulties from similar sources.

The Ezra memoirs (Ezra 7–10) first locate him in the lineage of Aaron, thus of priestly descent, and then report his return along with others (in 458 B.C.) under the auspices of Artaxerxes. Here the main focus is on rebuilding the religious community in and around Jerusalem in the midst of a conflict surrounding intermarriage, which is recognized as a main source of going astray after other gods.

The first of Nehemiah's memoirs (Neh 1–7) tells the story of the rebuilding of the walls of Jerusalem despite intense opposition by various groups, including even some Jews who had resettled or remained in the land (and were quite syncretistic); it concludes (7:6–73) by repeating the list of returnees found at the beginning of the book (Ezra 2).

This is followed by the high point of the narrative (Neh 8–10)—a covenant-renewal ceremony, which begins with a reinstitution of the Feast of Tabernacles and continues for twenty-four days (ch. 8), climaxing in a great national confession (ch. 9) and a community document signed by the leaders, committing themselves to obedience to specific aspects of "the Law of God given through Moses" (ch. 10).

After two more lists (of the repopulation of Jerusalem and its environs and of the priests and Levites, 11:1–12:26) the book concludes with the second part of Nehemiah's memoirs (12:27–13:31). These describe the consecration of the wall (12:27–47) and some final reforms (ch. 13).

SPECIFIC ADVICE FOR READING EZRA-NEHEMIAH

Before reading Ezra-Nehemiah, you may wish to review what was said about this historical period in "Specific Advice for Reading 1 and 2 Chronicles" (pp. 100–101), since the same basic historical and religious background lies behind this book as well. You should be looking for several emphases in the narrative that offer keys to making sense of things as you read.

Most important, and in keeping with all that has preceded him thus far, our author (reflecting his main sources, Ezra and Nehemiah) is intensely concerned with the purity of faith in Yahweh, the God of Israel. This purity is to be found in keeping the commandments in the "Book of the Law of God." All the reforms mentioned in the book are based on the Law, and the repentance in Ezra 10 and Nehemiah 9–10 is in both cases solely in light of what is said in the Law. This also accounts for the emphasis on the priests and Levites (as in Chronicles), because of their role both in teaching the Law and in maintaining purity of worship.

Crucial to this reform is the crisis over national identity: Who constitutes the true remnant of the people of God and thus is in genuine continuity with the past? It is in this context that you can best understand the urgent concern over intermarriage (Ezra 9–10; Neh 9:2; 10:28–30; 13:23–28). Thus the suggestion that Ezra-Nehemiah is mostly about community building is not far off the mark; it is indeed about rebuilding the community of God, based on the religious realities of the past.

This crisis over national identity is also the context in which to understand the passion for building the walls of Jerusalem. Walls do not simply keep unwanted people out; in ancient times they set boundaries and therefore gave *identity* to a city and its people. Nehemiah lived in a time when Jerusalem, the City of David and the place where God had chosen that his Name should dwell, had become the ultimate symbol of Israel's national and religious identity (a theme that pervades the book of Psalms and is crucial to the Revelation of John).

Finally, this concern over a pure people of God worshiping in a purified temple in a newly consecrated city (the word translated "dedicated" in Neh 3:1 is used most often for "consecrating" holy things) is also the context in which to understand the (somewhat ambivalent) attitude toward the Persian kings. On the one hand, the people, even those who have returned, are regularly referred to as "the exiles" (see esp. Ezra 10)—and they smart from their general lack of independent status as a people ("slaves," Ezra 9:9; Neh 9:36). On the other hand, they know full well that both their temple and the wall around Jerusalem are possible only because of the decree and protection of their Persian overlords—which gives them a margin of safety from local opposition. This is a primary reason for the recounting of the building of the temple in Ezra 1–6, since its construction under the decree of Cyrus serves as an introduction to the main project of Ezra-Nehemiah, namely, the building of the walls—this time on the basis of official letters from Artaxerxes (Neh 2:7–9).

A WALK THROUGH EZRA-NEHEMIAH

☐ **Ezra 1–6** *A Review of the Rebuilding of the Temple (538–516 B.C.)*

Watch for the narrative art of the author-compiler as you read this introduction to his book. Except for 4:6–23, he basically reviews the events surrounding the building of the temple, begun under Cyrus in 538/7 and completed under Darius in 516. In turn he describes Cyrus's decree (cf. 2 Chr 36:22–23) and his beneficence toward the project (Ezra 1); the list of the exiles who returned at that time (ch. 2), focusing especially on the priests and Levites (the interest is in the temple, after all!); the successful beginnings of the project, starting with the altar and then the foundations of the temple itself (ch. 3; don't miss the repetition in v. 11 of the theme from Chronicles); the opposition to the project that brought the rebuilding to a halt (4:1–5, 24) down to the time of Haggai and Zechariah (you might want to read at least the book of Haggai in connection with this part of Ezra); the renewed opposition in 520 that brought about the exchange of official letters (Ezra 5:1–6:12) and cleared the way for its completion (6:13–18), followed by a Passover celebration (6:19–22). What doesn't fit into this review chronologically, of course, is the insertion of the later opposition to an apparently abortive attempt to rebuild the walls (4:6–23 [ca. 448]), which is included here for literary purposes, anticipating the later opposition endured by Nehemiah.

☐ **Ezra 7–8** *The Return of Ezra and Others to Jerusalem (458 B.C.)*

Note how the author begins this section with an introduction to Ezra and his return, emphasizing his being a priest and a teacher of the Law of Moses given by Yahweh (7:1–10). This is followed by Ezra's own memoirs (7:11–8:36, note the shift to the first-person pronoun in 7:27–28), which tell of the circumstances of his leaving Babylon (7:11–28, note especially the role of the Persian king), those who accompanied him (8:1–14), and the circumstances of the return itself (8:15–36).

☐ Ezra 9–10 *The Crisis of Intermarriage*

With this section you come to the first major threat for our author, namely, that the returnees — even many priests and Levites (10:18–24) — "have mingled the holy race with the peoples around them" (9:2) by intermarrying with them. Note how Ezra's prayer (9:6–15) sets forth the main issues (and includes the tension between their present "slavery" and the kindness of the kings of Persia). Chapter 10 then describes the reform itself. Note also that all of this is from Ezra's memoirs.

☐ Nehemiah 1–7 *Rebuilding the Walls under Nehemiah's Governorship (444 B.C.)*

Using Nehemiah's memoirs, the narrator describes in some detail the circumstances surrounding the rebuilding of the wall. He begins with how Nehemiah, a prominent court figure, secured the king's permission and authority to return to Jerusalem (as governor, you learn in 5:14) to rebuild the walls (chs. 1–2). Chapter 3 describes in detail the who and the where of the participants in the project, while chapter 4 describes the opposition (thus recalling Ezra 4:6–23) and their rebuff. Note here also the surfacing of the holy-war theme (Neh 4:20). The interlude of chapter 5 relates Nehemiah's handling a conflict related to Jerusalem's poor — by reinstituting the "no usury" clause from the Mosaic Law (Exod 22:25; Deut 23:19–20). Further opposition and the completion of the project are recounted in Nehemiah 6:1–7:3. But note here the narrator's skill. Instead of going on to the dedication, which appears in 12:27–43, he brings this first long section of his narrative (Ezra 1–Neh 7) to completion by a nearly verbatim repeating of the list of returnees from Ezra 2. This enclosure, which also holds the narrative in suspension, is his way of calling special attention to the two events that follow.

☐ Nehemiah 8–10 *The Renewal of the Covenant*

With this account you come to the first of the two climactic moments in our author's narrative. Before the repopulation of Jerusalem and the dedication of its walls (chs. 11–12) comes the ceremony of primary significance for him — a time of national renewal of the covenant. It begins with a long celebratory reading of the Law (7:73b–8:12) and includes the great celebratory Feast of Tabernacles (8:13–18). This is followed by a time of community confession (ch. 9) in which the long history of disobedience is recounted (cf. Ps 106), and by the corporate signing of the renewal agreement (Neh 10).

☐ Nehemiah 11–12 *The Resettlement and Dedication of the Wall*

Note the narrative insight that puts this event *after* the covenant-renewal ceremony. Once covenant loyalty on the part of the renewed community is in place, then in turn are listed the new population (ch. 11) and the priestly community (12:1–26). With that the walls that give them definition and protection are dedicated (12:27–43)—in great ceremonial pageantry and with much music and praise (the reason for the Levites!).

☐ Nehemiah 13 *The Conclusion: Community Purity Reinforced*

Note that the final concern in the book is the one you have met throughout—that the renewed community of faith be pure with regard to the faith. Singled out are the exclusion of Ammonites from the sacred places (vv. 1–14), the purity of the Sabbath (vv. 15–22), and (not surprisingly) intermarriage (vv. 23–29).

Ezra-Nehemiah advances the biblical story by describing how the necessary reforms in Jerusalem were set in motion, which were later to serve as the basis for the Judaism out of which Jesus and the early church emerge.

Esther

ORIENTING DATA FOR ESTHER

- **Content:** the story of God's providential preservation of Jews throughout the Persian Empire through Mordecai and his niece, Esther

- **Historical coverage:** most of the story takes place during a single year during the reign of Xerxes (486–465 B.C.), a generation before the events recorded in Ezra-Nehemiah

- **Emphases:** God's providential care of the Jews in a context of a pogrom against them; Jewish remembrance of their survival through the feast of Purim

OVERVIEW OF ESTHER

As with the book of Ruth, Esther appears among the Writings in the Hebrew Bible, but in the Septuagint it was placed in its basic historical setting, although after Ezra-Nehemiah. With a marvelous display of wit and irony, and with obvious literary skill, the author tells the story of how Jews in the Persian Empire were saved from genocide instigated by a member of the royal court, who may himself have been a non-Persian— possibly an Amalekite who carried with him their ancient hatred for God's people.

The story revolves around the actions of its four main characters: (1) the Persian king Xerxes (mentioned by name 29x), an arrogant Eastern despot who serves as God's foil in the story; (2) the villain Haman (48x), a foreigner who has been elevated to the highest place in the empire, next to Xerxes himself—who is even more arrogant than Xerxes, and full of hatred for the Jews; (3) the Jewish hero Mordecai (54x), a lesser court official who uncovers a plot that saves the king's life, but whose refusal to bow to Haman sets in motion the basic intrigue of the plot—a plan to kill all Jews in the empire, which ultimately backfires on

Haman; and (4) the heroine, Mordecai's younger cousin, Hadassah, given the Persian name Esther (48x), who by winning a beauty contest becomes Xerxes' queen and the one responsible for unraveling Haman's plot, thus saving the Jews from annihilation.

The story line itself is easy to follow. It begins with a lavish feast given by Xerxes and the deposal of his queen Vashti, who had refused to come and be put on display; this leads in turn to Esther's becoming queen (1:1–2:18). The basic plot of the story, with its various intrigues, unfolds in the central section (2:19–7:10), which climaxes at two private feasts that Esther holds for Xerxes and Haman. The rest of the story primarily has to do with the Jewish defeat of their enemies (the holy war again) and their celebration that eventually becomes the feast of Purim (chs. 8–9). Inside this basic plot is the story of Mordecai, who represents God's favor toward his people, so that the book concludes with Mordecai's exaltation to Haman's position, where he achieved much good for the Jewish people (ch. 10; cf. Daniel's role the century before).

SPECIFIC ADVICE FOR READING ESTHER

As you read this story of Jewish survival, you will want to be looking for two factors that help make the story work. The first is *literary*. The author is a master storyteller, evidenced not only by the way he unfolds the characters and plot but especially by his inclusion of details that provide humor and irony. Who wouldn't smile at the thought of a king whose response to his wife's defiance is an empirewide decree that "every man should be ruler over his own household" (1:22)—as though that would solve the king's own problem! After all, he had been advised that, on the basis of this decree, "all the women will respect their husbands, from the least to the greatest" (1:20)!

You will hardly be able to miss other, although less humorous, touches of irony: Haman, who intends to destroy the Jews, ends up destroying himself and his family; the gallows erected for Mordecai are those on which Haman himself is hanged; Haman's edict was intended to plunder the wealth of the Jews—instead his own estate falls into Jewish hands; Haman, in writing the script for his own honor and recognition, in fact writes the script for Mordecai, and instead of receiving honor Haman must lead Mordecai through the streets of Susa on horseback. And these are not all of them, so be looking for other such moments as you read.

The second factor is *religious*. Although the book of Esther is known for the fact that God is never mentioned in the book (cf. Song of Songs), the author nonetheless expects his intended readers to see God at work at every turn in the story. First, Xerxes himself is portrayed as God's foil: He who displayed "the vast wealth of his kingdom and the splendor and glory of his majesty" (Esth 1:4) turns out to be something of a puppet, manipulated at will by those around him — while the reader knows that the God of eternal glory and majesty is behind everything that happens in the story. Thus, what the unschooled reader might regard as "just happening" is to be recognized instead as God's own sovereignty lying behind, for example, Esther's being chosen as queen (2:15 – 18), the king's sleepless night in which he discovers that he had failed to honor Mordecai (6:1 – 3), the fact that after a three-day fast Esther receives the gold scepter when she approaches the king unbidden (4:11; 5:1 – 2), and so on throughout the book.

The other religious factor you will want to watch for is the author's recognition that the action of Mordecai and Esther — and the Jews who are spared from annihilation — is an expression of the holy war. This comes out first in the conflict between Haman and Mordecai, who carry on the centuries-old conflict between the Israelites and the Amalekites. As the first to attack Israel after her deliverance from Egypt (Exod 17:8 – 16), the Amalekites came to be viewed as the epitome of the surrounding nations that stood against her. But especially this story needs to be read against the background of 1 Samuel 15. It is probably not incidental to this story that Haman is regularly called an Agagite (an intentional link to the Amalekite king in 1 Sam 15 whom Saul refused to slay?), whereas Mordecai — as Saul was — is a Benjamite who also belongs to the line of another Kish (1 Sam 9:1 – 2). This "son of Kish" (Esth 2:5) does indeed land the telling blow on this "Agag."

This is how you are also to understand the narrative in chapters 8 – 10. In a way similar to the narrative of Joshua, the Jews assemble in all the cities of the empire and "no one could stand against them" (9:2). That they saw this as a continuation of the holy war is highlighted by the author in his repeated notation that they would not touch the plunder (9:10, 15, 16; cf. Saul's action in 1 Sam 15:7 – 9), even though the king had decreed that they should have it (Esth 8:11). In the holy war the firstfruits of the plunder belong to God (cf. Deut 13:16).

A WALK THROUGH ESTHER

☐ **1:1 – 2:18** *The Setting: Xerxes, Vashti, Mordecai, and Esther*

The story begins in the palace complex at Susa, where Xerxes gives a great state banquet as a display of his wealth and splendor, while his queen, Vashti, is giving a banquet for the women. Her refusal to also be put on display leads to her being deposed as queen, which sets the stage for Esther. Enter the hero and heroine (2:5 – 7). Mordecai's — and Esther's — actions in this matter are not without their ethical flaws, but both Esther's beauty and her keeping her origins quiet are crucial to the story that follows. Note how this first section ends with yet another banquet, this time in Esther's honor — but especially as a way for the king to show off his new queen.

☐ **2:19 – 3:15** *The Plot Thickens: Mordecai and Haman*

Observe how this section begins by repeating Esther's readiness to follow her cousin's instructions. The plot itself begins with Mordecai using Esther's position as his way of warning the king about an assassination plot. Enter the villain (3:1), who is elevated to his high position and thus demands homage of all others, but Mordecai will not bow down or pay him honor. With his pride pricked, Haman sets in motion the plot to exterminate Mordecai and his people from the empire. Note how this "chapter" concludes with the king and Haman sitting down to drink (in contrast to the Jews, who will proclaim a fast).

☐ **4:1 – 7:10** *The Plot Unfolds: Mordecai and Esther, Haman and Xerxes*

Again Mordecai turns to Esther for help, this time urging that she has "come to royal position for such a time as this" (4:14). Note especially the literary skill of the author in chapters 5 – 7, where he encloses the irony of Mordecai's and Haman's reversals, including Xerxes' sleepless night and the recall of the matter in 2:21 – 23, within the framework of Esther's two banquets. At the end of the second banquet, the ultimate irony is narrated: Haman is hanged on the gallows he had prepared for Mordecai!

☐ **8:1 – 17** *Xerxes' Edict in Behalf of the Jews*

Since Xerxes cannot repeal his former edict, he does the next best thing: Mordecai assists in framing a new decree in which the Jews are allowed to defend themselves against all attacks on the day of the *pur* (the day "the lot" fell for the extermination of the Jews; see 3:7). Notice how the decree is sent to all the provinces in their own languages and that the end result is the conversion of many Gentiles (further fulfilling the Abrahamic covenant, Gen 12:3).

☐ 9:1 – 10:3 *The Triumph of the Jews*

Here you will see the three ways the story is wrapped up: (1) The Jews engage in the holy war and slay many of their enemies, (2) the final feast in the book is narrated—the feast of Purim that will be celebrated annually on the fourteenth and fifteenth days of Adar—and (3) Mordecai is promoted to a position where he is able directly (not through the less certain means of the queen) to benefit the Jews.

The book of Esther tells the story of God's providential protection of his people during a bleak moment in the Persian Empire, thus preserving them for the future gift of the Messiah.

The Writings
of Israel
in the Biblical Story

The books known as the Writings in the Jewish tradition stand in the final position in the Hebrew Bible, after the Law and the Prophets. In the Writings the Psalter is in first position, followed by the four books that belong to the Wisdom tradition plus Ruth—Job, Proverbs, Ruth, Song of Songs, and Ecclesiastes—concluding with Lamentations, Esther, Daniel, Ezra-Nehemiah, and Chronicles. But when the Greek translations of the biblical books were brought together into one collection (the Septuagint), the Writings were rearranged into what seems to be a mostly chronological and/or authorial order, to which then our English Bibles fell heir. Thus, in the current arrangement, only five of these books remain together, even though the traditional Jewish order has much to commend it.

These diverse books play an important role in the biblical story. For here, in a variety of forms, you find inspired human responses to the words and deeds of God that are recorded in the Law and the Prophets. Thus, even though many instructional moments appear in the psalms, for the most part they are prayers addressed to God, with the primary traditions in the biblical story (the promises, the exodus, the giving of the law, etc.) as the bedrock foundation from which these prayers are made—and thereafter recited and sung in the believing community. So one of the things you will regularly want to look for as you read the psalms are the various moments that echo the biblical story—both the revelation of God and his character, and the story of Israel. The same is true of Lamentations, which we have placed in this section so that you will read it in light of what is here said about the book of Psalms.

The Wisdom tradition, on the other hand, is quite different. These books contain few references to these primary traditions. Instead, here are writings whose authors or compilers are wrestling with many of the issues found in the wisdom traditions of *other* cultures. Thus, even though their content assumes Israel's God and story as the basis for their reflections, their method is very similar to what one finds in these other traditions. By and large, Wisdom concentrates on human conduct in society before God. And the assumed reader is "my son," which could refer, of course, to the teacher's own progeny or student but could also refer to anyone in the next generation who needs this instruction.

What makes the biblical books essentially different from the other traditions is their fundamental assumption that "the fear of the LORD [Yahweh] is the beginning of wisdom" (Prov 1:7 and throughout). While this is said less often in the two books that belong to the "speculative" Wisdom tradition (Job and Ecclesiastes), God and his story are nonetheless foundational for their wrestling with the larger questions of life—how to understand the undeserved suffering of the innocent (Job) and how one should live the brief span of years (mere "vapor," as it were) God has given (Ecclesiastes). And at the heart of both of these books is the reminder that true wisdom has to do with the fear of God (Job 28:28; Eccl 12:13–14).

The "odd book out" in all of this is Song of Songs, which does not even mention God and which reflects the Wisdom tradition in a much more specialized way. Nonetheless, even here, where the emphasis is on the delight of monogamous love and human sexuality, the presupposition of the story is Genesis 1–2, where God created man and woman to be precisely like this in their married relationships.

Thus, rather than wonder why God would have included books that speak to us "from our own level," as it were, you can find wonder precisely in the fact that he did so. The delight of these books is that they constantly remind us that God's love and faithfulness, which lie at the heart of the story, demand responses of various kinds from his people—the rich variety of these books both eliciting and guiding your own responses to this love and faithfulness.

Job

ORIENTING DATA FOR JOB

- **Content:** a brilliant wrestling with the issue of the suffering of the righteous and the justice of God, while also speaking to the larger question, "Where is wisdom found?"

- **Date:** the story takes place in the period of the patriarchs; various suggestions have been offered regarding the composition itself

- **Emphases:** wisdom is ultimately found in God alone; human wisdom cannot on its own fathom the ways of God; undeserved suffering has no easy answer; God is not obligated to fallen human beings to explain all things; the fear of the Lord is the path to true wisdom

OVERVIEW OF JOB

The book of Job is one of the literary treasures of the world. The central issue is the struggle over the ways of God, especially his justice when the godly suffer not from human hands but from "acts of God." At the same time, the author raises the question, "Where is wisdom found?" which in the end is powerfully answered in terms of God alone, as each of the participants—the three friends, the younger Elihu, and Job himself—in turn is silenced before the ultimate wisdom of God.

The structure of the book, important to the author's purposes, is easily discernible. The two larger parts (chs. 3–27; 29–42:6) consist of three sets of speeches. Part 1 is a series of *dialogues*. Framed by Job's lament (ch. 3) and closing discourse (ch. 27), the dialogues are also arranged in a three-cycle pattern—speeches by Eliphaz, Bildad, and Zophar, with a response to each by Job. The dialogue cycle gets shorter by a third each time—as they run out of anything new to say and as they all become increasingly blunt in disagreement. Part 2 consists of three

119

monologues: by Job (chs. 29–31), Elihu (chs. 32–37), and God (chs. 38–41)—who has the last word. All of this, except for the narrative framework, is expressed in superb poetry.

The poems are skillfully framed by their narrative setting (chs. 1–2; 42:7–17), which gives the reader an access to what's going on that is not given the participants themselves: Job's suffering is the result of a contest in the heavenly court, where Satan has argued that people are righteous only if they get "paid" for it—the crucial theological issue being put to the test. A second framing device can be found in the central position of the author's own wisdom discourse (ch. 28), which anticipates the answers given in the speeches by God at the end, with respect to "where is wisdom found?" Thus:

chapters 1–2	prologue
chapters 4–27	the three dialogue-disputes
chapter 28	the discourse on "Where does wisdom come from?"
chapters 29–41	the three monologues
chapter 42	epilogue

The four who dispute with Job all express a stark form of conventional wisdom—that a just God would not allow the righteous to suffer unjustly and that Job's suffering, therefore, is the direct result of specific sin. Job knows better, but in the end he has protested too many other things as well. So God speaks out of the storm and calls him—and the whole world—to a humble recognition that human wisdom amounts to nothing before God.

SPECIFIC ADVICE FOR READING JOB

Crucial for your reading of Job is to understand what the author is ultimately about, through both his arrangement of things and the content of the various speeches. His concern lies at two points: (1) the challenge to God by Satan (1:9): "Will [a person] fear God for nothing?" and (2) the question the author himself asks (28:12, 20): "Where can wisdom be found?" The issues are two: As creatures wholly dependent on God for well-being, will the godly love God for himself or only for his benefits? As creatures endowed with creaturely wisdom, are the godly willing to live within the bounds of creaturely wisdom (which is to be one who "fears God and shuns evil," 1:8; 2:3; 28:28), or will they demand to participate as equals in God's wisdom? Thus creaturely *dependence* and creaturely *wisdom* are the points at issue. What will bring these questions to the fore—and will dominate most of the human speeches—is the question of *theodicy,* namely, how to reconcile *undeserved* suffering with a God who is both almighty and just. Each of the participants has a significant role to play in this divine-human drama.

Satan plays the crucial role of putting God on trial, as it were, about the basic relationship between God and his human creatures—whether their reciprocal joy in each other is only the result of what the human creature gets out of it. *Job's wife* plays Satan's role on earth by urging Job to "curse God and die!" (2:9). You can imagine Satan whispering, "Do it, do it!" At issue is whether human beings love God, not for his own sake, but for what they get out of the relationship—which puts them in the driver's seat. But whatever else Job does or says, he will not curse God, as God in his wisdom knows.

Eliphaz, Bildad, and *Zophar* play the (likewise) crucial role of one form of "conventional wisdom"—the unbending, have-it-all-together theologians who believe their wisdom sufficient to understand the ways of God in the world: God is both almighty and just; suffering is the result of human sin; therefore, there is no such thing as undeserved suffering, and Job should own up and confess his (hidden) sins so that he will be restored.

Elihu plays the role of the overconfidence of youth, who think they really are wiser than their elders. At the same time, ironically, he does in fact have an additional point to make that the other three do not—that beyond Job's obviously deserved punishment there is a chastening value to such punishment that Job ought to be willing to accept.

Job plays the central role. For him it is all a frustrating enigma. He believes that his calamities ultimately come from God, yet there is no clear cause-and-effect correlation. But that is also his problem, since at issue for him is his integrity—recognized by God in the opening narrative. He is thus both the innocent sufferer and the one for whom the easy answers do not work anymore. Although he knows that no one is without sin (9:2), nonetheless, in his case, there is no correlation between the enormity of what has happened to him and his sin, and to confess sins not actually committed would be to lose his integrity—and thus take from him something far more than life itself. So he continually seeks an explanation for his suffering, and many of his speeches are pleas for the right to defend himself before God.

Yahweh, of course, plays the ultimate role. As the initiator of the story, he is thus in charge from the beginning, including getting Satan to think about Job—not the other way around. In the end, the tables are completely turned: (1) The question of where wisdom is found is answered not only in terms of God alone but also by silencing all human voices that would insist that God must explain himself to them, and (2) the question of whether one will serve God without receiving benefits is answered with a resounding *yes!*—the crucial role Job will play in the story. The brilliance of this book lies in the fact that although it looks as though it were a theodicy (human beings putting God on trial, insisting on explanations for his actions), it turns out in fact to be a theology (God putting human beings on trial as to whether they will trust him not only when they receive no immediate benefits but also when he does not give them the explanations they demand—and thus as to whether they will live within the bounds of creaturely wisdom). The whole point of the final speeches to Job is that God's wisdom evidenced in the created order is both visible to the eye and yet beyond human understanding (with no explanations given). If that be so, then Job should trust God and his wisdom in the matter of his suffering as well—to which Job offers the ultimate response of humility and repentance.

One final matter. With regard to the long speeches by the five disputants (including Job), we need to be reminded that these are *not* to be thought of as a word from God. Even though Job is more on target than the others (42:8), they all say things that carry enough truth to be dangerous. But their speeches are not God's words; he speaks only at the end, when all human voices have been silenced. Your concern as you read these dialogues is to be aware of their measure of truth, but also of their false suppositions.

You might try reading the poetry aloud. It is much too good for you to let your eye skip over it lightly. The speakers are wrestling with deep issues, and they also have a sense of the power of words, so they often both phrase and rephrase their thoughts. Note, for example, how often a point of comparison is made and then elaborated considerably, even though the elaboration is not strictly required to make the point at hand. Thus, in complaining that his friends are of no help (6:14–23), Job likens them to intermittent streams (v. 15), which he then elaborates richly and eloquently for several lines before returning to their non-help (v. 21). All of it is a wonderful read, even in the midst of so much pain and anguish.

A WALK THROUGH JOB

☐ **1:1 – 2:13** *Prologue*

This opening narrative is *not* the point of the book; it is rather the essential framework within which you are to understand the speeches that follow. Note that it has four parts (marked off by the NIV headings): 1:1–5 gives the essential information that makes the story work; Job is then tested as to whether he will serve God if his possessions are stripped from him (vv. 6–22); when Satan loses that round, he tries again (2:1–10)—and loses, even though Job's wife sides with Satan; the visit by the three friends (vv. 11–13) then sets the stage for the dialogues.

☐ **3:1 – 26** *Job's Lament*

Job finally breaks his silence with a curse against both the day and night of his birth (vv. 3–10); note how the whys in the following lament (vv. 11–26) tie it closely to the curse. Job may wish he had not been born, but neither will he take his own life. Thus pain is his only option.

☐ **4:1 – 14:22** *First Cycle of Speeches*

Job's lament launches the first cycle of speeches, in which each friend speaks in turn and in turn hears Job's response. Note that Eliphaz's speech is the longest of the three, while Job's speeches increase in length as Bildad's and Zophar's get shorter.

Chapters 4 – 5. *Eliphaz* begins the dialogue with an eloquent recital of the basic theology of "the wise." Not yet accusatory (see 4:1–6), this speech prepares the way for the rest. Divine retribution is certain (4:7–11), since no one is innocent before God (4:12–21). Job should therefore appeal to God for help (5:1–16); he is further urged to recognize his calamity as correction and to seek God for his benefits (5:17–26)—thus siding with Satan! Note Eliphaz's supreme confidence in his own wisdom (5:27).

Chapters 6 – 7. *Job* responds by defending his opening lament (6:1–13), accusing his friends of being no comfort to him (vv. 14–23), protesting his innocence (vs. 24–30), and finally appealing directly to God for the comfort lacking in his friends (7:1–21), concluding again with "whys."

Chapter 8. *Bildad* takes up Eliphaz's position, arguing that God is just, and thus calamity is punishment for wrongdoing (vv. 1–7), basing it on traditional teaching (vv. 8–10) and the laws of nature (vv. 11–22). Note how verse 20 states his basic position: Good and evil are clearly defined by what happens to people.

Chapters 9–10. Job's friends are no help, so *Job* agonizes over bringing his case before God, because he is unsure of its outcome (ch. 9); thus he bursts into lament (ch. 10). Note in passing that much of 9:1–10 anticipates chapters 38–39.

Chapter 11. The truth that *Zophar* finally speaks about forgiveness (vv. 13–20) unfortunately follows from his assumption that Job's calamity must be the result of Job's sin (vv. 1–12). How harsh the "righteous" can sometimes be!

Chapters 12–14. *Job* has been stung (12:1–3); to follow their advice (which continually sides with Satan) means to cash in his own integrity. So after defending his skill in wisdom equal to theirs (12:4–13:12), he mulls over bringing a legal case before God, which is his only hope (13:13–14:22), but again it is an agonizing alternative.

☐ 15:1–21:34 *Second Cycle of Speeches*

In this second round of speeches, the three accusers all play variations on a single theme—the present torment and final fate of the wicked. Job's responses show faint glimpses of hope, which are dashed by the others, so he points out finally that the wicked do not always suffer.

Chapter 15. *Eliphaz* appeals once more to their traditional wisdom: It is the wicked who suffer torment, so Job must be wicked, and his own mouth condemns him automatically when he questions his suffering.

Chapters 16–17. *Job* agrees that his affliction is from God, but he is also at a loss as to why. His only hope lies in a heavenly advocate (16:18–21).

Chapter 18. *Bildad* can hardly take it (vv. 1–4), so he picks up from Eliphaz by pointing out the terrible fate of the wicked—like Job!—and thus God will not hear him (vv. 5–21).

Chapter 19. *Job* complains about his friends (vv. 1–6) and about God's treating him as an enemy (vv. 7–12) with the result that his alienation is total (vv. 13–20). His plea for help is accompanied by another note of hope (vv. 21–27) before warning his friends (vv. 28–29).

Chapter 20. *Zophar* rejects Job's note of hope, repeating the refrain about the fate of evildoers.

Chapter 21. *Job* now calls into question his counselors' insistence on God's speedy retribution of the wicked (vv. 7–33), complaining about his friends on either side (vv. 1–6, 34).

☐ 22:1–26:14 *Third Cycle of Speeches*

The debate is now winding down. Note (1) that this final cycle is a third the length of the first one, (2) that there is no speech from Zophar, and (3) how much repetition there is of former arguments.

Chapter 22. Note *Eliphaz's* false accusations against Job (vv. 6–9; cf. 31:13–23), assumed to be true because Eliphaz's theology demands it; so after instructing Job on God's ways once more (22:12–20), he again calls him to repentance (vv. 21–30).

Chapters 23–24. *Job* again expresses a desire to plead his case before God (23:1–7), indicating both hesitant confidence (vv. 8–12) and trembling fear (vv. 13–17). In any case, Eliphaz is simply wrong. The world is full of injustice (24:1–17); may the wicked be cursed (24:18–25).

Chapter 25. *Bildad* utters the counselors' final word: God is too great for Job to question him.

Chapter 26. *Job* agrees about God's majesty, but (in what follows) not the implications they draw from it.

☐ 27:1–23 *Job's Closing Discourse*

Note the introductory formula (v. 1), indicating that these verses will serve (with ch. 3) to bookend the discourses. After arguing that integrity demands that he protest his innocence (27:1–6), Job then turns the tables on his friends, who have become his enemies (vv. 7–12), finally—and ironically—reminding them of the fate of the wicked (vv. 13–23)!

☐ 28:1–28 *Raising the Question of True Wisdom*

Read this pivotal chapter carefully. Here the author—not Job or his "friends"—raises the essential questions: Where can wisdom be found (v. 12)? Where does it come from, and where does it dwell (v. 20)? The answer of course is "in God" (vv. 23–27), and human wisdom is to be found in the fear of the Lord (v. 28). This insertion between the two sets of discourses clearly anticipates the final answer of chapters 38–41.

☐ **29:1–31:40   *Job's Call for Vindication***

In this first of the series of three monologues, Job presents his final case before God. He points out first his past honor and blessing (ch. 29) and then his present dishonor and suffering (ch. 30) before turning to a specific listing of his uprightness with regard to truth and marriage (31:1–12). He concludes with deeds on behalf of the people God himself cares for—widows and orphans (vv. 13–34; over against Eliphaz's accusation in 22:6–9)—before making his final appeal (31:35–40).

☐ **32:1–37:24   *The Elihu Speeches***

After an introduction (32:1–5), Elihu speaks (overconfidently) for the young, making four speeches whose basic point is found in the first one (chs. 32–33, esp. ch. 33)—that rather than protest his innocence, Job should learn about the disciplinary nature of suffering. With this insight, Elihu advances several steps beyond Eliphaz, Bildad, and Zophar, acknowledging at least that the righteous do sometimes suffer. But in his second speech (ch. 34), he agrees with his three elders that God governs a fair universe without exception; so in the third speech (ch. 35), he points out the uselessness of Job's appeals of innocence. In the fourth (chs. 36–37), he concludes by returning to the theme of his first speech (36:6–26) before extolling the majesty of God (ch. 37), which (ironically) prepares Job for what comes next.

☐ **38:1–42:6   *God Speaks and Job Responds***

Here you come to the climax of the book. God speaks out of the storm, breaking silence in fulfillment of Job's deep yearnings. But rather than vindicate Job (as Job had hoped) or reprove him (as his friends expected), God simply calls human wisdom into account, powerfully demonstrating over and over again from creation—both its origins and his care for it—that wisdom lies with him alone.

In the first speech (chs. 38–39), God begins with the basic question for all human wisdom: "Who is this that darkens my counsel with words without knowledge?" (38:2). The rest is a litany of questions about creation intended to give Job (and his friends) perspective: "Where were you when all of this was set in place and carefully watched over?" At the end Job properly responds with shame and silence (40:3–5).

The second speech (40:6–41:34) recounts God's mighty powers and then challenges Job to demonstrate his own prowess—as if he could—

by defeating the two beasts, behemoth and leviathan. The great issue raised by the book finds its answer in Job's twofold response (42:1–6), namely, his admission that he has spoken without understanding, and his repentance once he has truly "seen" Yahweh! And this, of course, is what the author intends that others should do as well.

☐ 42:7–17 *Epilogue*

Note that the epilogue is in two parts: First (vv. 7–9), God pronounces his verdict in favor of Job over against his friends; second (vv. 10–17), God finally vindicates Job—who has maintained trust in God whether he receives benefits or not—with a double portion of everything.

———————————————

The book of Job has an important place in the biblical story, not only by calling us to total trust in God even in the most trying of situations but also by preparing the way for Jesus Christ, who as the incarnate God gives the ultimate answer to Job's question by assuming the role of innocent sufferer—only in his case to bear the sins of the entire world.

Psalms

ORIENTING DATA FOR PSALMS

- **Content:** 150 psalms of rich diversity, which in their present arrangement served as the "hymnbook" for postexilic (Second Temple) Judaism

- **Date of composition:** the psalms themselves date from the early monarchy to a time after the exile (ca. 1000 to 400 B.C.); the collection in its present form may be part of the reform movement reflected in Chronicles and Ezra-Nehemiah

- **Emphases:** trust in and praise to Yahweh for his goodness; lament over wickedness and injustices; Yahweh as king of the universe and the nations; Israel's king as Yahweh's representative in Israel; Israel (and individual Israelites) as God's covenant people; Zion (and its temple) as the special place of Yahweh's presence on earth

OVERVIEW OF PSALMS

The 150 pieces that make up the book of Psalms were originally 147 different psalms (one occurs twice—14 and 53; two are broken into two—9 and 10, 42 and 43). Each was originally composed independently; thus each has integrity and meaning on its own. But the psalms were not randomly collected; rather they have been ordered and grouped in such a way that the whole together carries meaning that further enhances the affirmations each makes on its own. Therefore in the Psalter you can look for meaning both in the individual psalms and in their ordered relationship with each other. The latter is what we especially emphasize in this chapter and encourage you to be aware of as you read.

Although the present arrangement of the Psalter comes from the postexilic period, it also maintains the integrity of smaller collections that were already in use as part of Israel's ongoing history. Besides three collections of Davidic psalms (3–41; 51–70; 138–145), there are also two collections of "Asaph/sons of Korah" psalms (42–50; 73–88), plus four topical collections (God's kingship, 93–100; psalms of praise, 103–107; songs of ascent [pilgrimage songs], 120–134; and Hallelujah psalms, 111–113 and 146–150).

The collection in its present form was brought together as five books, probably with the Pentateuch in view (thus "David" corresponds to "Moses"):

Book 1 Psalms 1–41: All but 1, 2, and 33 titled "of David"

Book 2 Psalms 42–72: Psalms 42–50 "of the sons of Korah" or "of Asaph"; Psalms 51–70 "of David"; concluding with one "of Solomon" (72; note that 71 is untitled), with a coda at the end, "This concludes the prayers of David son of Jesse"

Book 3 Psalms 73–89: All titled, mostly "of Asaph" or "of the sons of Korah"

Book 4 Psalms 90–106: Mostly untitled, except for 101 and 103 ("of David")

Book 5 Psalms 107–150: Mostly untitled, but fifteen are "of David," including Psalms 138–145; also includes fifteen "songs of ascent" (120–134) and concludes with five "Hallelujah" psalms (146–150)

You will note that each book concludes with a similar doxology (41:13; 72:18–19; 89:52; 106:48; and the whole of 150). In the first four instances these are not a part of the original psalm; rather they are the work of the final compiler, and they function to conclude the books themselves. It is also important to observe that, although the vast majority of the psalms are addressed to God, within many of them there are words that address the people themselves (thus assuming a corporate setting), while some of the psalms function primarily as instruction (especially the Torah-Wisdom psalms; e.g., 1; 33; 37). In this regard, compare Colossians 3:16 and Ephesians 5:19 (hymns about Christ sung in thanksgiving to God also function to instruct the people).

SPECIFIC ADVICE FOR READING PSALMS

The psalms were written first of all to be sung—one by one and not necessarily in their canonical order; this is also how they are most often read—as songs. Since chapter 11 in *How to 1* is intended to help you read them this way, the contents of that chapter will be presupposed throughout this discussion, especially the information about the various kinds and forms of psalms and the nature of Hebrew poetry. The present concern is twofold: (1) to help you make some sense of the canonical arrangement of the Psalter and (2) to offer a minimal guide to reading the psalms as part of the biblical story. At the same time you should be constantly watching for their basic theological assumptions, viewed in terms of how the psalms fit into the story. (The analogy would be a Christian hymnbook, which is not intended to be read through, but is in fact carefully arranged, usually along theological/church-year lines.)

It is important to be aware that, even though the majority of the psalms are themselves preexilic, the collection as we have it was the hymnbook of Second Temple (postexilic) Judaism. When you recall the emphasis in Chronicles and Ezra-Nehemiah on the musicians associated with the temple, you can easily imagine the present Psalter taking shape during that period and that the arrangement itself had meaning for them.

The five books are carefully arranged so that they mirror the story of Israel from the time of David until after the exile. Books 1 and 2 basically assume the time of the early monarchy, as David speaks words of lament and praise, both for himself and for the people, based on Yahweh's unending goodness and righteousness. Together they are bookended by two coronation psalms (2 and 72) that extol the king as Yahweh's anointed one for the sake of his people. In book 2, especially in the Korahite collection inserted at the beginning, you also find a goodly number of royal and Zion hymns, which focus on the king but now especially emphasize Jerusalem and its temple as the place of God's presence and reign. Thus both books concentrate on David as king under Yahweh's ultimate kingship.

Book 3, on the other hand, has only one Davidic psalm; instead, by the presence of some prominent exilic and postexilic laments, it assumes the fall of Jerusalem. Picking up the mournful note of Psalm 44, the psalmists repeatedly ask "Why?" and "How long?" regarding Yahweh's rejecting them. This book thus begins with a Wisdom psalm that wonders aloud about the "prosperity of the wicked" (73:3); it ends first with the "darkest" psalm in the Psalter (Ps 88), whose only note of hope is the opening address ("the God who saves me"), and then with a poignant lament over the present (apparent) demise of the Davidic covenant (Ps 89).

In response book 4 begins by going back to Moses with a psalm that reminds Israel that God has been her dwelling place throughout all generations. Then, after two psalms of trust and thanksgiving (91–92), comes the collection of Yahweh's kingship (93–100). Despite the present state of the Davidic monarchy, Yahweh reigns! This book then ends with psalms of praise (101–106), whose last word is an appeal for Yahweh to gather the exiles (106:47).

Book 5 begins with a psalm of praise that assumes the gathering of the exiles (107:2–3), followed by Psalm 108, which acclaims God's rule over all the nations. The rest of this book, more heterogeneous than the others, looks forward in a variety of ways to God's great future for his people. Included are some royal psalms (110; 118) that were used in anticipation of the coming of the great future king, so one is not surprised by the significant role that these psalms played in the earliest Christians' understanding of Christ. Likewise, the psalms of ascent would have been used for present (and in anticipation of future) pilgrimages of God's people to Zion—while the final five "Hallelujahs" (146–150) remind them of God's ultimate sovereignty over all things. Thus in the final arrangement of things, the first three books contain predominantly laments, while the final two are predominantly praise and thanksgiving.

In light of this overall arrangement, you will want to read with an awareness of the undergirding *theological* bases on which these poems (songs, prayers, and teachings) were written. First, even though many of them are individual laments or hymns of praise, the collection itself assumes that even these have a "people of God" dimension to them: The individual is always aware of being part of the people who together belong to God in covenant relationship and who share the same story.

As elsewhere, Yahweh is the center of everything, and the psalmists are fully aware that their own lives are predicated on their covenant relationship to Yahweh. Thus their songs regularly remind those who sing them that Yahweh is the Creator of all that is and therefore Lord of all the earth, including all the nations—reminders that usually also affirm Yahweh's character, especially his love and faithfulness (cf. Exod 34:4–6), but also his mercy, goodness, and righteousness. At the same time they repeatedly echo the significant moments in their sacred history as God's people. Indeed several psalms relate the larger story itself, either in part or in whole, and for different reasons (Pss 78; 105–106; 136). So as you read, be looking for these affirmations about God (including the marvelous metaphors) and for the echoes of the story itself: creation, election, deliverance, the holy war, inheritance of the land, the role of Zion/Jerusalem as the place of God's presence and the abode of his vice-regent the king, and Israel's role in blessing the nations.

Finally, it is important to note that Psalms 1 and 2, which are untitled and framed by the expression "Blessed are ..." (1:1; 2:12), serve to introduce the whole Psalter. Psalm 1 (a Torah-Wisdom psalm) has pride of place because it sets out the basic theological presupposition on which everything else rests, namely, that God blesses those who delight in the law and thus commit themselves to covenant loyalty, while the opposite prevails for the wicked. This serves as grounds for most of the laments, as well as for the songs of praise and thanksgiving, since it is true even when one's experience suggests otherwise. Psalm 2 then introduces the role of the king, who as God's "Anointed One" and "Son" (Israel as Yahweh's son [Exod 4:22–23] now focuses on its king) is Yahweh's protector of his people. Psalm 2 thus serves as the basis not only for the Zion and kingship dimensions of the Psalter—not to mention the agony of Psalm 89—but eventually becomes the key to New Testament messianism as these psalms are recognized as fulfilled in Jesus Christ.

A WALK THROUGH THE PSALMS

Book I (Psalms I to 41)

☐ Psalms 1–2   Introduction to the Psalter

Even though these two psalms introduce the whole Psalter (see above), Psalm 1 also introduces the main thrust of book 1 in particular, while Psalm 2 introduces the main concerns of book 2.

☐ Psalms 3–7   Five Laments (Pleas for Help)

Since book 1 is predominantly lament, it is fitting that three statements of evening and morning trust (3:5; 4:8; 5:3) stand at the beginning of the collection. Typically, these laments combine prayer to Yahweh with affirmations about and trust in Yahweh, also the subject of the address to others in Psalm 4:2–5 (cf. 6:8–9). Psalms 3, 5, and 7 plead for deliverance from foes, while 4 pleads for relief in time of drought and 6 for healing. Note also the theological presuppositions (God's role in the holy war; Yahweh's presence on Zion [3:4; 4:5; 5:7]; God's character [merciful, righteous]) and that each of them presupposes the basic assumptions of Psalm 1.

☐ Psalm 8   *Praise to the Creator*

This hymn revels in Yahweh and his majesty as Creator, and it marvels at his condescension toward humanity and their role in the created order, thus echoing Genesis 1 and 2.

☐ Psalm 9 – 13   *Lament for Deliverance of the "Righteous Poor"*

Together these five (or four) psalms are of exactly equal length to the first five laments (3 – 7). Psalms 9 and 10 together form an acrostic prayer for deliverance, each line beginning with successive letters of the Hebrew alphabet (see Ps 119). The first half (Ps 9) is a plea for deliverance from wicked nations; the second (Ps 10) assumes the stance of the righteous poor, the helpless person who is the recipient of social injustice (see Exod 22:22 – 27; Amos; Isaiah; and Micah). After an affirmation of trust in Yahweh's righteous rule (Ps 11), two further laments appeal for help and deliverance (12; 13). As you read, watch for the various expressed and assumed affirmations about God that mark these psalms.

☐ Psalm 14   *The Folly of Humankind (see Psalm 53)*

Note how this psalm serves to conclude this second set of laments, as Psalm 8 did the first, by pointing out the utter folly and wickedness of humanity that does not acknowledge God (thus echoing Genesis 3), while affirming the righteous poor.

☐ Psalms 15 – 24   *On Access to the Temple*

Together this series of psalms forms a chiastic pattern. In the outer frame, Psalms 15 and 24 ask the same basic question: Who has access to the temple of Yahweh (15:1; 24:3)? The answer, of course, is those who are righteous in keeping with Psalm 1 (note how each affirms different aspects of the law). In the next frame, Psalms 16 and 23 express trust in Yahweh, both concluding on a note of joy for being in Yahweh's presence (16:11; 23:6). Psalms 17 and 22 are then pleas for deliverance, which especially express trust in Yahweh. In the inner frame, Psalms 18 and 20 – 21 together express prayer and praise for the king's deliverance from his enemies (hence picking up on Ps 2). The centerpiece in this group is Psalm 19, which glories in creation (Ps 8)—especially the summer sun as it moves across the sky—and the law (Ps 1). Again, as you read, be looking for the basic theological affirmations (Yahweh's love, Yahweh as Divine Warrior, etc.) and the echoes of Israel's story (the Law, inheritance of the land, election [the point of 22:22–31], their role among the nations, etc.).

□ **Psalms 25–33** *Prayer, Praise, and Trust in the King of Creation*

As with the prior grouping, one can detect a chiastic pattern here as well. In the outer frame (both acrostics), Psalm 25 offers prayer and praise for Yahweh's covenant mercies, while (the untitled) Psalm 33 is a hymn of praise for Yahweh's gracious rule. In the next frame, Psalm 26 is the prayer of one who is "blameless" before Yahweh's covenant law, while Psalm 32 expresses the blessedness of the one whom Yahweh has forgiven. Psalms 27 and 31 both appeal to Yahweh against false accusers (note how they conclude with nearly identical admonitions: "Be strong and take heart"). In the next frame, Psalm 28 is the prayer of one going "down to the pit" (v. 2), while Psalm 30 is praise from one spared from "going down into the pit" (v. 3). As with the preceding group, the centerpiece (Ps 29) praises the King of creation, this time in light of a thunderstorm. Again, mark the various theological affirmations expressed in these hymns.

□ **Psalms 34–37** *Instruction in Godly Wisdom and Appeals against the Wicked*

This group of four psalms also forms a chiasm. Psalms 34 and 37 are alphabetic acrostics, both of which teach godly wisdom (again reflecting Ps 1), while the enclosed psalms appeal to Yahweh as Divine Warrior against malicious slanderers (35) and against the godless wicked (36, which has its own chiastic pattern: vv. 1–4, 5–9, 10–12). Note that in keeping with the Wisdom tradition (see "Overview of Proverbs," p. 145), the "fear of the LORD" lies at the heart of Psalm 34 (see vv. 7, 9, 11), while this is exactly what the godless lack (36:1).

□ **Psalms 38–41** *Four Laments: Prayer and Confession of Sin*

These final laments in book 1 have a fourfold common denominator: (1) The psalmist is in deep trouble (illness in three cases), which he perceives as the result of sin (again, Ps 1); (2) he is mocked by enemies; (3) while appealing for mercy he confesses his sin; and (4) the appeal is based on his trust in Yahweh. It is of some interest that in the original Davidic collection, Psalm 51 would be the next in order, which carries on the theme of confession of sin.

Book 2 (Psalms 42–72)

This book features Zion, the temple, and the king—all of them in relation to Yahweh, who dwells in the temple on Zion and whose king-ship over Israel is represented by the human king—although you will note in this book that the generic name "God" *(Elohim)* occurs with greater frequency than Yahweh ("LORD"). It begins and ends with a series of three prayers followed by a royal psalm (42–44 and 45; 69–71 and 72), whose inner frame is a collection of Zion psalms (46–48) and the marvelous psalm celebrating Yahweh's own enthrone-ment in the temple on Zion (68).

☐ Psalms 42–45   *Three Prayers and a Royal Psalm*

You will observe that Psalms 42 and 43 belong together as one (note the thrice-repeated refrain in 42:5; 42:11; 43:5). Their place at the head of book 2 lies with the psalmist's longing to join in the pilgrimage to Zion (42:4; 43:3–4), while Psalm 44 anticipates book 3 by mourning over a national defeat of considerable proportions (but with no mention of the devastation of Jerusalem as in Ps 74). Note especially the appeals to Israel's history and covenant loyalty. The royal psalm that comes next (45) was composed to celebrate the king's wedding.

☐ Psalms 46–48   *In Celebration of Zion*

This trio of Zion psalms is central to book 2, celebrating the people's security in Zion (46 and 48) and Yahweh's kingship over all the earth (47). No matter how they may have felt about the Davidic dynasty, the singers of Israel well remembered that the real "palace" on Zion was the temple of Yahweh Almighty.

☐ Psalms 49–53   *On the Proper Stance before God*

Watch for the echoes of Yahweh's rule from Zion in this group of psalms (50:1–15; 51:18–19; 52:8–9; 53:6), even as they focus on other matters. As a group they contrast proper and improper approaches to

God—not to trust in wealth (49), but to bring sacrifices based on covenant loyalty (50), especially a penitent spirit (51), because God rejects the wicked (52) and exposes their folly (53).

☐ Psalms 54–59 *Six Laments: Prayers for Help*

Note what is common to these laments, namely, that they assume the king's presence in Jerusalem, that they assume Yahweh's presence in Jerusalem, that they are all complaints against enemies, and that the chief weapon of their attacks is the mouth (slander, lies, etc.).

☐ Psalms 60–64 *Five Prayers with Common Themes*

These five psalms are enclosed by a community lament (60) and an individual lament against enemies (64). Watch how they all continue some of the previous themes: They are spoken by the king; Yahweh's presence on Zion lies at the heart of both prayer and praise; they look to Yahweh for protection or deliverance from enemies.

☐ Psalms 65–68 *In Praise of God's Awesome Deeds and Presence*

The main theme of book 2 comes into full focus with this group of hymns and thanksgivings that exalt Yahweh's kingship by recalling his "awesome" deeds, first on behalf of the whole earth (65 and 67) and then on behalf of Israel (66 and 68). Psalm 68 is especially crucial, both to book 2 and to the whole Psalter, as it celebrates Yahweh's enthronement on Zion—note how he has moved from Sinai to Zion, and thus is King over Israel and the nations, not to mention the whole earth. Psalm 72, which concludes book 2, must be read in light of this psalm.

☐ Psalms 69–72 *Three Prayers and a Royal Psalm*

Book 2 now concludes in a way similar to how it began—with three pleas for help that conclude with a royal psalm. Note how the plea in Psalm 69 especially assumes David's role as king in relation to the people. Note further that Psalms 70 and 71 rework/restate portions of Psalms 40:13–17 and 31:1–5. The final psalm (72) is crucial to the larger concerns of the Psalter: An enthronement psalm attributed to David's son, Solomon, it functions with Psalm 2 to frame the royal dimension of books 1 and 2; at the same time, it stands in bold relief to the conclusion of book 3 (89), which mourns the present demise of the Davidic dynasty.

Book 3 (Psalms 73–89)

The several prominent exilic and postexilic laments in this collection (including several community laments) reflect the time after Zion had been laid waste, the temple desecrated, and the Davidic dynasty, with its "everlasting covenant" (see 2 Sam 7:14–16), was now without a king. Thus, even the several preexilic psalms (e.g., 76; 78; 83; 84; 87) are best understood in this light; namely, that they contain the memory that the surrounding psalms now lament.

☐ Psalms 73–78   On Rejection and Hope for Zion

As in book 1, a Wisdom psalm opens book 3, pondering the puzzle of the prosperity of the wicked and thus setting the tone for what follows. Along with Psalm 78 (another Wisdom psalm), it frames two prayers (74; 77) that cry out the basic question of book 3 (Why have you rejected us?/Will the Lord reject us forever?). These in turn frame a thanksgiving and a Zion psalm (75/76), which highlight the reasons for the laments. Note that Psalm 78 is one of four psalms that retell Israel's story in some detail (cf. 105; 106; 136), in this case recalling past rebellions and their dire consequences as a warning to what could—and did—happen again, on an even larger scale.

☐ Psalms 79–83   On Rejection and Hope for Zion, Again

This group of five is framed by two sets of psalms that again express the basic theme of book 3. Although Psalms 79 and 80 reflect two different times (after and before the fall of Jerusalem), they have in common the basic question "How long?" (79:5; 80:4). Likewise Psalms 82 and 83 have in common the plea that concludes the first one (82:8) and begins the second (83:1): "Rise up" and "do not keep silent." Together these enclose an exhortation to Israel that suggests the reason for her fall (81).

☐ Psalms 84–89   In Celebration of Zion, and Lament
over Its Demise

This final group is in two sets of three, each set having a similar pattern. They begin (84) with a celebration of, and yearning for, the courts of Yahweh. This is followed by another psalm that asks the theme question ("Will you be angry with us forever?" 85:5), which is followed in turn by the only Davidic psalm in book 3 (Ps 86)—a plea for mercy based on the great revelation of Yahweh on Sinai, that he is a "compassionate and gracious God, slow to anger, abounding in love and faithfulness" (v. 15; cf. Exod 34:4–6).

The second set follows the same pattern—beginning with a celebration of Zion (Ps 87), followed by the dark lament of Psalm 88, and concluding with a three-part psalm (89) that echoes concerns from Psalm 86. The first part (89:1–18) celebrates Yahweh's love and faithfulness to his people, especially evidenced by the covenant with David (vv. 19–37); together these become the basis for the lament over the present demise of the Davidic dynasty (vv. 38–51). Note that the concluding section of Psalm 89 contains the theme question: "How long, O Lord?" (v. 46).

Book 4 (Psalms 90–106)

In direct response to the devastation of Jerusalem and the present void in the Davidic dynasty, book 4 begins with the reminder that Yahweh has been Israel's "dwelling place" throughout all generations. The heart of this collection, therefore, is the series of psalms that celebrate Yahweh's kingship—over both Israel and all the nations. The book ends with a series of responses to Yahweh's reign, concluding with two that retell Israel's story from two different perspectives.

☐ Psalms 90–92 *Yahweh Our Dwelling Place*

Reaching back to the one psalm that is titled "of Moses," the collector placed this psalm at the head of book 4, with its opening assurance that God has been Israel's "dwelling place throughout all generations." This is followed by a psalm of trust, which has making "the Most High your dwelling" as its centerpiece (91:9), and by a psalm of praise to "O Most High" (92:1) for his many benefits, including the defeat of adversaries.

☐ Psalms 93–99 *Yahweh Reigns, Let the People Rejoice*

The common theme of this group of psalms is their celebration—in a variety of ways and for a variety of reasons—that Yahweh reigns over Israel, the nations, and the whole earth. The one apparent exception (94) nonetheless assumes Yahweh's reign as it calls for justice on those who reject Yahweh's law. Note also the inherent warning in 95:7–11, which picks up the concerns of Psalm 78 and anticipates the concluding psalm of this book (106), and is the basis for the exhortation in Hebrews 3:7–4:11.

☐ Psalms 100–106 *In Praise of Yahweh and in Hope of Restoration*

This final group in book 4 forms a kind of mini-Psalter, as these psalms reflect various responses to Yahweh's reign: celebration (100); a pledge to live faithfully (101); a prayer for the future rebuilding of Zion (102; note especially v. 12, which assumes Yahweh's reign but pleads for him also to return to Zion); praise for Yahweh's great love (103); and praise of Yahweh as Creator (104). The concluding two psalms retell Israel's story from two points of view: a call to remember all his mercies in that story (105) and a warning not to repeat the rebellion side of the story (106). Note how book 4 ends with a prayer of deliverance from exile (106:47, reflecting Deut 30:1–10).

Book 5 (Psalms 107–150)

This final book in the Psalter is much more varied, both in form and content, than the first four. It begins with a thanksgiving psalm that opens (107:1–3) in direct response to the prayer in Psalm 106:47; it ends with the five Hallelujah psalms. Besides the central role of Psalm 119, which echoes the concerns of Psalm 1, the major part is composed of three sets of psalms: (1) 110–118, which begin and end with psalms that, in this setting at least, look forward to the renewal of the Davidic kingship; (2) 120–134, the songs of ascent—now sung in the context of the second temple, but also with a future orientation; and (3) 138–145, a Davidic collection that functions as a kind of reprise, looking back to books 1 and 2, and concluding on the note of the eternal nature of God's kingdom and his faithfulness to his promises (145:11–13). Thus, on the whole, this book contains psalms that reflect the current situation and the future longings of postexilic Judaism.

☐ Psalms 107–109 *In Praise of God's Rescue of His People, and Two Davidic Laments*

Although not written with the return of the exiled community in mind, the opening hymn of thanksgiving for deliverance begins with the "gathering" motif (107:1–3) and thus serves to introduce book 5. Note how readily Psalm 108 responds to this, combining praise (vv. 1–5) with an appeal for Yahweh to give aid against Israel's enemies (vv. 6–13)—a psalm constructed from 57:7–11 and 60:5–12—while Psalm 109 picks up that plea, spelling out the enemy's sins in great detail and asking the divine Judge for justice in kind.

☐ **Psalms 110–118** *The Coming King, and Festival Psalms*

This group of psalms is framed by two royal psalms (110; 118) that in postexilic Judaism were recognized as messianic, which explains why together they played such an important role in Jesus' own ministry (Mark 11:4–12:12, 35–37) and in the early church (Ps 110 in particular; Acts 2:34–35; Rom 8:34; 1 Cor 15:25; Col 3:1; Heb 1:13). They enclose a series of psalms (excepting 114) that either begin or end with "Hallelujah," which were used in Israel's great festivals. Psalm 114 is one of Israel's great celebrations of the exodus—with marvelous imagery (the sea "looked and fled," Mount Sinai "skipped like rams").

☐ **Psalm 119** *In Celebration of the Law, Yahweh's Faithful Word*

This great poem in celebration of the Law forms the centerpiece of book 5, thus taking us back to the introductory Psalm 1. An alphabetic acrostic (eight lines of poetry for each letter of the Hebrew alphabet), it was composed by someone who recognized the benefits of, and gloried in, God's covenantal gift to his people.

☐ **Psalms 120–134** *Songs of Ascent*

This collection, all titled, belongs to the tradition of making the pilgrimage to Zion for the three annual feasts. In the setting of postexilic Judaism, they almost certainly also carry a forward-looking dimension. Be looking for the many different theological and "story of Israel" themes that are found in these psalms.

☐ **Psalms 135–137** *In Response to the Ascents*

Psalms 135 and 136, as different as they are, both assume the pilgrims' arrival at Yahweh's sanctuary for worship. Note how the first one praises him for creation and election (over against those whose gods are idols), and the second is another retelling of Israel's story, with antiphonal response. The final one (137) bemoans the reality of the exile when pilgrimage was not possible.

☐ Psalms 138–145 *The Final Davidic Collection*

The main body of the Psalter appropriately concludes with a final collection of psalms attributed to David. They begin with praise (138), move to an acknowledgment of Yahweh's greatness as the all-knowing, ever-present God—expressed in wonder, not fear (139)—followed by five prayers for deliverance (140–144). They conclude with another alphabetic acrostic (145) praising Yahweh for his awesome works and his character (goodness, compassion, faithfulness, righteousness). Note especially verses 11–13, which anticipate God's everlasting kingdom.

☐ Psalms 146–150 *Fivefold Hallelujah*

These concluding "Hallelujahs" punctuate the main point of the Psalter: God is to be praised—for his being the Helper of the helpless (146); as Creator and Restorer of his people (147; note how these two themes are interwoven); from heaven above and earth below (148); with dancing, with the mouth, and with sword in hand (149); and with calls to praise with all manner of music and dancing (150). This last psalm seems to have been composed deliberately to conclude both book 5 and the entire Psalter. We do well to heed this call on a continuing basis. God is worthy. Hallelujah!

The collection of psalms, which is the voice of Yahweh's people singing to him in praise and prayer, functions also to remind them—and us—of the central role of worship in the biblical story, worship that focuses on the living God by recalling his essential goodness and love and his wondrous deeds on their behalf.

Proverbs

ORIENTING DATA FOR PROVERBS

- **Content:** a series of opening poems praising wisdom and warning against folly, followed by several collections of proverbs from sages who taught wisdom to Israel, starting with Solomon

- **Author(s):** collections of proverbs originating with Solomon, various wise men, Agur, and Lemuel's mother—gathered and arranged for later generations by someone otherwise unknown

- **Emphases:** wisdom begins with the fear of and trust in Yahweh; at the practical level, it consists of making wise choices between good and evil behavior; such wisdom is to be desired above all else in order to live a full and godly life

OVERVIEW OF PROVERBS

The larger part of the book of Proverbs is made up of six collections of proverbs/aphorisms, that is, wisdom sayings, mostly couplets (two-liners) that offer guidance to the young—although their value is by no means limited to any age group—on how to live morally and beneficially in the world. On either side of these collections is a prologue of several poems (1:8–9:18) that stress the importance of listening to the sages, and an epilogue of one poem (31:10–31) that idealizes a wife who is characterized by wisdom. A preamble (1:1–7) sets forth the book's title, purpose, and theme.

The groupings of proverbs and aphorisms are all identified within the book itself:

Proverbs of Solomon I (10:1–22:16)
Sayings of the Wise I (22:17–24:22)
Sayings of the Wise II (24:23–34)

Proverbs of Solomon II (25:1 – 29:27)
Sayings of Agur (30:1 – 33)
Sayings of Lemuel (31:1 – 31)

All of these are intended to be read and studied in light of the prologue, with its emphasis on the need to attain wisdom and to reject folly
(to walk in righteousness and to shun evil). Here you also find the book's
fundamental theological perspective: "The fear of the LORD is the beginning of wisdom, and knowledge of the Holy One is understanding"
(9:10; cf. 1:7). For even though many of the proverbs are common to
other cultures, these have been especially tailored for life in the covenant
community of Israel. They presuppose not only the covenant of law
(6:16 – 19) — indeed, to fear Yahweh is to hate evil (8:13) — but also the
life of the people of God in their promised land (2:21 – 22; cf. 10:27 – 30).

SPECIFIC ADVICE FOR READING PROVERBS

As with the book of Psalms, reading through the book of Proverbs is
not the ordinary way of handling the proverbs (who would read a collection of familiar quotations?). On the other hand, the preamble, the
prologue, and the macrostructure of the whole indicate a rather careful
overall arrangement, probably intended to be memorized by the young
(see 3:3; 4:21; 7:3; 22:17 – 18). So two matters are of importance in
order for you to read the book well.

First, some observations about *structure*. The preamble (1:1 – 7) prepares you for reading the book as a whole, setting forth its theme (v. 2,
attaining wisdom), its purpose (vv. 3 – 5), the basic contrasts between
wisdom and folly (v. 7), and its theological foundation (v. 7). At the
same time verse 6 offers an outline of the book, according to its main
"authors" (proverbs belonging to Solomon and the sayings of the wise).

It is important to observe that the contrast between wisdom and folly
is also a contrast (primarily) between righteousness and wickedness.
These contrasts become the predominant theme in the poems of the prologue (1:8 – 9:18), where the two main illustrative themes are *easy money*
(money taken by corrupt means) and *easy sex* (being seduced by another
man's wife). At the end of the prologue, wisdom and folly are personified as women calling the young men to follow them. It is therefore no
surprise that the central section of these poems (chs. 5 – 7) admonishes
the young man to a lifelong love of his wife (5:15 – 19) and not to be

tempted by a wayward wife, which in turn also serve as analogies for loving wisdom rather than folly (chs. 8–9). This also helps to make sense of the acrostic poem with which the entire collection ends (31:10–31), where the idealized wife is a model of wisdom, while serving as an analogue for Lady Wisdom. It is also not surprising that these poems are primarily in the form of admonitions.

These contrasts between wisdom and folly carry through the first half of Solomon I (10:1–15:29), now with mostly antithetical couplets (the second line in sharp contrast to the first) rather than with admonitions. Here wisdom/righteousness means diligence in work and care of the land, prudent use of money (resources), caring relationships with neighbor and in family, proper use of the tongue, and proper attitudes and actions (being humble, avoiding anger, etc.); while folly is pictured as its opposites. The second half of Solomon I (15:30–22:16) continues these themes, now using predominantly synthetic couplets (the second line completes or builds on the first), with the noteworthy addition of several proverbs that focus on the king and his court.

Second, a few comments about proverbs themselves and what makes them work. First, their *form* is that of poetry. But the poetry is *Hebrew* poetry, which means that some things translate into English, and some do not. Think about how difficult it might be to put the following English aphorisms into another language: "A stitch in time saves nine," or "A penny saved is a penny earned," or "An apple a day keeps the doctor away." Common to these are their rhythmic nature and "sound alike" pattern, which are what makes them memorable. Another language cannot always capture these qualities, even though the gist of the proverb may be plain. So it is with these Hebrew proverbs, which are pithy (typically only three or four Hebrew words to a line) and full of alliterations, catchwords, poetic meter, etc.—not to mention allusions and metaphors that belong to their cultural setting, not all of which are easily captured in English.

Their *function* is to offer practical instruction for the young, with the focus on how to live uprightly and well in a society that understands itself to be under God. It is important to remember that these proverbs functioned primarily in the home to reinforce the benefits of living prudently and well in everyday life; they are not religious instruction as such. Nonetheless, their goal is to mold the character of the young in ways that conform to the law, even if the law itself is not mentioned.

Their *method* is the same as with proverbs universally—to express important truths for practical living in ways that are memorable and thus repeatable. This is done by overstatement, by "all or none" kinds of phrases, or by catchphrases that are not intended to be analyzed for their precision. Sometimes it is the overstatement—which speaks truth but not the whole truth—that makes the point. Take, for example, the American proverb, "A penny saved is a penny earned." While true, its point is thrift, *not* that one should never spend. Or take its reverse, "A fool and his money are soon parted," which reminds one of the need for thrift in a different way. The latter has an earlier counterpart in Proverbs 17:16, "Of what use is money in the hand of a fool, since he has no desire to get wisdom?" Thus what is at stake for you in reading the proverbs is to determine their point by looking carefully at their content and poetic form, but to be careful also not to make them "walk on all fours"—and not to ignore counterproverbs, which also speak truth. (See *How to 1*, pp. 231–41.)

A WALK THROUGH PROVERBS

The Preamble (1:1–7)

Several important matters for reading the whole collection are presented here. The proverbs originate with Solomon, who is significantly noted as the son of David, king of Israel (v. 1); their purpose is given (vv. 2–5)—to attain a prudent life that is also righteous and just; they are addressed to the young and "simple" (v. 4, the latter word meaning something like "gullible"—those who are easily led astray); their content is anticipated (v. 6); and their basic perspective and basic contrasts are spelled out (v. 7).

The Prologue (1:8–9:18)

To understand the collection of proverbs that begins in 10:1, it is important for you to pay close attention to this prologue. You will see that it comes as a series of ten lessons from a father to his son(s), especially picking up the antitheses set out in 1:7; you will also see that most of this material comes as admonition. Each new lesson begins with an introduction of several couplets ("Listen, my son, to your father's instruction," etc.), followed by the lesson itself. The lessons themselves are carefully structured and arranged, building toward the climax of chapter 9, where wisdom and folly make their final appeals.

☐ **1:8–33** *Lesson 1 (and Interlude 1): Warning and Rebuke*

Note that this first introduction (vv. 8–9) includes both the father and mother (cf. the beginning of the collection at 10:1). You will see that this lesson is a strong warning against the enticements of wicked men (vv. 10–19) who plot evil against others for easy money ("ill-gotten gain").

You will also see that in the interlude (vv. 20–33), personified wisdom speaks, rebuking not the "son" but the "simple ones" and "mockers," those who would entice the son away from his parents' wisdom. Her rebuke basically describes the just end of such people.

☐ **2:1–22** *Lesson 2: Safeguard against the Wicked*

Watch for the four distinct parts of this lesson. A longer introduction urges the son to seek wisdom (vv. 1–4); then he will "understand the fear of the LORD and find the knowledge of God" (vv. 5–6), which in turn will protect his way (vv. 7–8) and enter his heart to guard him (vv. 9–11). What follows, then, are the two main ways in the prologue the son needs protection: (1) from "wicked men" (vv. 12–15) and (2) from the "wayward wife" (vv. 16–19). Verses 20–22 then return to his walking in the paths of the righteous.

☐ **3:1–35** *Lessons 3 and 4: The Value of Wisdom*

Lesson 3 (verses 1–10) sets forth God's promises and the son's obligations: love and faithfulness = favor with God and people (vv. 3–4); trust in the Lord = straight paths (vv. 5–6); humility = good health (vv. 7–8); tithes and offerings = abundant crops (vv. 9–10).

Lesson 4 (verses 13–26) presents three poems that highlight the value of wisdom (note the 6–2–6 couplet arrangement)—its blessings and value (vv. 13–18; note the "blessed" at the beginning and end); its role in creation (vv. 19–20), picking up on "the tree of life" from verse 18; and its blessings again (vv. 21–26), now picking up especially the theme of peace and prosperity from verse 2.

Now watch how verses 27–35 at the end of lesson 4 correspond to lesson 3 by offering negative admonitions and warnings.

☐ **4:1–27** *Lesson 5–7: The Supremacy of Wisdom*

The first of these three lessons (vv. 1–9) emphasizes the family's heritage of wisdom and thus urges the sons to continue in it. Lesson 6 then urges the son to stay off the wrong way, the way of wickedness (vv. 10–19), while lesson 7 urges him not to swerve off the right way, the way of righteousness (vv. 20–27).

☐ 5:1–6:19 *Lesson 8: Warnings against Adultery, Folly, and Wickedness*

Picking up from 2:16–19, this lesson warns against adultery (5:3–14, 20), which also includes an admonition to marital fidelity (vv. 15–19); this is followed by a further warning against the wicked (vv. 21–23) and against two kinds of folly (securing strangers, 6:1–5; sloth, vv. 6–11). It concludes with the final warning in the prologue against the wicked (6:12–19).

☐ 6:20–35 *Lesson 9: Further Warning against Adultery*

Note how this introduction begins as the others did (vv. 20–23), but concludes on the warning note (vv. 24–25) that will then be elaborated. With a threefold series of couplets (vv. 26–29, 30–33, and 34–35), the lesson points out the fearful consequences of adultery (punishment, disgrace, a vengeful husband).

☐ 7:1–8:36 *Lesson 10 (and Interlude 2): The Unfaithful Wife, and Wisdom's Call*

This final lesson corresponds to lesson 8, focusing now on the seductive tactics of the unfaithful, adulterous wife. Note that she will also serve as an analogue for the invitation of Folly at the end of the prologue (9:13–18; cf. 9:18 with 7:27; and 9:14 with 5:8).

Notice how the second interlude (8:1–36) corresponds to the first one (1:20–33), which followed the warning against the "wicked men." This time Wisdom offers self-praise to the "simple" and "foolish" (v. 5) to recognize her value both to kings and the prosperous (vv. 12–21), not to mention to Yahweh himself (vv. 22–31). And at the end (vv. 32–36), she steps into the father's shoes and invites the sons to watch daily at her doorway (vis-à-vis the seductress).

☐ 9:1–18 *Epilogue: Rival Banquets of Wisdom and Folly*

Note how this final series begins and ends with rival invitations to "all who are simple" to banquet at the houses of Wisdom and Folly (vv. 1–6; 13–18), and note especially how Folly both mimics Wisdom and echoes the seductions of the unfaithful wife. Between the two final invitations you will find two brief lessons (vv. 7–9, 10–12) contrasting the wise and mockers—all of this to lead you into reading the proverbs themselves with diligence and thoughtfulness.

Proverbs of Solomon I (10:1–22:16)

☐ **10:1–15:29   Solomon I, Part I**

Our division of Solomon I into two parts is intended to highlight the fact that most of the couplets in this section are antithetical, thus following hard on the antitheses of the prologue. But in contrast to the prologue, there is scarcely an admonition among them. They begin with a couplet (10:1) that not only picks up the "instruction" of the young from the prologue, but also puts both parents in the picture, along with the contrast between the wise and foolish child.

As you read through this collection, note how certain themes characterizing wisdom/folly and righteousness/wickedness are replayed over and over in different ways and with different images. Scholars are only recently discovering various patterns that hold smaller groupings together, often in relationship to groupings that precede and follow. But many of these are difficult to trace in English translation. So two things may help you here as you set out to read through the proverbs.

First, be aware of the many educative proverbs that look very much like the introductions to the lessons in the prologue (e.g., 10:17; 12:1; 13:13). These usually mark "seams" in the collection, so you should look more closely at the smaller groupings before and after these educative proverbs.

Second, you might find it helpful to use a set of colored pencils and mark out some of the recurring themes. Along with the more generic wise/foolish and righteous/wicked themes, note the frequency of themes such as wealth/poverty, work/sloth, speech (truth/lying, etc.), relationships (neighbors, family, king), and attitudes (anger, love/hatred, etc.).

For example, the following may be marked out among the thirty-two couplets in chapter 10: Contrasts between the righteous and the wicked (either expressly or implied) occur 18x, both generically (10x, where this is the point of the proverb [vv. 3, 6–7, 9, 24–25, 27–30]) and in conjunction with other themes (8x, vv. 2, 11, 16, 20–21, 23, 31–32); contrasts between wisdom and folly occur 2x generically (vv. 1, 23) and 8x in conjunction with other themes (vv. 5, 8, 13–14, 18–19, 21, 31); contrasts between proper and improper speech occur 11x (vv. 8, 10–11,

13–14, 18–21, 31–32) and constitute the main theme in most of their occurrences; contrasts between work and sloth are the subject 3x (vv. 4–5, 26); and contrasts between wealth and poverty occur 3x (vv. 15–16, 22), occurring in conjunction with work/sloth in verse 4. The only proverb in this chapter that does not belong to these concerns is verse 17, which deals with discipline (cf. also v. 13). The fact that many of these are related and grouped suggests that the arrangement is not simply haphazard. You may wish to try this for yourself on other small groupings that emerge as you read.

☐ 15:30–22:16   *Solomon I, Part 2*

While this section of Solomon I continues the themes and emphases of part 1, they are noticeably different in two ways. First, you will see that, even though antithetical couplets still occur, the majority of couplets are now synthetic, so that both lines add up to one point. Second, there is an increase in couplets that reflect the king and his court (and other forms of "vertical" relationships, which began at 14:28, 35 in part 1).

The Sayings of the Wise (22:17–24:34)

☐ 22:17–24:22   *First Collection of the Sayings of the Wise*

Two things mark this collection to distinguish it from Solomon I: (1) The verses are not uniform, having from two to several lines each, and (2) they return to the admonitions that marked the prologue. Note also that they are introduced and numbered as "thirty" (22:20), which probably includes the introduction (22:17–21) as the first of these. Watch for the interesting and broad range of topics covered here.

☐ 24:23–34   *Second Collection of the Sayings of the Wise*

This collection is separate, because "thirty sayings" (22:20) sets limits to the preceding collection. The five sayings of this second collection are diverse both in form and content, dealing with relationships with neighbors and diligence in work.

Proverbs of Solomon II (25:1–29:27)

Observe how this collection of Solomonic proverbs moves away from the admonitory style that has just preceded it. These were collected by

Hezekiah's "men." Two collections are in evidence (chs. 25–27; 28–29), while the whole is less uniform in style than Solomon I.

☐ 25:1–27:27   Solomon II, Part I

You will find that in this first part the proverbs are more vivid and diverse in nature, with explicit comparisons becoming more frequent (note the number of verses that begin with "like"). The collection begins with a series relating to the king's court (25:2–8), which also sets a pattern for several longer units (sometimes called "proverb poems": 25:16–17, 21–22; 26:23–26; 27:23–27). Otherwise most of them repeat themes found in the first collection.

☐ 28:1–29:27   Solomon II, Part 2

This second collection is a series of fifty-five (mostly antithetical) couplets that focus primarily on the wicked and the righteous. Note how the first, middle, and final couplets make this theme explicit (28:1, 28; 29:27; but see also 28:12; 29:2, 7, 16), and that they frame couplets that are basically concerned with rulers, teaching, and justice for the poor.

More Sayings of the Wise (30:1–31:31)

☐ 30:1–33   Sayings of Agur

This diverse collection is full of interest, in terms of both form and content. Note especially the following: how verses 2–4 echo material in Job 38:5–11; the prayer in verses 7–9 (the only one in Proverbs); the four classes of wrongdoers singled out in verses 11–14; and the numerical sayings/riddles in verses 15–31, which seem to contain simply various kinds of observations about life as opposed to specific moral teaching.

☐ 31:1–9   Sayings of Lemuel

This final collection is unique in that it relates sayings of a king taught to him by the queen mother. Both parts of this concluding chapter, therefore, offer examples of wise women—thus serving to bookend the instruction of Lady Wisdom in chapters 1–9.

☐ 31:10–31 *Epilogue: A Wise/Ideal Wife*

This final, idealistic portrait of "a wife of noble character" is probably to be understood as another saying that Lemuel's mother taught him. It is an acrostic poem (each verse begins with a succeeding letter of the twenty-two-letter Hebrew alphabet). Note how it idealizes the wife in terms of the values that have been taught throughout the book—a fitting conclusion to the collection.

The book of Proverbs fits into the biblical story by giving practical instruction to the young (and all others listening in) in order to help them follow in the ways of the Lord and have a beneficial, fruitful life on earth.

Ecclesiastes

ORIENTING DATA FOR ECCLESIASTES

- **Content:** the ponderings of a Wisdom teacher who wrestles with life's realities; what is to be gained by achieving wealth or wisdom when in the end death claims both rich and poor, wise and foolish; but specially set in a context of knowing the fear of God

- **Date of composition:** unknown; scholarly guesses cover a broad range

- **Emphases:** the transitory nature of present life; how to live wisely in a world where the only certainty is death and judgment; the futility of human pursuits that do not take the fear of God into account

OVERVIEW OF ECCLESIASTES

Ecclesiastes comes to us from an editor (12:9–14) who has compiled the teachings and proverbs of an Israelite king who calls himself Qohelet ("assembler"), a title that alludes to his role as a teacher of wisdom in an assembly—presumably of God's people (12:9). A prologue (1:1–11) sets forth the basic concern that drives Qohelet's whole enterprise, namely, the *hebel* (= "breath," "vapor"; NIV, "meaningless") nature of human life in a world that continues as it was before and after anyone's own life span. The book concludes with the words of the editor-compiler, who encourages contemplation of Qohelet's words as goads for the young, but also warns that there is a proper limit to such speculation (12:12)—and in the end he makes sure that all is placed within the ultimate setting of biblical wisdom: Fearing God by keeping his commandments gives meaning to human life.

The words of Qohelet himself are enclosed (1:2; 12:8) by the melancholy refrain: *Hebel, hebel!* says Qohelet; *Hebel* of *hebel!* Everything is *hebel*. The rest is an inquiry into how one should live in such a world, since reality isn't as neat as some expressions of traditional wisdom might lead one to think. And the structure of the book mirrors its content, for there is no immediately apparent order to it. What the author does is to play and replay certain themes, all the while moving toward his concluding advice to the young (11:9–12:7): to enjoy life while they are young, but to do so remembering their Creator. If Qohelet's material can be divided into coherent subdivisions at all, they would seem to be 1:12–6:12 and 7:1–12:7, the first playing and replaying Qohelet's primary concerns, the second, while keeping these themes alive, sounding much more like proverbial wisdom.

SPECIFIC ADVICE FOR READING ECCLESIASTES

Traditionally, no other book in the Bible has been such a difficult read. This is because of (1) the somewhat rambling nature of many of Qohelet's observations—at least to the Western mind—(2) some strikingly antithetical statements existing together in the same book, and (3) the negative side of some of these statements, which seem so contradictory to the rest of the Bible. But if you try to read the book from the editor-compiler's perspective—that of a teacher of wisdom who, living before the full revelation of resurrection, recognized the value of Qohelet's assertion that life in the present world doesn't always add up—then you will be able to see that the final message of the book is not at all the hedonist or fatalist tract that some have made it out to be. Crucial to understanding this is to appreciate Qohelet's own context(s).

First, whatever else, Qohelet was written within Israel's Wisdom tradition (see the introduction to the Writings, p. 120), a tradition that was not trying to speak for God in the same way the prophets did, but one that was musing carefully on life in order to teach the young how to live well before God. And somewhat like the author of Job, but in contrast to the way some might mechanistically apply the book of Proverbs, Qohelet is convinced that the ways of the Creator are past finding out. Although he maintains a sturdy trust in God throughout (2:24; 3:11–14; 5:7b, 19; 9:7) and believes God to be just (3:17; 8:12–13), he nonetheless finds the real world not nearly as predictable as, for example, Job's "comforters" do, who see a sure cause and effect to everything and thus represent a kind of "wisdom" that Qohelet is likewise reacting strongly against.

Four realities dominate Qohelet's overall perspective: (1) God is the single indisputable reality, the Creator of all and the one from whom all life comes as gift (e.g., 3:12–14), including its—for Qohelet—usually burdensome nature. (2) God's ways are not always, if ever, understandable (3:11; 8:17). (3) On the human side, what is "done under the sun" (2:17) simply is not tidy; indeed, much of it doesn't add up right at all. The way things should be (the righteous get the good, the wicked get the bad) is not in fact the way things are—at least not consistently in this present life. (4) The great equalizer is death, which happens to rich and poor, wise and foolish alike. Given Qohelet's lack of hope in a resurrection, then once you're dead that's it—without memory, forgotten, no matter what your life may once have meant (9:5–6). And it is this reality that makes life seem *hebel* (a word that occurs thirty-seven times, just over half of its seventy-three OT occurrences).

At issue is what this word means for Qohelet, since it literally means "wisp of air" or "vapor." Most of the time he uses it as a metaphor for the nature of human existence. But what metaphorical freight does it carry? A tradition that goes back to the Septuagint translates it "emptiness" (cf. the KJV, "vanity," that is, "in vain"), pointing to the "vaporous" nature of our human lives (along with its companion, "chasing after the wind"). Another tradition, followed by the NIV, goes for "meaningless." While either of these work fine in some instances, they do not help in others. In most cases the sense seems to be the passing/ transitory or unsubstantial nature of things, like vapor itself. This seems especially to be its sense in the prologue, where human life, in contrast to the constancy and "oldness" of the world, e*vapor*ates very quickly. Moreover, the "vapor" that is our life is also elusive, lying outside our own control; it is like "chasing after the wind" (an ironic play on *hebel* = "wisp of air").

So what should one make of such a "vapor," these "few and *hebel* days" we pass through like a shadow (6:12; cf. 2:3; 5:18), especially in light of life's inequalities and, for the one who lives apart from God ("the fool"), its utter meaninglessness? Qohelet's answer is not, as some have accused him, "milk it for all you can, because you only go around once" (a misunderstanding of his repetition of the "eat and drink" theme, 2:24; 3:13; 5:18; 8:15; 9:7). Rather, his point seems to be that, even if one knows so little except the certainty of the grave, one should live life, *hebel* as it usually is, as a gift from God. This is because, in the end, joy and pleasure come not in "getting" (securing "profit" from what one does)—because that will evaporate—but in the journey itself, the life God has given. Death comes to all alike, but not all live alike; in such a world, joy and satisfaction are to be found in living the rhythms of life without trying to be in control or to "make gain" of what is itself merely transitory.

Even read from this perspective, Qohelet's wisdom is not altogether comforting. But overall it is an orthodox book. If one misses any mention of the great events of Jewish history, that is quite in keeping with the Wisdom tradition, and if one feels squeamish about great but contradictory realities being set side by side, that is probably because we too, like Job's "comforters," prefer things to be tidier than they are. But in the end even Qohelet does not leave the young dangling. One way is clearly to be preferred to the other, and the so-called contradictions serve to highlight that fact. The Christian believer, who now reads from the perspective of joyous hope in the resurrection and the certainty of divine judgment, should all the more be prepared to appreciate Qohelet's embracing of life in the present, despite its *hebel* nature.

A WALK THROUGH ECCLESIASTES

☐ **1:1–11** *Introduction to the Theme*

After the heading, where Qohelet is identified as a Davidic king (yet purposely not named), verses 2–11 introduce the main themes of the book: Everything is like a vapor; nothing human is permanent or new. The basic question to be answered comes up front (v. 3): What, then, is the profit of human toil? The reason for this is verse 4: Human beings come and go, but the earth is permanent—which is then illustrated in several ways (vv. 5–7), before concluding on the note of human finitude in the face of the massive reality of history (vv. 8–11).

☐ **1:12–2:26** *Various Ways of Trying to Gain from Labor*

From the perspective of his role as king (who should have profited most in life), Qohelet picks up the question from verse 3 about "gain/profit" from human toil. He starts with his special concern, namely, wisdom (1:12–18). Useful as it is, it only brings more sorrow, because one now understands the *hebel* nature of things. He then moves to the pursuit of pleasure (2:1–3) and the accumulation of wealth and possessions (2:4–11), but these too are ephemeral, and thus of no gain, since the same fate—death—overtakes all (2:12–16). The fact that one's gain must be left to someone else spoils everything (2:17–23)—unless one is prepared to make some adjustments, namely, to enjoy the gift of life as from God rather than to use it to make gain (2:24–26).

☐ 3:1–22 *A Time for Everything*

Qohelet now lyrically describes the nature of the reality that his reader should appreciate: The world God has made has its rhythms and seasons (vv. 1–8) that put it outside the reach of profit (v. 9), but bring joy when one adjusts to it (vv. 10–22). Note Qohelet's insistence that this is a gift from God (vv. 11–14) and that he takes this position even though he lives in a world that has no certainty about the future of the individual (v. 21). At the same time, he returns to earlier themes (human wickedness; death as the great leveler).

☐ 4:1–16 *Success, Oppression, and Solitariness*

Picking up the theme of wickedness (3:16–17), Qohelet notes that the desire for gain results in oppression of others, which is such a sorry sight for him that nonexistence would actually be better (4:1–3); labor and achievement (success), he goes on, spring from envy (vv. 4–6). Such striving is antineighbor and thus lonely (vv. 7–8); the better alternative is to live in community (vv. 9–12). Using an illustration from kingship (vv. 13–16), he concludes that poverty with wisdom is better than success with folly: The youthful "successor" to an old king eventually suffers the same fate as the one he succeeded.

☐ 5:1–7 *On Approaching God*

Qohelet breaks into his litany against gain and oppression by urging a proper stance toward the worship of God—being a listener whose speech is brief and correct, as one who stands in awe of God.

☐ 5:8–6:12 *Wealth and Oppression*

Returning to the theme of oppression and the quest for and hoarding of wealth, Qohelet focuses now on the love of money itself (5:8–13); in the same vein, he ponders wealth that is lost through misfortune, thus leaving no inheritance (5:14–17; cf. 1 Tim 6:6–10, where Paul reflects on this passage), before returning again to God-given contentment (Eccl 5:18–20). Then, typically, Qohelet acknowledges how few have received this gift (6:1–2), the example of which—in that culture—is the enormously blessed man who does not receive proper burial (6:3–6), the madness of which is summed up in verse 7. The first half of the book is then summarized in 6:8–12.

☐ 7:1–29 *The Advantage of Wisdom*

In 12:9 Qohelet is called a collector of proverbs; here at last is such a collection—of "better than" proverbs that echo previous concerns. Note how he steers a middle path regarding wisdom, neither idolizing nor hating it, but living in full light of it, since even in our transient existence, wisdom is better than folly—and this includes embracing the reality of death (vv. 2–4). At the heart of things is the contentment argued for earlier (vv. 7–24). But even if wisdom per se is still elusive (vv. 23–25), some wise things can be learned, such as the need to avoid the woman who sets a snare (v. 26; cf. Prov 2:16–19; 5:1–23) and the reality that human beings have gone astray, despite how they were created (vv. 27–29).

☐ 8:1–17 *Dealing with an Unjust World*

Note how Qohelet "explains" the question of verse 1 as referring to the wise man in the king's court (vv. 2–6), who will withdraw rather than confront the king. This observation is then applied to the wise person, who cannot change things as they are (vv. 7–8). In verses 9–15, he returns to the theme of wickedness and injustice, insisting that it is better to fear God and enjoy the life he has given, but concluding on the enigma of life (vv. 16–17).

☐ 9:1–12 *Living in the Face of Death*

Note how many previous themes are picked up once again: the certainty of death for all (vv. 1–6); that meaning lies in enjoying whatever life God has given (vv. 7–10), even though the outcome is unpredictable and often unpleasant (vv. 11–12).

☐ 9:13–10:20 *The Way of Wisdom*

Here Qohelet once more ponders the advantages of the way of wisdom over against folly; note especially the repetition of "better than" in 9:13–18, while most of chapter 10 reaffirms this with a collection of proverbial material, especially on how to survive bad government.

☐ 11:1–8 *On Not Understanding the Ways of God*

Once more Qohelet returns to a former theme, this time emphasizing our lack of control of the times, based on our limited understanding (vv. 1–6), and concluding on the reality of life as bittersweet (vv. 7–8).

☐ 11:9–12:8 *A Final Word to the Young*

Having repeatedly advocated the enjoyment of this brief life to the extent possible and while it lasts, Qohelet concludes by focusing on the young man (the wise man's son, 12:12). The brevity of youth gives him an even shorter time in which to make the most of his opportunities. He is thus urged to live life to the full (11:9–10) in light of the slow but steady intrusion of death into life as people age (12:1–7). This is what it means to "remember your Creator" (12:1, 6). Note how verse 8 serves to enclose the whole book (1:2): Life is transitory and elusive.

☐ 12:9–14 *Epilogue: Qohelet As a Wise Man*

The compiler, whose voice was heard previously in 1:1–2 and 7:27, now adds an epilogue, highlighting the value of Qohelet's arguments but summarizing his own orthodox perspective in verses 13–14 (cf. Qohelet's in 8:12–13). Qohelet's musings are quite true; life's emptiness *without* the fear of God and keeping his commandments should impel the truly wise to think on these "just the right words" (12:10).

The book of Ecclesiastes fits into the biblical story as a constant reminder of the brevity of human life in light of eternity, emphasizing our need to fear God while also paving the way for the greater revelation of our certain resurrection through Jesus Christ.

Song of Songs

ORIENTING DATA FOR SONG OF SONGS

- **Content:** a love poem of several episodes, celebrating the sexual love between a woman and a man

- **Date of composition:** unknown; scholarly guesses cover a broad range

- **Emphases:** the proper love of a woman and a man for one another; the unquenchable nature of pure love; the delight in and longing for each other that pure love engenders

OVERVIEW OF SONG OF SONGS

Song of Songs is a unique biblical book. Without mention of God and written in marvelous poetry, full of evocative and vivid images, it is a celebration of sexual love — and marital fidelity — between a woman and a man. Although it may have originated as several separate love poems, its title, Song of Songs (singular), indicates that in its canonical form it is intended to be read as several episodes/scenes of one poem, thus a "narrative" only in the sense that such poetry is trying to create a picture.

SPECIFIC ADVICE FOR READING SONG OF SONGS

Crucial for a good reading of the Song is to recognize that it comes to us basically in three voices: the woman, who plays the leading role throughout; the man, who especially celebrates the beauty of, and his love for, the woman; and the woman's companions, called the "daughters of Jerusalem." (The NIV headings "Lover" [the man], "Beloved" [the woman], and "Friends" [the woman's companions] are not in the Hebrew text; they are an attempt to help you see when there is a change of speakers.) Other characters are present basically as helpful props (the shepherds, 1:7–8; the city watchmen, 3:3; 5:7; the woman's brothers, 1:6; 8:8–9).

What is most difficult to determine is the role of Solomon. While it is possible to read 3:6–11 as suggesting that the man in the poem is Solomon himself and that this paragraph presents him as the bridegroom, it is not necessary to hold this view to appreciate the message of the Song. Indeed, there is little else that supports such a view, other than the possibility that "Shulammite," the woman's title in 6:13, means something like "Mrs. Solomon." The superscription (1:1) is quite ambiguous in Hebrew, since the preposition *le* could be either possessive (as NIV) or a form of dedication to Solomon as the original commissioner of the Song for one of his weddings—but with the intention that it could be used to encourage pure love in any marriage. At the same time 3:6–11 is unique to the poem—a third-person description of a named person—and the allusion to his harem in 6:8 and 8:11–12 looks like an intentional contrast between Solomon's "vineyard" being let out to tenants (8:11) while the woman's "vineyard" is her own to give (8:12).

This ambiguity has created several different readings of the text; the one offered here assumes an intended contrast, suggesting that the Song was never intended to apply only to Solomon, but to make every married couple who share pure love each other's "king" and "queen." That is, the "Lover" in most of the Song is not specifically Solomon, who as an oriental king might not invite love but take it as the privilege of position—and it is harder to imagine the primary role of the woman as taking place if she were part of his harem. On the other hand, such factors as the explicit association with Solomon and the proverbial nature of the conclusion (8:6–7) brought about its inclusion in the Jewish Wisdom tradition.

The constant shift of speakers and the richness of the poetry can make the structure difficult to discern. The clues seem to lie with some repeated refrains that conclude several of the scenes (e.g., the charge to the daughters of Jerusalem, 2:7; 3:5; 8:4). The poetry itself is full of rich and powerful images intended to evoke the imagination. They cover a large range of human activity—the world of nature (gardens, mountains, forests, animals, plants, spices, etc.), architecture (towers, walls, cities, etc.), clothing/jewelry, and warfare. The woman, whose body and love are described three times as the lover speaks to her (4:1–15; 6:4–7; 7:1–9), is especially seen in terms of a garden and vineyard full of precious spices and wine for the man's pleasure. The man's body is described but once—by the woman to the daughters of Jerusalem—with a whole range of images (5:10–16).

The forthrightness and evocative nature of these descriptions has historically been a point of difficulty for many, especially male readers/interpreters, both Jewish and Christian. The result has usually been to allegorize it—so much so that an early church council (A.D. 550) forbade any interpretation that was not allegorical! But such a reading seems to be a capitulation to human fallenness and to the way sexual love has often been twisted so as to become exploitative, manipulative, and destructive—up to the present day. This poem should be read in light of Genesis 1 and 2. Following the command to "be fruitful and increase in number" (Gen 1:28), God plants a *garden* (2:8) in which he placed the man and woman he created in his own image. The narrative concludes with the words: "A man will ... be united to his wife, and they will become one flesh. The man and his wife were both naked, and *they felt no shame*" (2:24–25, emphasis added). The picture of sexual love in this book recaptures that scene, where the woman and the man take utter delight and pleasure in each other's bodies and do so without shame. This is thus God's way of recapturing both the fidelity and the unity and intimacy of marriage, which the enemy has tried to take away from God's people by making it seem either titillating outside of marriage or something shameful and unmentionable within marriage. This inspired author has a different view.

A WALK THROUGH SONG OF SONGS

☐ **1:1–6** *The Lovers Presented*

Note that, typical within the book, the woman takes the lead role, so that in this opening scene where each is introduced, she sets the stage for the rest—her desire for and delight in him, with an invitation to be taken away by him. If "the king" is literal, then Solomon is intended; otherwise it is a metaphor, using royal imagery to evoke love's grandeur.

☐ **1:7–2:7** *First Scene: The Lovers Together*

As you read this first scene, note that verse 8 could just as easily be the man's own response to the beloved's question. That would mean that the whole scene is an exchange between the two lovers. She first searches for him among the shepherds (vv. 7–8), followed by an interchange of description (vv. 9–11, 12–14) and of delight in each other (vv. 15–16), before turning to a description of the scene of love (v. 17, a forest). She then evokes the imagery of flowers (2:1–2), while he is an "apple tree" in whose shade she rests and whose fruit she enjoys (vv. 3–6). Her last words are to the daughters of Jerusalem to let love take its own course (v. 7).

□ 2:8–3:5 *Second Scene: Hope, Invitation, and Dream*

This scene is characterized by longing; he is a gazelle leaping across mountains, then gazing through the window (2:8–9). She then recites his words of invitation—it's spring, the time for love (vv. 10–13). He calls her out of hiding (vv. 14–15) and for the "foxes" (those who would oppose their love) to be caught so as not to ruin the "vineyards" (their bodies; cf. 1:6, 14) that are in bloom. With the total mutuality and exclusive fidelity of love (2:16), her lover then "browses among the lilies," but is (apparently) sent away at the close of day (v. 17). That leads to what is probably a dream scene (3:1–4) in which she seeks and finds her lover, concluding again with the admonition to the daughters of Jerusalem (v. 5). Note also the minor, passive role of the watchmen.

□ 3:6–11 *Solomon's Wealth and Extravagance*

This enigmatic section may be intended to provide contrast to the woman's lover, since the descriptions of him thus far have been from nature, not from pomp and circumstance; otherwise Solomon is the lover and the section introduces their lovemaking in the next scene. Note that it is the only thing that borders on narration in the entire poem, and the picture educed is one of wealth, power, and opulence (thus echoing 1 Kgs 10:14–11:6).

□ 4:1–5:1 *Third Scene: Admiration and Invitation*

This is the first scene in which the man takes the lead. He begins with a description of the beloved's body from head to breasts (4:1–5). Picking up her language from 2:17, he will go to the mountain of myrrh (vv. 6–7, echoing 1:13). He then describes her as a lover, a garden of delights and spices (vv. 8–15). Her response is to invite the winds to enhance her fragrance and thus to invite him into the garden (v. 16), to which his response after love (5:1) echoes language from the preceding description (myrrh and spice [4:14], honeycomb and honey [4:11], wine [4:10] and milk [4:11]). To this the daughters of Jerusalem respond by encouraging them to eat and drink their fill (5:1c).

☐ 5:2–6:3   *Fourth Scene: Dream and Search*

The woman is again in the lead. In what appears to be another dream scene, her lover comes and beckons her and then disappears (5:2–6); again she searches for him, but this time the watchmen abuse her (v. 7). In response to the short dialogue with the daughters of Jerusalem (vv. 8–9), she gives her only description of him (vv. 10–16), moving from head to legs, but concluding, as at the beginning (1:2) by recalling his kisses. To their second question (6:1), she answers first (v. 2) by echoing language from the preceding love scene and then (v. 3) by repeating the word of mutuality and exclusive fidelity (cf. 2:16).

☐ 6:4–8:4   *Fifth Scene: The Delights of Love*

Note that in this scene the man and woman both speak at length. The scene begins with him in the lead, describing the beauty of her head (6:4–7)—in contrast to the king's wives and concubines (vv. 8–9b), who also admire her (vv. 9c–10). After an interchange with them (vv. 11–13), he then launches into his final description of her body, this time from feet to hair (7:1–6), before returning to her breasts and mouth (vv. 7–9a). She then picks up the imagery of her mouth as wine, urging that it go straight to him who desires her, with further invitation to lovemaking (vv. 9b–13). Her love for him is such that she would gladly express it in public, against all cultural norms (8:1–2a); her desire again echoes previous language (vv. 2b–3) before she concludes with the refrain to the daughters of Jerusalem (v. 4).

☐ 8:5–14   *Conclusion(s): Love Strong As Death*

The poem concludes with a series of brief sketches that suggest the unquenchable nature of their love (8:5–7), despite opposition (vv. 8–9, 10–12), concluding with their final interchange of invitation (vv. 13–14).

Song of Songs fits into God's story as a reminder that the sexual love he created is good and should be embraced with godly fidelity and delight.

Lamentations

ORIENTING DATA FOR LAMENTATIONS

- **Content:** a series of five laments over the fall of Jerusalem
- **Date of composition:** unknown, probably soon after the fall of Jerusalem (586 B.C.)
- **Emphases:** the deep personal suffering and spiritual agony experienced at the fall of Jerusalem; the justice of God in carrying out the overthrow of Zion; hope lies finally in God's character alone

OVERVIEW OF LAMENTATIONS

Lamentations consists of five laments written in response to the fall of Jerusalem in 586 B.C. The laments, which correspond to the five chapters, are carefully composed pieces of literature, similar in form and content to Psalms 74 and 79 (cf. Ps 89). Together they express deep anguish over Zion's desolation and Israel's exile—recognized to be well deserved—and mourn the sorry plight of those who were left in the now desolate and dangerous city, while raising some larger questions about justice and the future. The whole is written basically from the perspective of those who have been left behind.

At least three voices can be identified: the narrator-author, Zion (personified Jerusalem), and the people of Zion (Yahweh himself never speaks). In the first two (closely related) poems, the narrator and Zion are the speakers; they mourn over the fall of the city itself, recognizing that it happened because of her sins, so that Yahweh himself had become her enemy. In the final two (again closely related) poems, the speakers are the narrator and the people of Zion, who agonize for the people in occupied Jerusalem. In the central poem (ch. 3) Jerusalem is essentially personified, that is, the only identifiable speaker is the author, whose personal agony is so closely tied to that of Jerusalem that in various ways they become one; here you also find the single expression of hope, as well as a brief discussion of the meaning of suffering.

SPECIFIC ADVICE FOR READING LAMENTATIONS

In order to read Lamentations well, you need to be aware of its basic literary features, as well as its historical background and theological perspective. The most striking literary feature of these poems is that they are a series of acrostics (cf. Pss 34; 119), where the first letter of each verse starts with a succeeding letter of the (twenty-two-letter) Hebrew alphabet. The first two poems thus have twenty-two stanzas of three lines each, the first line in each case being the acrostic. The third poem also has twenty-two stanzas, but in this case all three lines in each stanza begin with the same letter. The fourth poem returns to the form of the first two, but now with stanzas of two lines each, while the fifth, although not an acrostic, is nonetheless composed of twenty-two lines. Thus the pattern builds to the agonizing climactic descriptions of chapter 3, then diminishes somewhat in chapter 4, and ends with a whimper in chapter 5, a pattern that mirrors the city's destruction and its aftermath. While not all these features can be carried over into English, the acrostic pattern does affect verse numbering (22, 22, 66, 22, 22) and to some degree explains why these poems contain some abrupt shifts of topic (the alphabet often controls what may be said at any point). But throughout the whole, the lament form itself (see *How to 1*, pp. 212, 215–218) implicitly encourages hope — though nothing is guaranteed — in the midst of suffering.

As to its historical and theological perspective, it is hard for us at our point in history to appreciate the utter devastation of the fall of Jerusalem for the people of Judah. First, there was the terrible suffering of the historical event itself, narrated in 2 Kings 25. The siege lasted for two years, as tens of thousands huddled in Jerusalem, hoping that Yahweh would intervene. Instead, the Babylonian troops finally breached her walls, raped her women, and slaughtered many of her inhabitants. In light of subsequent conditions in Jerusalem, our author wonders rhetorically whether death might not have been the better option. All of these horrible realities — famine, thirst, cannibalism, rape, slaughter — are echoed in these poems.

But beyond that there was the larger question of Israel's calling and role as the people of God. Here was a people whose history was singularly bound up with the God who had redeemed them from slavery in Egypt, created them as a people for his Name, made covenant with them at Sinai, and eventually fulfilled his promise that Abraham's offspring would inherit the land. At the heart of their self-understanding was the fact that their God—who was God alone, the living God, and Creator of all that is—had chosen to dwell personally in their midst, first in the tabernacle in the desert and finally in the place he chose "as a dwelling for his Name" (Deut 12:11; Neh 1:9), Jerusalem itself. Thus both the land and the city held a significance for Israel in terms of identity unlike most other peoples in history. Indeed, because of this, many wrongly thought Zion inviolable (cf. Jer 7; 26; 28; Ezek 13–14). It is this total identification of the people with their city as God's own dwelling place that lies behind the utter anguish of these poems and that makes the appeals over the present plight of her people so poignant. And even though the author is fully aware that their punishment is just, his agonized descriptions indicate how hard it was to handle the reality and enormity of the desolation and suffering (e.g., Lam 2:20–22).

At the same time, however, the author wrestles with the issues also raised by Habakkuk and Obadiah, for example. What about Israel's enemies, who were equally deserving of God's anger? This is what lies behind the frequent imprecations (Lam 1:21–22; 3:61–66; 4:21–22). And in the end, even though Moses and the prophets foretold such disaster as a result of unfaithfulness to the covenant, our author struggles with it right up to the last words, where the promised future is only a distant shadow. But in the crucial central poem he also holds out the one all-important ray of hope—the character of Yahweh himself, who has revealed himself to Moses on Sinai as full of love and faithfulness (Exod 34:5–7; cf. the appeal in Ps 89).

A WALK THROUGH LAMENTATIONS

☐ 1:1–22 *First Lament: Zion Laments over Her Destruction*

In the first part of this poem (vv. 1–11b), the narrator sets out the basic matters, which are repeated throughout: Zion and her temple have been laid waste, her people taken into exile; during the siege her friends deserted her, while her enemies mocked and her foes are now her masters. Those who remain, both priests and people, are in dire straits, the pilgrimage feasts a thing of the past; for them there is only weeping and groaning. And all of this is because of Judah's many sins.

Toward the end of this first part, Zion herself calls out to Yahweh to look on her affliction (v. 9c), which is then repeated at the beginning of her own lament (vv. 11c–22). Calling out to any "who pass by" (v. 12), she basically repeats the matters from verses 1–11, but now in more detail and with increased pain and distress, concluding with an imprecation against her enemies (vv. 21–22). Note especially the role that Yahweh played in her destruction; note also that her lament is momentarily relieved halfway through by the poet's own voice (v. 17).

☐ 2:1–22   *Second Lament: Zion's Lament and Appeal*

With still further intensification, the poet speaks again, spelling out in great detail the ultimate cause of Jerusalem's destruction, namely, Yahweh's anger. The Divine Warrior, who in the past had fought *for* Israel, had now become their enemy—city, land, leaders, and people alike (vv. 1–9). The poet then concentrates on those left behind (vv. 10–17). Note here how he speaks in the first person (vv. 11, 13), and finally calls on Zion herself to call out to Yahweh (vv. 18–19), which she does in the poignant words of verses 20–22, reminding Yahweh of both the famine and the subsequent slaughter (of priest and prophet, young and old together).

☐ 3:1–66   *Third Lament: Despair, Hope, and Imprecation*

In this central poem, the author makes Jerusalem's despair his own and vice versa (vv. 1–18, already alluded to in 2:11). What seems to be at issue here is that the fall of Jerusalem meant the suffering of many who were faithful to Yahweh and innocent of her corporate crimes, but who yet felt relentlessly pursued by Yahweh. In the end, his only hope lies in the covenant faithfulness of Yahweh, whose love and faithfulness (echoing the words of Exod 34:6) are new every morning (vv. 19–24). These then are followed by a kind of personal dialogue about the meaning of suffering and its relationship to Yahweh, concluding with a call to repentance (vv. 25–42). Note that at the end the lament is then renewed (vv. 43–51), focusing finally on his enemies who are responsible for his suffering (vv. 52–62) and concluding with an imprecation against them (vv. 63–66).

☐ 4:1–22   *Fourth Lament: Groping in the Streets*

With this lament the author turns his attention to the present horrible conditions in Jerusalem, comparing them with the years of the siege and offering his belief that the dead are the lucky ones (vv. 1–11). He then focuses on the plight—and guilt—of the prophets and priests (vv. 12–16). Note that verse 17 begins the lament of the people themselves, in this case looking back to the last bitter days of the siege (including the flight and capture of the king, Jer 52:7–11), while the author himself concludes with an imprecation against Edom (Lam 4:21–22).

☐ 5:1–22   *Fifth Lament: The Remnant of Zion Weeps*

In this final poem, only the people speak, calling out to Yahweh to look on their present affliction, reflecting especially that occupied Judah is an unhappy and dangerous place in which to live (vv. 1–18). The poem and book then conclude with a prayer for restoration, which begins with an affirmation of Yahweh's eternal reign but is concerned, in characteristic lament fashion, with whether or not they have been forgotten (vv. 19–22).

The book of Lamentations reflects a significant turning point in the biblical story—the fall of Jerusalem—thus reminding us that God is true to his word about standing in judgment against unfaithfulness, while still holding out hope for the future based on his character.

The Prophets
of Israel
in the Biblical Story

The next part of the biblical story comes in the form of sixteen books that we call the Prophets. In Jewish tradition they are known as the Latter Prophets and were usually counted as four books, in this order: Isaiah, Jeremiah, Ezekiel, and the Book of the Twelve (the so-called Minor Prophets; Lamentations and Daniel were included among the Writings). The prophetic tradition had a long history in Israel, going back as far as Moses and including Samuel. But those whose words were eventually written down in scrolls bearing their names flourished from the middle of the eighth century B.C. (ca. 760) until the middle of the fifth century B.C. (ca. 460).

The prophets have an especially crucial role to play in the "story of Israel" part of the grand story. Indeed, they cannot be properly understood apart from their function in relation to the Law and the Former Prophets (Joshua through 2 Kings). As God's appointed spokesmen, they call Yahweh's people back to their covenant roots, announcing both the curses and blessings for covenant disloyalty or loyalty (see esp. Deut 27–30). The exilic prophets also helped the people through their twofold loss—of the divine presence and of the promised land—thus playing the role of Moses and Joshua in reverse.

Thus the prophets constantly call God's people back to divine realities: They belong to God, God does not belong to them; God has called

169

them into being for his purposes of redeeming what was lost in the Fall and of blessing the nations. At the heart of the prophets' message, therefore, is deep concern that Israel reflect God's character by walking in his ways and keeping covenant with him. At the same time, they are constantly reminded that Yahweh is not a local Israelite deity, but is the sovereign God of the universe—Creator and Sustainer of all things and therefore also sovereign over all the other nations.

The nations, accordingly, play a very important role in the prophets' part of the grand story. On the one hand, the nations are included in the Abrahamic promise (Gen 12:2–3), so Israel is often reminded of her failure to be God's "blessing" for them. This dimension of the promise is thus regularly seen as part of God's final fulfillment of his promises (see Isaiah in particular), a part of the tradition that becomes central to the New Testament. On the other hand, since the Abrahamic promise included God's "cursing" those who "curse you," the prophets also regularly pronounce God's judgment on the nations. Thus Israel is not alone in coming under God's righteous judgments—indeed, Obadiah and Nahum are exclusively oracles against the nations (Edom and Assyria, respectively).

Much of what is said as you are guided through these books presupposes chapter 10 in *How to 1* as to the nature and function of the prophetic oracles (lawsuit, woe, promise, etc.). But three matters raised there are especially crucial and need to be repeated here in order to help you make sense of these (sometimes difficult) books as you read them.

1. In much the same way as the New Testament Letters, these writings were addressing ad hoc situations; therefore some awareness of the social-religious-political situation into which they were speaking is essential in order for you to read well. So in the section on "Specific Advice," the nature of the specific situation for each prophet will be pointed out.

For now, recall the three important matters that apply across the board for this time in Israel's history: that it was a time of (1) significant political, military, economic, and social upheaval, (2) a very high level of unfaithfulness and disregard for the Mosaic covenant, and (3) enormous shifts in the balance(s) of power on the international scene.

It is especially important to note that all of these prophets spoke at a time when Israel had been permanently divided into north (Israel/Ephraim) and south (Judah). Most of them address Judah, some of them speak into the situation of the exile, and several of them speak after the exile when a small remnant had returned to their historic land. Because it will be useful for you to relate these books to the sections of 1–2 Kings and 1–2 Chronicles to which they correspond, the relevant passages will regularly be called to your attention.

2. As you read, you will want to be aware of the frequent tension that exists in the prophets between the near future and the ultimate future, since the final consummation of the biblical story often serves as the backdrop for what is said about the near future. Thus Haggai, for example, is speaking directly to the situation of the rebuilding of the temple after the return from exile. Yet in encouraging the people to return to this work, he speaks both of the greater future of the temple and of the near future of Zerubbabel as the Davidic heir. And so it is with most of these books in their final form.

3. It is important also for you to be reminded that most prophetic speech takes the form of poetry. Here it would benefit you greatly to read pages 197–99 in *How to 1,* as well as perhaps an entry on Hebrew poetry in a recent Bible dictionary, so that you can appreciate the kinds of parallelism involved. Also, because these books are poetry, you will want to pause at times to notice the powerful and evocative images and metaphors that the prophets regularly use to capture the people's attention.

Here is God speaking in ways that are loud and clear (the latter more so than some are apt to think!). As you read, be aware not only of what God was saying to the people of the prophets' times but also of how much it is equally relevant to our own times and history. (Had Amos, you may find yourself asking, been reading the *New York Times*?)

Isaiah

ORIENTING DATA FOR ISAIAH

- **Content:** Yahweh's sovereign majesty and redemptive love, revealed in his dealings with his chosen people the Israelites, who are destined for both judgment and salvation, in which the nations will also be included

- **Prophet:** Isaiah of Jerusalem

- **Date of prophetic activity:** from about 740 to 687 B.C. (see 1:1)

- **Emphases:** the holiness, majesty, and righteousness of Yahweh; the compassion and saving mercy of Yahweh; the central role of Israel in Yahweh's plans for the nations and the world; the central role of Zion in these plans; the redemptive role of God's suffering servant; the glorious final future God has in store for those who are his

OVERVIEW OF ISAIAH

The book of Isaiah in many ways is the centerpiece of the story of Israel in the biblical story. Standing at the beginning of the Latter Prophets, even though not first chronologically, it serves to guide your reading of the rest of this tradition. But beyond that, its theological scope is all-embracing, constantly reminding Israel that Yahweh is the living God, the Creator and majestic Sovereign—and Judge—of all that is, as well as the compassionate Redeemer of Israel. Thus Isaiah looks forward to Israel's judgment, to her redemption from exile through a second exodus, and, through her coming Servant King, to the fulfillment of the Abrahamic covenant that includes the nations in Yahweh's salvation. And in the end it pictures the final redemption of Israel and the nations in a new heaven and new earth, when Zion, the place where Yahweh and people meet, is restored to its ultimate glory. Isaiah, therefore, had enormous influence on the New Testament writers, being cited or alluded to more often than any other Old Testament book except the Psalter.

The book itself presents this glorious panorama as a carefully crafted whole, which comes in two basic parts: Chapters 1–39 deal primarily with Jerusalem during the period of the Assyrian threat, but at the end Isaiah prophesies the future threat of exile in Babylon. Chapters 40–66 focus on the future of Israel and Jerusalem toward the end of the Babylonian captivity and beyond, climaxing with the hope of a new heaven and new earth and a final eschatological Zion.

Each of these parts has its own structures and rhythms. Chapters 1–5 introduce the major concerns of part 1—that Judah and Zion have failed in their calling to be Yahweh's people for him and the nations, so they must be judged (while 2:1–5 looks forward to the fulfillment of that calling). The failure is threefold: (1) lack of trust in Yahweh, which is expressed in (2) their constant flirtation with idols and (3) their lack of social justice. Isaiah's call (ch. 6) introduces the rest of part 1. His vision of the "Holy One of Israel" leads to his own cleansing and his commission to announce God's judgment on a people who are exactly like their idols—they have ears that do not hear and eyes that do not see. The rest of part 1 is framed by two sets of narratives (chs. 7–9; 36–39), one at the beginning (with Ahaz) and one at the end (with Hezekiah) of Isaiah's long career—both are during outside threats and both mention the same piece of geography (7:3; 36:2). In both cases at issue is trust in Yahweh: Ahaz does not, Hezekiah does. But Hezekiah then shows lack of trust with regard to envoys from Babylon, which leads to the second part of the book. Much of the inner frame of part 1 is a series of oracles against the nations, including nations on whom Israel has leaned for support rather than trusting Yahweh.

Part 2 is basically in two parts, each of which is also in two parts. Chapters 40–55 move the story ahead to a time toward the end of the Babylonian exile; chapters 40–48 are both consolation and confrontation—the latter to a people who are settled in Babylon and of no mind to take part in the new exodus—while chapters 49–55 reflect that the (now postponed) new exodus will finally be brought about by Yahweh's servant, who will thereby also gather the nations. Chapters 56–66 reflect the continuing failure of Israel (chs. 56–59), but then speak to the grand future that God has for his people and for the nations (chs. 60–66).

SPECIFIC ADVICE FOR READING ISAIAH

To read Isaiah well, you need to have some sense of the history it reflects, as well as of the theological concerns that energize the book from beginning to end.

The *history* reflected in chapters 1–39 is dominated by the role of Assyria on the international scene. Isaiah's call comes in the last year of Uzziah's long reign in Jerusalem (792–740 B.C.; see 2 Kgs 15:1–7), which had been a time of Assyrian decline and thus of relative peace in Judah and Israel. But by the time of Uzziah's death, Assyria had reasserted her power in the Near Eastern world through a new series of kings (Tiglath-Pileser III [744–727], Shalmaneser V [726–722], Sargon II [721–705], and Sennacherib [704–681]). Much of the political intrigue in Samaria and Jerusalem had to do with Israelite and Judean kings paying or withholding tribute to Assyria. It is these intrigues that lie behind the two sets of narratives in Isaiah 7–9 and 36–39. In each case Isaiah announces the deliverance of Zion, but he also foretells the exile to Babylon (39:5–7).

The siege and fall of Jerusalem and the twofold exile to Babylon is the story of Jeremiah and Ezekiel. The historical setting envisioned in Isaiah 40–55 is the later part of this exile, that is, the time after the message of Jeremiah and Ezekiel has been heeded and the exiles have settled into a new life in Babylon. The whole of this section of Isaiah is dominated by the expectation of a new exodus—from exile, across the desert with promises of water and safe passage back to Zion, the place where Yahweh will reestablish his dwelling. But the exiles will not receive this message of consolation—they cannot believe that Yahweh will use the Persian Cyrus to accomplish his purposes—and so the second exodus becomes part of a more distant future.

The *theological passions* of Isaiah find their focus at four points: (1) Yahweh as the "Holy One of Israel" (a term found thirty times in Isaiah and only six times in the rest of the OT); (2) Israel as Yahweh's "Holy People" (62:12); (3) Zion (Jerusalem) as God's "holy city" (48:2) and "holy mountain" (11:9; 27:13); and (4) the inclusion of the nations (Gentiles) in his people (2:2; 52:15).

Yahweh as the "Holy One of Israel" lies at the heart of everything— Isaiah's vision (ch. 6), Yahweh's justice and judgments (5:19–25), and Yahweh's mercy and compassion as Israel's Redeemer (41:14; 43:3–15; 62:12). Thus in Isaiah the term *holy* carries both of its essential characteristics: (1) Yahweh's absolute "otherness"—the Creator and Sustainer of all things and all nations, the one who has no rivals, since no other gods exist. You will not be able to miss this theme as you read, especially when it takes the form of scathing rebuke on the "lifeless" nature of such idols, who have eyes that cannot see and ears that cannot hear (see esp. 44:6–20). (2) Yahweh's absolute holiness in the moral/ethical sense. As a holy God, he requires holiness of his people—they are to bear his likeness (compassion, love, goodness, faithfulness) rather than that of their idols. After all, idolatry inevitably leads to injustice: The lifeless gods are unjust; their worshipers become like them.

At the center of Isaiah's story is Israel, redeemed but wayward, stubborn but loved, and it is Yahweh's relationship with them, told over and over again by pointing back to the exodus and the Davidic covenant, that reveals his mercy and compassion. Judge them he must, but give them up he will not—and it is here that the theme of Yahweh's saving a "remnant" belongs to the story. The story of this redemption thus climaxes with a servant Messiah who will redeem both Israel and the nations by dying for them—a story that finds its fulfillment in Jesus Christ and the cross.

The essential symbol of the relationship between Yahweh and his people is his presence with them in Jerusalem on Mount Zion. Here is where Israel has desecrated the relationship (1:10–25), yet here also is where Yahweh plans to restore the relationship (1:26–31) so that the nations will join them in worship on Zion (2:1–5). Thus the book begins with a desecrated Zion that is promised to be restored, and it ends (chs. 65–66) with the promised final expression of the Holy City and its Holy People, which includes the Gentiles.

There is much else that makes up this marvelous telling of the biblical story, but watching for these several themes, as well as being sensitive to the powerful imagery and cadences of the poetry, should help you catch something of the book's splendor, as well as its important place in the biblical story.

A WALK THROUGH ISAIAH

Yahweh's Complaint with Judah, and Isaiah's Call (chs. 1–6)

☐ **1:1–2:5 Introduction: The Corruption and Future
of the Holy People and Holy Place**

This section introduces both chapters 1–5 and the whole book; be watching for the pervading themes. Here Yahweh's complaint takes the form of a lawsuit against Jerusalem's ongoing *rebellion* against *the Holy*

One of Israel that has brought on his *judgment* (vv. 2–9, 24–25); their *religion* is useless (vv. 10–15d) because of their sins—*social injustice* (vv. 15e–17; cf. Amos) and *idolatry* (v. 29)—but there is also the offer of *mercy* (vv. 18–20) and a bright *future* (vv. 26–28). In 2:1–4 Yahweh makes plain his commitment to redeem his creation, with Mount Zion functioning as the new Mount Sinai to which all *the nations* come (thus fulfilling Israel's true purposes in keeping with his covenant with Abraham). Note how the section ends with an invitation to Israel to thus walk in the light of Yahweh.

□ 2:6–5:30   *The Coming Day of the Lord*

In the first oracle (2:6–22) the key issues are arrogant trust in idols and lack of trust in Yahweh; also watch for some repeated themes that give power to the poetry. The coming disaster prophesied in 3:1–4:1 is directed especially at the leaders, and again the issue is *social justice*—the wealthy abusing the poor and the land (including the graphic portrayal in 3:16–4:1). But after disaster there is *hope* (4:2–6), the first expression of "second exodus" themes in Isaiah. Likewise, the song of the vineyard (5:1–7; picked up in Jer 12:10; Ezek 19:10–14; and by Jesus [Mark 12:1–12; John 15:1–8]) focuses on social injustice (Isa 5:7), as do the six woes that follow (vv. 8–25); hence, instead of the nations now coming to worship on Zion (2:2–4), they are summoned to destroy it (5:26–30).

□ 6:1–13   *Isaiah's Vision and Commission*

Uzziah has died (symbolic of what is happening to the Davidic dynasty). In the temple, the place of Yahweh's presence, Isaiah sees a vision of Israel's true King, the Holy One of Israel. Crushed because of his own and his people's uncleanness, Isaiah is pardoned and then commissioned to pronounce God's judgments on a people who have become like the idols they worship, that is, neither seeing nor hearing.

A Crisis of Trust: Ahaz and the Syro-Ephraimite Coalition (chs. 7–12)

At issue in chapters 7–39 is whether or not Jerusalem, represented by her king, will trust in Yahweh or in entangling alliances (a form of idolatry). Note that the narratives about Ahaz's (7:1–8:10) and Hezekiah's (ch. 39) failures to trust Yahweh bookend this larger section. And this is why there must be a future faithful king for Judah and the nations (9:1–7; 12:1–6; and throughout the oracles against the nations).

☐ 7:1–8:22   *Failed Kingship in Judah*

Watch how this opening narrative reveals Ahaz's wavering before a Syro-Ephraimite coalition. The names of Isaiah's two sons reflect Yahweh's response to Ahaz—the threat of Israel's being *plundered* (Maher-Shalal-Hash-Baz) and the mere *remnant* that will remain of the northern alliance after Yahweh judges them (Shear-Jashub)—while Immanuel, Yahweh's "sign" to Ahaz, reminds him of Yahweh's own presence in Zion (in this case, probably as a threat). Yahweh's word to Isaiah and Isaiah's response (8:11–22) indicate the issue at hand—trust in Yahweh.

☐ 9:1–12:6   *Future Kingship in Judah*

Central here is kingship in Israel. So note how Ahaz's failure to trust Yahweh is responded to by the announcement of a coming great Davidic king (9:1–7; 11:1–16). Together these oracles bookend (1) the announced fall of Samaria (9:8–10:4, who sided with Damascus against Judah), (2) the punishment of her destroyer, Assyria (10:5–19), and (3) the preservation of Judah (10:20–34). After the second announcement of the coming king (11:1–16), the section concludes with Yahweh on Zion as Judah's true king (ch. 12).

Yahweh's Complaint with the Nations (chs. 13–27)

☐ 13:1–14:27   *Against Babylon and Assyria*

Note that both oracles against these two historic enemies of Judah are distinguished at their heart by words of hope for Judah (14:1–3, 25). Babylon probably stands first in the series because eventually she would turn out to be *the* world power, whose collapse would be of monumental significance. Two things are noteworthy about this oracle: (1) It contains the imagery of the holy war, as Yahweh himself musters the army that will destroy Babylon (13:4–22), and (2) the king in particular is singled out because of his arrogance against Yahweh (14:12–21).

☐ 14:28–17:14   *Against Judah's Neighbors: Philistia, Moab, Damascus*

These oracles each put emphasis on the coming disaster, not on these nations' sins as such; in each case, as with the preceding two, look for the word of hope about the future of Zion and her people (14:32; 16:5; 17:6–7).

☐ **18:1–20:6** *Against Cush and Egypt*

Note how the two more general oracles (chs. 18–19) are concluded with a historically specific oracle against both Egyptian realms (ch. 20). In the two oracles, note that, as before, emphasis lies more on the announcement of judgment than on the reasons for it, and again it will result in the exaltation of Yahweh as king (18:7; 19:19–21). The length of the oracle against Egypt is probably related to the way it concludes: Judah's having sought help from Egypt.

☐ **21:1–23:18** *Against Babylon and Her Allies*

The oracle against Jerusalem (ch. 22) fits within these final oracles against Babylon and her allies (ch. 21), because Jerusalem's ruin will come at the hands of Babylon. Note the repeated motifs—emphasis on the doom, not the sins as such; turning from Yahweh on the part of Jerusalem, but with a future for the house of David (22:20–24); Yahweh's judgment of the arrogant (23:9).

☐ **24:1–27:13** *The Distress of the Nations, and Feasting on Yahweh's Holy Mountain*

The preceding oracles seem to imply that Yahweh is merely reacting to what the nations are doing; however, this next series makes it clear that he is the Sovereign Lord of the nations. In the first oracle, the coming destruction of Jerusalem (24:10–13) is appropriately placed in a context of the ultimate devastation of the earth. The nations respond by joining his people in a great eschatological feast on Mount Zion (ch. 25), while Judah's response (ch. 26) is to renew commitment to her trust in Yahweh and to enjoy his peace after discipline—to which Yahweh, having atoned for her guilt, responds by a renewed song of the vineyard, as Jacob takes root once more (ch. 27).

A Crisis of Trust: Hezekiah and the Babylonian Threat (chs. 28–39)

☐ **28:1–33:24** *Woe to Ephraim and Judah, Who Trust in Egypt*

Back to present reality in Judah once more; note how these oracles pick up themes from chapters 6–12. Again it is a crisis of trust regarding Yahweh. Watch for the sins that call forth this series of woes, first against Samaria (28:1–6) and then against Judah and her leaders (28:7–31:9)—especially the sins of injustice (the rich lying around getting drunk off the labor of the poor), mockery of God's prophet, and idolatry, all of which reflect Judah's arrogance, both in worship and foreign policy, with its accompanying failure to trust Yahweh, for which exhibit A is their going to Egypt for help (ch. 31). But note also how these threats are interlaced with words of hope that focus on the future of Zion and God's righteous king. Future hope then becomes the primary theme of chapters 32–33, interlaced with threats of judgment. Note especially that when Yahweh's righteous king reigns, the blind finally will see and the deaf hear (32:3–4; cf. 6:9–10).

Also be on the lookout for the many wordplays that mark these oracles (Samaria as a fading "flower" to be replaced by Yahweh as their "wreath" [28:1–5]; Judah's mockery is turned into God's mockery of them [28:9–13; cf. v. 22]; the deaf will soon hear from the scroll [29:11–12, 18]; etc.).

☐ 34:1–35:10 *Once More: Judgment on the Nations, and the Future of Zion*

The final two oracles of this part of Isaiah conclude with Yahweh's love for Zion, first by announcing the Divine Warrior's judgment against the nations, especially Edom (ch. 34; cf. the similar phenomenon in Ezek 35–36), and second by announcing the coming new exodus (Isa 35:1–10); note how the judgment of 6:9–10 against the blind and the deaf, who have become like their idols, is finally reversed forever (35:5) and the ransomed of the Lord enter Zion with joy (v. 10). This final oracle also paves the way for chapters 40–55.

☐ 36:1–39:8 *Trusting Yahweh regarding Assyria, and Failure regarding Babylon*

Most of this narrative is repeated in 2 Kings 18:13, 17–20:19. In contrast to Ahaz earlier, Hezekiah listens to Isaiah and puts his trust in Yahweh, who miraculously delivers Judah from Assyria. Note again the emphasis on Zion and the remnant of Yahweh. But then Hezekiah fails to trust Yahweh by dallying with Babylon, not recognizing, as Isaiah does prophetically, that Zion's real threat lies in that quarter. So this narrative also serves as a transition to the oracles that come next.

Consolation and Confrontation (chs. 40–48)

☐ 40:1–11 *Introduction*

Watch how the theme of Israel's second, even greater exodus, which lies at the heart of the oracles contained in this section, is introduced here. Jerusalem's "hard service" in exile is coming to an end (vv. 1–2), as the desert is to be prepared like a highway, and Yahweh's glory will be revealed once more (vv. 3–5). All of this is the result of God's unbreakable word (vv. 6–8). Thus the prophet announces "good tidings to Zion"—that Yahweh will once more come with power and "shepherd" his people, bringing them safely home (vv. 9–11; note how v. 9 responds to 35:4).

☐ **40:12–41:29** *The Consolation of Israel*

But is exiled Jerusalem ready for this? Note how the oracles begin with Yahweh's contending with his people that he is the Sovereign Lord who can be trusted absolutely. His wisdom is unsearchable (40:12–14); no nation or idol can compare with him (vv. 15–26), so he will strengthen them for the journey (vv. 27–31; cf. v. 31 and Exod 19:4). Then Yahweh contends with the nations and their idols (41:1–7 [which have to be created in order to join the dispute!], vv. 21–29) to point out that he alone has raised up "one from the east" (v. 2, Cyrus), who comes on Babylon from the north (vv. 21–29). These oracles are obviously for Israel's consolation, since they bookend Yahweh's encouragement to Israel his "servant" that he is with them (as in the former exodus) and will provide for them through the desert (vv. 8–20).

☐ **42:1–44:23** *Israel As God's Reluctant Servant to the Nations*

As you read this series of stirring oracles, watch for the following repeated themes—that God's gracious redemption of Israel is so that she might become his servant for the nations; that Israel, still deaf and blind (cf. 6:9–10), is reluctant to receive this redemption; that Yahweh thus contends with them that he alone is God and that there is no other; that he will bring about a second exodus that will cause them to forget the first; and that all of this is for his own glory, he who is the gracious Redeemer of Israel.

☐ **44:24–45:25** *Yahweh's Chosen Deliverer, Cyrus*

Note the renewed emphasis on Yahweh's unbreakable word that accomplishes what he intends, including the raising up of Cyrus his servant for the sake of Israel his servant; especially note the repeated emphasis on "I am the LORD [Yahweh], and there is no other" (45:5, 6, 18; cf. 43:11; 45:14, 21, 22). Tucked into all this is also the note of

Israel's reluctance (45:9–10). Nonetheless Yahweh intends to use Israel's redemption as an appeal to the nations (vv. 14–25).

☐ 46:1–48:22   *Yahweh's Disputation with Stubborn Israel*

In this series of oracles Yahweh at last announces the actual fall of Babylon (46:1–2; 47:1–15). But his contention is with citizens of stubborn Israel, who are resistant to what Yahweh has planned for them (46:3–13; 48:1–19); he concludes with a final plea to flee Babylon (48:20–22).

Yahweh's Coming Servant Who Will Bring Salvation (chs. 49–55)

☐ 49:1–50:11   *Yahweh's Servant and the Salvation of Israel*

Note in these oracles how Yahweh's "servant, Israel," narrows down to one servant who will stand in for Israel and redeem both Israel and the nations. Note also that the new exodus is more clearly located in the relatively distant future. The first oracle paves the way: Yahweh's servant, Israel, becomes the one who brings Israel—and the nations—back to Yahweh (49:1–7). This is followed by the renewed announcement of the new exodus (49:8–13), along with Israel's continued reluctance (49:14, 24) and Yahweh's responses (49:15–23, 25–26), climaxing with the servant's own response to his commission (50:1–9) and the prophet's invitation for Israel to obey Yahweh (50:10–11).

☐ 51:1–52:12   *The Glorious Future of Zion*

After Yahweh appeals to the faithful in Israel who will inherit the promises (51:1–8), the prophet calls for Yahweh to lead the new exodus (51:9–11). Yahweh responds with words of consolation to Israel (51:12–16), so the prophet calls for Israel to respond (51:17–21), since their cup of wrath is to be passed on to Babylon (vv. 22–23). Zion must therefore prepare herself for the great exodus to come (52:1–6), which climaxes with Yahweh's return to Zion (vv. 7–10) and a final appeal to flee Babylon as they did Egypt, but not in haste this time (vv. 11–12).

☐ 52:13–53:12   *The Servant Atones for Israel's Sins*

How will this new exodus be achieved? Through the redeeming work of Yahweh's suffering servant, whose effective ministry is presented in 52:13–15, its means in 53:1–9, and its divine origins and assessment in 53:10–12. No wonder the New Testament sees the fulfillment of this passage in Jesus Christ (Mark 10:45; Acts 8:30–35; 1 Pet 2:21–25).

□ **54:1–17** *The Glorious Future of Zion*

The climax of the servant's work is now expressed by means of echoes of three former covenants—Abraham (54:1–3), Sinai (vv. 4–8), and Noah (vv. 9–10)—as Zion's future glory is expressed with lavish imagery (vv. 11–17). Note especially that the exiles in chapter 52 are still in Babylon, but here they appear on Zion (v. 11). How did they get there? Through the suffering servant of 52:13–53:12!

□ **55:1–13** *Yahweh's Invitation to Israel and the Nations*

Yahweh's final word in this section is one of invitation—to Israel and to the nations—to receive freely of God's gracious provision (55:1–7). Appealing once more to his sovereignty and unbreakable word (vv. 8–11), Yahweh announces the great reversal of fortunes for those who respond (vv. 12–13).

Present Failure, and Zion's Glorious Future (chs. 56–66)

□ **56:1–59:21** *True Sabbath Keeping and True Fasting*

This final section of Isaiah begins with a kind of reprise—a return to the themes with which the book began. An opening oracle (56:1–8) sets the tone, with its concerns for Yahweh's soon-coming salvation, Israel's keeping covenant, Sabbath keeping in a context of justice, and the gathering of the nations on the holy mountain.

The series of oracles that follows picks up these themes, plus condemnation of Israel's leaders (56:9–57:4) and idolatry (57:5–13). But inserted between this condemnation of idolatry and of religion without justice (58:1–14) is an oracle of salvation for the humble (57:14–21). Note how all these themes echo 1:2–2:5.

The section concludes with an announcement of the sins that have kept Yahweh at a distance (59:1–8), a prayer of repentance by the people (vv. 9–15) and Yahweh's response of coming salvation (vv. 16–21), which echoes 1:18–20. Note especially how it ends by announcing the coming Redeemer and the Spirit (59:20–21).

□ **60:1–63:6** *The Future Glory of Zion, and Yahweh's Anointed One*

This collection of oracles is the centerpiece of the final section of Isaiah. It starts with a marvelous picture of the future glory of Zion (ch. 60), which, as throughout Isaiah, includes the nations (vv. 10–14). Then comes the announcement of the coming Redeemer (ch. 61), who has remarkable resemblances to the servant of chapters 42–53—a passage that Jesus announces as fulfilled in himself and his ministry (Luke 4:16–21). Note also that the redeemed are the humble poor of the preceding oracles. This is followed by yet another oracle about Zion's glorious future (Isa 62), concluding with the Redeemer's eschatological judgment of the nations (63:1–6), a passage picked up by John (Rev 14:17–20).

☐ 63:7–64:12 *Yahweh's People Pray*

This prayer brings us back to present realities, as God's people await their great future. Note how it begins by recalling the first exodus—that Yahweh was present by his Spirit and in mercy redeemed them despite their rebellion (63:7–14)—which leads to the prayer for God to act again on their behalf (63:15–64:12), constituting one of the more poignant moments in Isaiah.

☐ 65:1–16 *Judgment and Salvation*

Yahweh's response to their prayer is to remind them of their waywardness (vv. 1–7), but also of his consistently promised redemption (vv. 8–16).

☐ 65:17–66:24 *Future Zion in a New Heaven and New Earth*

Isaiah now concludes with one more look at the future glory of Zion—what Yahweh has always been after—placed in an eschatological setting of a new heaven and a new earth, with a reminder of final judgment to come. Note how the end echoes 2:2–4: God's salvation encompasses a renewed Zion that will include the nations (66:18–21).

———————————

The book of Isaiah stands in the middle of the Old Testament as a reminder that Yahweh is the living God who will both judge the world in righteousness and will in mercy save his people and the nations through his "suffering servant" Messiah. It thus gathers up the whole of the Old Testament story and prepares the way for the New.

Jeremiah

ORIENTING DATA FOR JEREMIAH

- **Content:** oracles of judgment against Judah and the nations, along with oracles of future hope, interwoven with narratives of Jeremiah's role in the concluding days of Judah

- **Prophet:** Jeremiah, of priestly lineage from the village of Anathoth, about three miles south of Jerusalem

- **Date of prophetic activity:** from 627 to 585 B.C. (see 1:2–3)

- **Emphases:** Judah's unfaithfulness to Yahweh will end in its destruction; in keeping with the promises of Deuteronomy, God has a bright future for his people—a time of restoration and a new covenant; Yahweh's own heart for his people revealed through the heart of Jeremiah

OVERVIEW OF JEREMIAH

The book of Jeremiah is a collection of his many oracles—mostly in poetry and mostly against Judah and Jerusalem—plus a large number of narratives in which he is the leading player. The collection itself, perhaps "published" by Baruch (Jer 36:32; 45:1–5), comes in four major parts. Chapters 1–25 contain oracles and interpreted symbolic actions that announce the coming doom of Judah and Jerusalem. A large part of this material appears in the form of conversation/dialogue between the prophet and Yahweh. In chapters 26–36 two collections of (nonchronological) narratives enclose the highly important message of hope in chapters 30–33. Chapters 37–45 contain a series of narratives in chronological order, having to do with events that fulfill prophecies in part 1. Chapters 46–51 contain oracles against the nations, while chapter 52 is a historical epilogue, vindicating Jeremiah as a prophet. Thus:

A Prophecies of Judgment against Jerusalem (chs. 1–25)
  B Narratives Holding Out Hope for the Future (chs. 26–36)
  B* Narratives regarding the Fall of Jerusalem (chs. 37–45)
A* Prophecies of Judgment against the Nations (chs. 46–51)
Epilogue (ch. 52)

It is important to note that the narratives in chapters 26–36 have many correspondences with the preceding oracles. For example, the *content* of the famous temple sermon appears in 7:1–29, while the *reaction* to it appears as the first narrative (ch. 26); the policy to yield to Babylon and go into exile in 21:8–10 becomes the major focus of the narratives in chapters 27–29; and the reasons for judgments against Judah's kings and prophets given in chapters 22–23 find narrative expression in chapters 26–29 and 34–36. This suggests that the reason for the (nonchronological) first collection of narratives is topical—and intentional.

SPECIFIC ADVICE FOR READING JEREMIAH

To read Jeremiah well, you need to have some inkling about the man and his times, as well as the nature of the materials that make up the book.

First, a few comments about the times in which Jeremiah lived. Although Jeremiah received his call during the thirteenth year (of thirty-one years) of the reign of Josiah, only one of his oracles is dated to that period (3:6–10). Most of them come from the tumultuous years in Jerusalem after Josiah's death, during the reigns of two sons (Jehoiakim, 609–598 B.C., and Zedekiah, 597–586). Josiah himself had reigned during a lull on the international scene, as Assyria was in serious decline and both Egypt and Babylon were vying for supremacy in the coastal area that included Judah. Josiah had died in battle against the Egyptian pharaoh Neco (609), but Neco in turn was defeated by Nebuchadnezzar of Babylon in 605. The rest of Judah's final years are related to the political events that followed.

Josiah's sons (and one grandson, Jehoiachin) spent their few ruling years as political footballs between Egypt and Babylon, always under Babylonian control but repeatedly turning to Egypt for help to throw off the Babylonian yoke and gain a measure of independence. These policies eventually resulted in a siege by Nebuchadnezzar in 598 that brought Jehoiachin's brief reign of three months to an end, as he and most of the leading people of Jerusalem were sent into exile to Babylon (2 Kgs 24:8–17; Jer 29:2; see Ezekiel). Nonetheless, the final king of Judah, Zedekiah, returned to these hopeless policies, which eventually led to a second siege and the total destruction of Jerusalem (586). A still further rebellion by a remnant of those who remained in Judah finally resulted in a flight to Egypt in which both Jeremiah and Baruch were taken along.

It is not possible to make sense of Jeremiah apart from this history, since he played a major role in speaking into these political affairs over the twenty-two years of Jehoiakim's and Zedekiah's reigns. The narratives reveal a great deal about political intrigue, as both hawks and doves are represented, along with pro-Egyptian and pro-Babylonian voices. And because Jeremiah's oracles and narratives (until the events of the end, chs. 37–45) are not in their chronological order, you will do well to keep these names, dates, and political policies near at hand as you read.

Second, Jeremiah was given a most unenviable task, namely, to stand in opposition to the royal house of David and to the prophets, priests, and people by announcing the coming destruction of Jerusalem and urging them to accept exile in Babylon if they wished to live and have any future at all. At issue is Jeremiah's pro-Babylonian policy (following the first exile under Jehoiachin in 598), a view that had two things militating against it in the royal court: Many believed (1) that Jerusalem was secure because of the Davidic covenant and the presence of Yahweh's temple (see 7:4–11) and (2) that the present exile of Jehoiachin would be short-lived (see 28:1–4). Jeremiah's message is clear: Yield to Babylon and you will live—even if the return is a lifetime away(!); resist and you will die. Lying behind this resistance is a conviction, stemming from Yahweh's rescue of Jerusalem from the Assyrians (see Isa 36–37), that Zion was inviolable—because of its temple, Yahweh's resting/dwelling place.

Third, a few comments about Jeremiah's book. You need to note that chapters 1–25 form the heart of Jeremiah's prophetic word and probably represent much of the scroll that was burned by Jehoiakim and rewritten with the help of Baruch (ch. 36). The beginning oracles announce the coming judgment and the reasons for it (primarily unfaithfulness to Yahweh in the form of idolatry), while at the same time they are full of appeals to Judah, urging that if her people repent, Yahweh will relent. But the appeals go unheeded and eventually give way to the certainty of coming judgment. Included in this collection are the many intriguing moments of Jeremiah's own interactions with Yahweh (by argument, dialogue, lament, and complaint) over the coming disaster or over his own ill-treatment. You may find the going a bit easier when reading this collection if you mark carefully the changes of speakers. Also included are several interpreted symbolic actions, which serve to illustrate what Yahweh has to say to Judah.

Of the several influences on Jeremiah himself, the most obvious are Hosea and Deuteronomy. Jeremiah makes considerable use of the former's vivid imagery of Israel as a faithless bride-turned-prostitute, dearly loved by Yahweh, but whose unfaithfulness will cause him to give her over to her "lovers." This in turn reflects several Deuteronomic influences, especially the appeal to the stipulations of the covenant, including the curses for unfaithfulness at the key point of whether they will serve Yahweh alone (Jer 11:1–13; cf. 17:5–8). Related is the imagery of the un/circumcised heart (4:4; 9:25; cf. Deut 10:16; 30:6) and the promised restoration after exile with a new covenant (Jer 30–33). As in Deuteronomy, the issue is not merely idolatry, but syncretism—worshiping and serving Baal alongside Yahweh. But Yahweh is God alone and therefore a jealous God who cannot abide their idolatry, yet he is also compassionate and loving toward his people. It is this mixture of realities that finds poignant expression in Jeremiah.

A WALK THROUGH JEREMIAH

Oracles of Judgment against Judah and Jerusalem (chs. 1–25)

□ 1:1–19   *Introduction*

Watch for several important clues to the rest of the book as you read this introduction. The *heading* (vv. 1–3) places Jeremiah socially (from a priestly family in a village) and historically. The *call* itself (vv. 4–10) initiates the pattern of dialogue, as Jeremiah, in proper prophetic humility, resists his calling. The *first vision* (vv. 11–12) assures him of the certain fulfillment of God's word through him. The *second vision* (vv. 13–16) indicates the source of God's coming judgment (Babylon, from the north). The *final summons* (vv. 17–19) anticipates both his role and reception in these events.

☐ 2:1–6:30 *Oracles against Judah's Idolatry*

This first series sets up the rest of the book. Yahweh's charge against Judah/Jerusalem is given in 2:1–3:5. Watch for the following: the basic imagery of a formerly loving bride (2:2) who has turned to prostitution (2:20–25, 32–33; 3:1–5), mainly in the form of idolatry (but see also 2:34); the role of the leaders (kings, officials, priests, prophets; 2:8, 26; cf. chs. 21–23); and Yahweh's astonishment over such craziness (2:10–19).

In the next collection (3:6–4:4), watch for the many appeals to the faithless bride not to be like Samaria (who must also repent, 3:12–14), but to return to her husband, with the threat of sure doom if she fails to take heed. Next comes the announcement of disaster from the north (4:5–31, picking up from 1:14–16); note how this section alternates between direct words from Yahweh (4:5–6, 9, 11–12, 15–18, 22, 27–28) and Jeremiah's own words (vv. 7–8, 10, 13–14, 19–21, 23–26, 29–31).

Chapter 5 is a collection of short oracles, with two interventions by Jeremiah (vv. 3–6, 12–13) that alternately announce coming judgment (vv. 9–10, 15–17) and the reasons for it: Social injustice (vv. 26–28) again joins idolatry (vv. 7–8, 19). Note the thought echoed from Isaiah that the people have become like their idols (v. 21, eyes and ears that cannot see or hear).

Chapter 6 concludes this first collection by announcing the siege of Jerusalem. Note especially Jeremiah's own futile pleas with his people to take heed (vv. 10–11a, 24–26).

☐ 7:1–10:25 *More Oracles against Idolatry*

The first two sets of prose oracles (7:1–29; 7:30–8:3) spell out in stark detail Judah's syncretistic ways, all the while believing that the people's "devotion" to Yahweh and his presence will make them secure. You may wish to read chapter 26 in conjunction with the temple sermon (7:1–29), which narrates the response to it. The rest is a series of poetic oracles that picks up most of the themes from the first cycle (idolatry, forsaking the law, and judgment), but now heavily loaded with interventions by Jeremiah, mostly in the form of anguish over Jerusalem's coming destruction or in praise of the God whom Judah has spurned (note also the intervention by the people, 8:14–16). Note how it ends with a prayer (10:23–25) that echoes a common prophetic theme: Even though Judah deserves what it gets, so do the other nations, thus anticipating the oracles in chapters 46–51.

☐ **11:1–13:27** *The Broken Covenant*

Note how the first oracle (11:1–17) echoes what has gone before, but now in terms of the bride's breaking covenant with Yahweh. Look for Jeremiah's deep involvement in the rest of this section—a plot against him by his own people will result in their judgment (11:18–23); his renewed complaint about God's justice (12:1–4) is answered in terms of what Jeremiah's own people have done to him (12:5–13), yet justice will come to the nations as well (vv. 14–17); a symbolic action is then interpreted in terms of Judah's uselessness and coming destruction (13:1–14); and his own appeal to Judah (13:15–23) is answered again in terms of the unfaithful wife (vv. 24–27), thus returning to the theme of the broken covenant.

☐ **14:1–17:27** *Yahweh's Rejection of His People*

Note that this series continues the format of dialogue between Yahweh and Jeremiah: Yahweh announces judgment (14:1–6); Jeremiah prays for his people (vv. 7–9), but because their judgment is now set, he is told not to pray (vv. 10–16) but to weep over them (vv. 17–18). Jeremiah responds by reminding Yahweh of his covenant (vv. 19–22), to which Yahweh counters that even Moses and Samuel couldn't help them now (15:1–4, 5–9; cf. 15:12–14). Jeremiah responds with a lament (vv. 10, 15–18), and Yahweh with a call to repent and to stay with his calling, assuring him of deliverance (vv. 11, 19–21). After a series of personal prohibitions that are tied to judgments against the people (16:1–9), Jeremiah is commissioned to proclaim both judgment and hope (vv. 10–18), while another oracle of judgment (16:21–17:8) is followed by another dialogue (17:9–10) and personal lament (vv. 11–18). The concluding oracle announces judgment for breaking the Sabbath (vv. 19–27; cf. Exod 23:10–12; 31:12–17; 35:1–3).

☐ **18:1–20:18** *Symbols and Laments*

Two interpreted symbolic actions (18:1–17; 19:1–15) frame another personal lament (18:18–23), the second resulting in Jeremiah's being beaten (20:1–3), which in turn serves as another announcement of judgment (vv. 4–6), followed by a final personal lament (vv. 7–18). Note that the terror from the north is finally identified: It is Babylon (v. 4).

☐ **21:1–24:10** *Judgment against Kings and Prophets*

Oracles against Zedekiah bookend this section, which picks up from 2:8 and 2:26. A request from Zedekiah (ch. 21) that took place at the

THE PROPHETS OF ISRAEL IN THE BIBLICAL STORY

beginning of the siege (588 B.C.) thus heads a series of oracles against Judah's kings (ch. 22, note Jehoiakim [v. 18] and Jehoiachin [v. 24]), who will someday be replaced with a true Branch from David's line (23:1–8). These are followed by oracles against false prophets and priests (23:33–40) and a final oracle against Zedekiah and his officials (ch. 24). Note especially the messianic oracle in 23:5–6, which echoes Isaiah 11:1, 10. It is repeated in 33:15–16 and picked up in Revelation 5:5.

☐ 25:1–38   *Summary of Part 1 and Anticipation of Part 4*

Note how the announcement of a seventy-year exile (vv. 1–14) is full of reasons for it that recall the preceding chapters. This is followed by an announcement of judgments against the nations (vv. 15–33), which will be spelled out in full in chapters 46–51, and a concluding word against the shepherds (vv. 34–38), bringing closure to chapters 21–24 as well. You will find the words against Babylon in 25:10 echoed in the final doom of John's "Babylon" in Revelation 18:21–23.

God's Word Offers Hope but Is Rejected (chs. 26–36)

☐ 26:1–24   *Reaction to Jeremiah's Temple Sermon*

The brief summary in verses 1–6 introduces the narrative about Jerusalem's reaction to Jeremiah's temple sermon in 7:1–29. After the initial reaction (26:7–9), there is a hastily convened trial (vv. 10–19) in which Jeremiah is saved by a split between priests/prophets and officials and by a comparison with Micah. The final account compares Jeremiah with a prophet who did not fare as well (vv. 20–23) and another one who did (v. 24).

☐ 27:1–29:32   *Jeremiah and the False Prophets*

This section is dominated by the conflict between Jeremiah and two false prophets (Hananiah and Shemaiah) over Jeremiah's pro-Babylonian policy. In contrast to Jeremiah himself (ch. 26) and over against his message of hope through exile, both of these men die. Note especially how the message of hope through exile prepares the way for the next section.

☐ 30:1–33:26   *Promised Restoration and a New Covenant*

Here you will find the basic reason for Jeremiah's pro-Babylon stance: In it lies the only hope for the future. Thus, chapters 30–31 are a collection of short oracles that prophesy the return from exile and the

190

restoration of Zion (see Deut 30:1–10); they are, however, interlaced with moments of judgment (Jer 30:5–7, 12–15, 23–24) in order to remind the people of what led to the exile. Note the various players in the restoration story—the people (of both Israel and Judah), the land, the city, the king, the priests, and especially the new covenant.

Jeremiah then buys a field in Anathoth (32:1–25) as down payment on this future that will come after his time! This is followed by another announcement of judgment at the time of the siege (32:26–35), followed by prose oracles of future restoration (32:36–33:26). Note how 33:15–16 picks up the promise of the Messiah from 23:5–6.

☐ 34:1–36:32   Zedekiah, Jehoiakim, and Jeremiah's Scroll

In response to chapters 30–33 these narratives illustrate covenant disloyalty (ch. 34) and then covenant loyalty (ch. 35), with the rejection of Jeremiah's words by Jehoiakim (ch. 36) concluding the section. True hope for Judah has been offered, but rejected.

The Fall of Jerusalem and Its Aftermath (chs. 37–45)

☐ 37:1–38:28   Jeremiah and Court Politics

The narratives in this final cycle are in chronological order, spelling out various episodes that marked the end of Jerusalem. The first (ch. 37) reflects the placing of false hope in Egypt by Zedekiah, resulting in Jeremiah's arrest; the second reflects Zedekiah's continuing anti-Babylonian policy (38:1–13), which results in Jeremiah's being thrown into a cistern; note that in the final episode (vv. 14–28), Jeremiah repeats the advice to yield to Babylon so as to live.

☐ 39:1–41:15   Jeremiah and the Fall of Jerusalem

This group of narratives tells the story of Jerusalem's fall, plus the sordid events that follow, including the assassination of Gedaliah.

☐ 41:16–45:5   Jeremiah and the Flight to Egypt

These final narratives contain Jeremiah's last oracles to the exiles in Egypt, who still resist Yahweh, plus a final word to Baruch.

Oracles against the Nations (chs. 46–51)

In keeping with the prophetic tradition, Jeremiah had over many years spoken oracles of Yahweh's judgment of the nations. These are placed at the end of his book—so that God's message of doom for Babylon would be the final word.

☐ 46:1–28 *The Doom of Egypt*

The promised oracles against the nations (see 1:10) now conclude the book. They begin with Judah's false hope, namely, Egypt. The defeat of Egypt's army (46:2–12) will be followed by the ruin of their land (vv. 13–24), with an appended note about Israel's hope (vv. 27–28).

☐ 47:1–49:39 *The Doom of Judah's Neighbors*

This series of oracles condemns Judah's closest neighbors, who are also historic enemies, judged primarily for pride and for their treatment of Israel. Starting in the south (Philistia), the focus moves to the east (Moab, Ammon, Edom), and then to the northeast (Damascus, Hazor, Elam). They are judged primarily for pride and for their treatment of Israel.

☐ 50:1–51:64 *The Doom of Babylon*

Although Jeremiah was pro-Babylon with regard to Israel's future, he also recognized that the destroyer must likewise be destroyed. Here especially you'll find the motif of Yahweh the Divine Warrior engaged in holy war against his enemies. Note in this collection of oracles announcing Babylon's doom how much is related to Israel's future, beginning with 50:2–7. Babylon's desolation will be even more complete than Jerusalem's, brought about by her cruelty to God's people, her arrogance, and her own idolatries. Several of these oracles will serve as the basis for John's announcement of doom on a later "Babylon"—the city of Rome (Rev 18).

An Epilogue (ch. 52)

Notice how this final historical epilogue serves to vindicate Jeremiah as a prophet. The king who rejected his words dies in ignominy (52:6–11); the king who accepted them, though imprisoned, lives on and dies in honor (vv. 31–34).

The book of Jeremiah is a constant reminder of God's faithfulness to his word in Deuteronomy that his elect will be cursed by exile for their unfaithfulness to Yahweh but will be restored at a later time with the hope of a new covenant—which was fulfilled through Jesus Christ, David's "righteous Branch" (Jer 23:5).

Ezekiel

ORIENTING DATA FOR EZEKIEL

- **Content:** a series of prophecies announcing the fall of Jerusalem, including the departure of Yahweh, followed by Israel's eventual restoration with the return of Yahweh

- **Prophet:** Ezekiel, an Israelite priest and prophet who was taken to Babylon among the first wave of captives from Judah in 598 B.C., and a younger contemporary of Jeremiah

- **Date of prophetic activity:** from 593 (Ezek 1:2) until 571 B.C. (29:17)

- **Emphases:** the inevitability of the fall of Jerusalem because of her sins, especially idolatry; the transcendent sovereignty of God as Lord of all the nations and all history; the loss and restoration of the land and of Yahweh's presence among the people of God; the promise of the life-giving Spirit as the key to covenant faithfulness

OVERVIEW OF EZEKIEL

The book of Ezekiel contains a variety of prophetic visions and oracles, which Ezekiel presented to the exiles in Babylon over a twenty-two-year period (593–571 B.C.), the most turbulent years in the history of Jerusalem. Except for the oracle and lament over Egypt (29:17–30:26), the oracles appear in chronological order.

The book is in three clear parts. Chapters 1–24 contain oracles from the five-year period preceding the siege of Jerusalem (588). These are primarily announcements to overconfident Judeans of God's certain judgment against the city and her temple. Next is a series of oracles against surrounding nations (chs. 25–32)—Babylon itself being notably excepted. The final oracles (chs. 33–48), which cover a sixteen-year period after the fall of Jerusalem, focus on hope for the future.

The structure of the book reflects Ezekiel's theology: Yahweh's *holy wrath* against his people's idolatries would cause Jerusalem to be destroyed, including her temple (the place of his presence)—despite disbelief and protest to the contrary (chs. 1–24). Yahweh is also *the sovereign God* over all the nations, so they, too, will experience judgment because of their idolatries and sins (chs. 25–32). But Yahweh is a God of *great mercy and compassion,* who intends to restore his people and be present with them once more (chs. 33–48).

SPECIFIC ADVICE FOR READING EZEKIEL

In order to read Ezekiel well, you need a measure of appreciation for the history of his times, some of which can be found in 2 Kings 22–25. Ezekiel was born into a priestly family in Jerusalem just before the reforms of Josiah (622 B.C.) and was presumably preparing for priestly duties to begin at age thirty (593). But in 598, disaster struck in the form of Nebuchadnezzar of Babylon. Over the span of Ezekiel's life, Judah's kings had made some bad political choices in the struggle between Egypt and Babylon over supremacy in the area. So Nebuchadnezzar eventually laid siege to Jerusalem; King Jehoiachin surrendered, and he and most of Jerusalem's prominent people, including Ezekiel's family, were taken into exile (see Jer 29:2) and placed in a refugee settlement south of Babylon near the Kebar River. Apparently many believed this exile was only a temporary blip on the screen of their glorious history as God's people (see Jer 28). But Jeremiah had already informed the exiles in writing (Jer 29:1–23) that they were going to be there for the long haul. Five years later Yahweh called Ezekiel to be a prophet who would announce God's judgment against Jerusalem, addressing his words to "the house of Israel"—primarily to the exiles in Babylon (Ezek 3:1, 11).

Lying at the heart of things was a theology to which both Ezekiel and the people were committed, although they had radically different views as to what it meant—the people of Israel as Yahweh's people, created and redeemed by him and ultimately defined by their *place* (the land, and especially Jerusalem) and by Yahweh's *presence* (symbolized by the temple in Jerusalem). Most people understood this theology to mean that Jerusalem was inviolable, a view reinforced by the miraculous salvation of Jerusalem after the fall of Samaria some 125 years earlier (see 2 Kgs 17–19). This theology had been continually fed to the people by the false court prophets (e.g., Hananiah, Jer 28), although opposed by Zephaniah and Jeremiah.

Ezekiel also understood that Israel was defined by place and presence (he was, after all, to become a priest in Jerusalem). But he also recognized that Judah had failed to keep covenant with Yahweh (see the arresting imagery of chs. 16; 23), thus they would forfeit the land and God's presence. Through a variety of visions, prophetic actions, and oracles, he announced over and over again that Jerusalem would soon be destroyed and that Yahweh would depart from his temple (ch. 10). This was both as unbelievable to the exiles in Babylon as it was excruciating for Ezekiel. But he also saw clearly that all of the best of the past was to be renewed in the future: king, land, people, covenant, and presence—which was eventually realized in Christ and his new-covenant people.

About the oracles themselves. You will observe that, in contrast to the prophets who preceded him, Ezekiel spoke his oracles primarily in prose rather than poetry. Indeed, reading Ezekiel is like entering into a verbal picture book, as one prophetic word after another comes either in the form of a symbolic action on his part or as a vision or allegorical picture, some of which are also interpreted. These latter cover a broad range, from the apocalyptic imagery in chapters 1 (cf. 10:1–22) and 37, to the interpreted symbolic visions of chapters 15 and 17, to the parable of chapter 16, which is so straightforward that it needs no separate interpretation.

You will want to be looking for other features that are also unique to Ezekiel, including his interest in the temple and things priestly. For example, watch for the frequency with which oracles are introduced by Yahweh's asking questions, and how often they conclude with the words "so you/they will know that I am the LORD [Yahweh]" ($58x$) or with "I the LORD [Yahweh] have spoken" ($18x$). His tendency to be repetitive may at times be burdensome to the modern reader, but for Ezekiel it was a way of reinforcing what he saw and reported. The repeated address to him as "son of man" is a Hebraism emphasizing his humanity in the presence of the eternal God.

Finally, you will meet many of Ezekiel's words and ideas when you come to the New Testament, especially in Paul's letters and John's Revelation. Many of John's own images are retakes of Ezekiel's as he joins them to some from Daniel and Isaiah to form a whole new set of images intended to express anew the unspeakable greatness of God and his ways.

A WALK THROUGH EZEKIEL

Oracles of Judgment against Israel (chs. 1–24)

☐ 1:1–3:27 Ezekiel's Call and Commissioning

Verses 1–2 place Ezekiel among the exiles and date the time of his call to his thirtieth year and to the fifth year of the exile (July 593 B.C.). His call begins with high drama (ch. 1), as Yahweh appears to him seated on a magnificent chariot throne borne by four cherubim (see 10:20), to which Ezekiel responds appropriately by falling facedown (cf. Dan 10:9; Rev 1:17). He is then commissioned and equipped (by the Spirit) for his exceedingly difficult assignment (Ezek 2:1–3:27). Note especially that his commission as a "watchman" (3:16–21) also stands at the beginning of the final series of visions/oracles (33:1–20).

☐ 4:1–7:27 The Coming Siege and Doom of Jerusalem

As you read this section, note that it is still part of the same sequence dated in 1:2. Thus, five years in advance, Ezekiel is to engage in three symbolic actions (4:1–3, 4–17; 5:1–4) by which Yahweh announces the coming siege and destruction of Jerusalem (5:5–17). These are followed by two straightforward oracles announcing the devastation of Jerusalem and the countryside alike (chs. 6–7); note that the first is addressed to "the mountains of Israel," a designation for the land (cf. 36:1–15), and that both conclude with "Then they will know that I am the LORD [Yahweh]." The singular reason for this devastation is idolatry, so the Israelites' dead bodies will be sacrifices to their idols (6:5).

☐ 8:1–12:20 Israel's Idolatry and Yahweh's Departure from Jerusalem

Over a year later (September 592), Ezekiel is taken by the Spirit to "see" Jerusalem's idolatry in the temple itself (ch. 8). This is one of the most poignant moments in the Bible. Can you feel Yahweh's utter dismay as the women weep over the god Tammuz and the men—with their backs toward Yahweh!—worship the sun in the place of the eternal God's very presence? Thus the people are symbolically marked for destruction (ch. 9) as Jerusalem is assigned to burning (10:2–8) and the glory of Yahweh leaves the temple (10:9–22) and eventually the city

(11:23). The judgment is especially against the present leaders in Jerusalem for their bad politics (11:1–15). But in anticipation of chapters 33–48, hope lies in the future (11:16–25) in keeping with Ezekiel's plea for a remnant to be spared (11:13). The final event prophesied in this sequence is the second deportation of exiles, announced by another symbolic action (12:1–20).

☐ 12:21–14:23 *False Prophets and Misguided Elders*

Like Jeremiah, Ezekiel is plagued by false prophets, who in this case say that either Ezekiel's prophecies will not come to pass (12:21–25) or they will be long delayed (vv. 26–28); so Ezekiel is told by Yahweh to prophesy against those who cover flimsy walls with whitewash and those who make and use charms for divination in Yahweh's name (ch. 13). When the elders come to see him, their idolatrous hearts and their false prophets are exposed (14:1–11); Ezekiel concludes with a true prophecy—the inevitability of the coming disaster in Jerusalem (vv. 12–23). Despite her "prophets," Zion is simply *not* inviolable.

☐ 15:1–19:14 *The Doom of Jerusalem and Her Kings*

These loosely related oracles—four allegories and a response to a proverb—variously reflect the situations of both the exiles in Babylon and current affairs in Jerusalem. The first two (chs. 15–16) focus again on Jerusalem's coming destruction, the first echoing Isaiah's song of the vineyard (Isa 5:1–7); note that it is the first of several oracles in the book that begin with Yahweh's asking questions. Ezekiel 16 graphically portrays the history of Israel's unfaithfulness to Yahweh (a prostitute who pays men to have her!)—by both her political intrigues and an insatiable appetite for idolatry. The allegories of eagles (ch. 17) and lions (ch. 19), the latter ironically taking the form of a lament, are directed especially at Zedekiah, present king in Jerusalem (17:15–21; 19:5–9; see 2 Kgs 25:6–7). These allegories enclose a complaint against God's injustice (the children pay for their parents' sins) brought to Ezekiel by the exiles (Ezek 18). Their proverb is rejected altogether and replaced with an offer to forgive if they repent. Note especially that their sins are expanded considerably beyond idolatry (cf. ch. 22).

☐ 20:1 – 24:27   *Countdown to Catastrophe*

This series, which begins August 591 (20:1), concludes (24:1) with the beginning of the siege of Jerusalem (January 588). The first oracle (20:1 – 44), picking up from chapter 16, puts Israel's history of unfaithfulness in plain terms, but concludes on a note of hope (anticipating chs. 36 – 37). In the brief oracle that follows (vv. 45 – 49), note that "south" is the direction to Judah from Babylon. God's "sword" for executing his judgment will be Babylon (ch. 21), again because of Judah's sins that demand judgment (ch. 22). The allegory of two sisters (ch. 23), also picking up from chapter 16, now sets Jerusalem's sins in light of fallen Samaria's, while the beginning of the siege is pictured in two ways as a cooking pot (24:3 – 8, 9 – 14). The siege coincides with the sudden death of Ezekiel's wife (24:15 – 27), and he is struck dumb by the enormity of his grief—a symbol for how the exiles will respond to the fall of Jerusalem.

Oracles of Judgment against the Nations (chs. 25 – 32)

Before the actual fall, at which point Ezekiel turns toward Yahweh's future for his people, he receives a series of oracles against the nations who were Judah's political allies, indicating that the same fate awaits them.

☐ 25:1 – 17   *Against Surrounding Nations*

This first set of oracles are against Judah's historic enemies, who became political allies only by the pressure of events, but who turned against her at the time of the siege.

☐ 26:1 – 28:26   *Against Tyre and Sidon*

Although not a political enemy, Tyre represents the economically exploitative powers; she lives in arrogance because of her position in the world's economic systems. The first oracle (ch. 26) is against the city herself, while the second (ch. 27) mockingly laments her coming demise. Here especially you get insight into the Phoenicians' role as merchants to the world, a passage from which John borrows heavily in his woe against Babylon (Rome) in Revelation 18. The third oracle (Ezek 28) focuses on the sheer arrogance of her king. But Yahweh alone is King of the nations, so Tyre must also fall.

☐ 29:1–32:32 *Against Egypt*

Here you find Ezekiel finally turning to the primary cause of so much of Judah's grief, namely, Egypt, from whom Judah's kings constantly sought help against Babylon. As with Tyre, there is an oracle of judgment (ch. 29) followed by a lament (ch. 30) and by an oracle against her king (ch. 31), but in this case concluding with a lament for this king as well (ch. 32).

Oracles of Hope and Consolation (chs. 33–48)

Watch for the clear sense of development you find in this final series of oracles. After positioning Ezekiel in the role of a watchman, Yahweh promises to restore, in turn, the Davidic kingship, the land, Yahweh's honor (by way of the new covenant), his people, his sovereignty over the nations, and finally his presence among the people in the land.

☐ 33:1–33 *Ezekiel's Role*

The word of hope begins by Ezekiel's returning to his role as watchman (33:1–20; cf. 3:16–21 to catch the new emphasis here). The news of Jerusalem's fall causes Ezekiel's mouth to open (33:22; cf. 24:25–27), and the first word is in keeping with Jeremiah's—that the *land* will be desolate for a long time (33:23–33).

☐ 34:1–31 *Restoring Yahweh's Role as Shepherd of Israel*

Note how the first word of hope focuses on *kingship,* since that has now failed in Israel. Using the imagery of shepherd (echoing David's kingship), Yahweh announces the failure of her past shepherds (vv. 1–10) and then his gathering of the scattered sheep whom "David" will once more shepherd in a future messianic age (vv. 11–31; cf. 11:16–17). Note especially the role of this passage in John 10, where Jesus announces himself as the fulfillment of this prophecy.

☐ 35:1–36:15 *Restoring Yahweh's Land*

You should not be surprised that the next focus for the future is on the *land.* This section begins with an oracle against Edom (ch. 35), who seized Judean lands after Jerusalem fell (cf. Obad 11–13). This is followed by an oracle to "the mountains of Israel" (Ezek 36:1–15; cf. 6:1–14)—that they shall produce abundantly in God's future for his people.

☐ 36:16–38 *Restoring Yahweh's Honor in Israel*

The next focus is on Yahweh's *honor.* Israel's past dishonor of his name will be reversed as the people are cleansed, and they will be given a new covenant and Yahweh's Spirit so that they can live by it (now written on their hearts; cf. Jer 31:31–33). Watch for Paul's development of this theme in 2 Corinthians 3:1–6. Finally, evidence of Yahweh's honor will be the productivity of the formerly desolate land to which he will bring them.

☐ 37:1–28 *Restoring Yahweh's People and His Covenant*

In order for all of this to happen, there must be a "resurrection" of the *people,* brought to life by Yahweh's word and Spirit (vv. 1–14), so that Israel again is *one nation* in the *land,* under their Davidic *king* and in the renewal of Yahweh's own *presence* among them (vv. 15–28).

☐ 38:1–39:29 *Restoring Yahweh's Supremacy*

Israel's restoration will be complete when Yahweh exercises his sovereignty over all her enemies, here symbolically represented by his defeat of Gog of Magog, from a distant land in the north (38:15). The point is that Yahweh will secure Israel's future restoration against all future enemies. Note how this section ends with Yahweh's victory banquet (39:17–20) and two summarizing promises of restoration (vv. 21–29) that prepare the way for the finale in chapters 40–48.

☐ 40:1–48:35 *Restoring Yahweh's Presence among His People and in the Land*

In April 573, fourteen years after the fall of Jerusalem, Ezekiel is given his final set of visions, which focus first on the restored temple and priesthood. What he sees is so grand that he includes its extraordinary measurements, thus symbolizing its grandeur and glory. All of the detail is a way of emphasizing the importance of the worship of Yahweh by the restored community of the future. And even if you do not share Ezekiel's own vested interest in the details, do not lose the central point, which Ezekiel himself makes by giving it center place in the vision — the return of Yahweh's presence among his people (43:1–9)! Also important for this great future for God's people is the redistribution of the transformed land (45:1–12), which is what the final two chapters (47–48) are all about. Note especially that the life-giving river is seen as flowing from the temple (47:1–12), the place of God's presence and of the people's worship, imagery that John picks up in his vision of the final city of God in Revelation 22:1–5. So the book ends with a new name for the city: "THE LORD IS THERE" (Ezek 48:35)!

The book of Ezekiel is a significant part of God's story as it tells of the final failure of the people of God as constituted by the first covenants, but looks forward to their being reconstituted by a new covenant that includes the true Shepherd and the gift of the Holy Spirit.

Daniel

ORIENTING DATA FOR DANIEL

- **Content:** a series of stories about how God brings honor to himself through Daniel and his three friends in Babylon, followed by four apocalyptic visions about future kingdoms and God's final kingdom

- **Prophet:** Daniel, one of the early exiles to Babylon, who was selected to serve as a provincial administrator in the Babylonian—and finally Persian—court

- **Date of composition:** unknown; presumably toward the end of the sixth century B.C. (ca. 520), although many have suggested it dates from the early second century B.C. (ca. 165)

- **Emphases:** God's sovereignty over all the nations and their rulers; God's care for the Jews in exile, with promises of final restoration; God's present overruling of and final victory over human evil

OVERVIEW OF DANIEL

The book of Daniel comes in two clear parts (chs. 1–6 and 7–12). The first half contains court stories, mostly about Daniel and three friends who remain absolutely loyal to Yahweh even while rising to positions of importance within the Babylonian Empire. The emphases are four: (1) on the four Hebrews' loyalty to God, (2) on God's miraculous deliverances of them, (3) on Gentile kings' acknowledging the greatness of Israel's God, and (4) on Daniel as the God-gifted interpreter of dreams—all of which emphasize God's sovereignty over all things, including the king who conquered and destroyed Jerusalem.

Part 2 is a series of apocalyptic visions about the rise and fall of succeeding empires, in each case involving a coming tyrannical ruler (7:8, 24–25; 8:23–25; 11:36–45)—most often understood to be Antiochus

IV (Epiphanes) of the Seleucid rulers of Palestine (175 – 164 B.C.), who because of his desolation of Jerusalem and sacrilege of the temple was to become the first in a series of antichrist figures in Jewish and Christian literature. But in each case the final focus is on God's judgment of the enemy and the glorious future kingdom awaiting his people.

SPECIFIC ADVICE FOR READING DANIEL

At the outset it is important to note that in the Hebrew Bible, Daniel is included among the Writings rather than the Prophets. In part this was due to its genre — stories about a "prophet" and apocalyptic visions, rather than prophetic oracles. Indeed, there is nothing else quite like Daniel in Jewish and Christian literature, with its combination of court stories and apocalyptic visions. Furthermore, its intent is to inspire and encourage God's people living under foreign domination, not to call them to repent in light of coming judgments. Daniel is thus never called a prophet, but one to whom God reveals mysteries.

It may be helpful, therefore, for you to review the brief description of apocalyptic in *How to 1* (pp. 251 – 52), since the dreams and visions in chapters 2 and 7 – 11 have most of the features of apocalyptic — the book was born in a time of oppression; it is a literary work altogether; it comes by means of visions and dreams that are given by angels; the images are those of fantasy symbolizing reality; and Daniel is told to seal up the visions for the last days (8:26; 9:24; 12:4).

Interestingly, chapters 1 and 8 – 12 are in Hebrew, while chapters 2 – 7 are in Aramaic, the lingua franca of the Near East from the sixth century onward through the time of Christ. Two things about this are important. First, the Aramaic portion consists of the stories, plus the first vision, suggesting that these are open reading for all, but the introduction and the interpreted visions are in Hebrew, implying perhaps that they are for God's people only. Second, the Aramaic portion is arranged in a chiastic pattern:

- Chapters 2 and 7 contain similar visions of future kingdoms, ending with God's final, eternal kingdom.
- Chapters 3 and 6 are stories of miraculous deliverance, where opposition has been directed against God.
- Chapters 4 and 5 are stories about the demise of two Babylonian kings, who both acknowledge the greatness of Israel's God.

Thus these stories tell us that God is in ultimate control of all human history (chs. 2; 7), illustrated both by the stories of miraculous deliverance (chs. 3; 6) and of the "overthrow" of the two Babylonian kings (chs. 4; 5). In each case they are marvelously narrated; to get their full benefit, you might try reading them aloud, as they were originally intended to be.

Also important for reading Daniel is to be aware of two historical contexts: (1) Daniel's own and (2) that predicted in his visions. Thus chapters 1–6 describe affairs within the Babylonian court from Nebuchadnezzar to the first of the Persian rulers of Babylon (ca. 605–530 B.C.)—from the time before the fall of Jerusalem, when the first captives from Judah were brought to Babylon, to that just beyond the demise of the Babylonian Empire in 539.

The visions (chs. 7–12) pick up at that point. Babylon was followed by the long-lived Persian Empire (539 to ca. 330). Then came the short-lived Greek Empire of Alexander (333–323), which at his death was divided among four generals (see 8:19–22). Of special interest for understanding intertestamental Jewish history is the long contest for Palestine between the Seleucids (of Antioch [the North]) and the Ptolemies (of Egypt [the South]), which is alluded to in the vision of Daniel 11 (see, e.g., the study notes in the NIV Study Bible). Crucial for Daniel is the rise of Antiochus IV, described in 11:21–32, who in fact set out to crush Jewishness in Jerusalem by forcing them to adopt his policy of Hellenizing his lands. Thus he forbade the keeping of the law and showed special favors to those who Hellenized (see 11:28). Eventually thwarted by Rome from seizing Egypt, he returned home by way of Jerusalem and poured out his fury on the Jews who resisted him, finally desecrating the Holy Place by erecting a statue of Zeus there in 167 (11:30–31). This event, which eventually led to the Maccabean revolt recorded in the Apocrypha's 1 and 2 Maccabees, is envisioned in Daniel 7–11. You can well imagine what it might have been like to read Daniel during this period—both the stories in chapters 1–6 (God honors loyalty and will humble arrogant kings!) and the visions themselves (God has foretold all this).

Finally, it is important to note that the coming of the messianic kingdom is pictured as taking place following the overthrow of Antiochus, which in fact it did a century and a half later—the only kingdom worth mentioning after Antiochus being not the Roman one, but that of Christ.

In keeping with the whole Hebrew prophetic tradition, these coming historical events were seen against the backdrop of God's great final eschatological future (see the introduction to the Prophets, p. 173).

A WALK THROUGH DANIEL

☐ **1:1–21** *Introductory Narrative: Daniel and Friends in Nebuchadnezzar's Court*

Watch for the ways this opening narrative introduces you not only to the stories that follow, but to a good reading of the whole book. Verses 1–2 give the historical setting, but also anticipate 5:1–2. Daniel and his fellows outshine all other provincials pressed into the king's service—and do so precisely because they maintain covenant loyalty with regard to the food laws (1:6–20), but note also the little insertion in v. 17, which anticipates the next story. And finally see that God is seen as directing these affairs (vv. 9, 17).

☐ **2:1–49** *Nebuchadnezzar's Dream Interpreted by Daniel*

This narrative serves three purposes: to exalt God over Nebuchadnezzar (vv. 27–28, 36–38, 44–45, 47), including God's exalting Daniel in the king's eyes (vv. 46, 48–49); to present Daniel as God's agent in interpreting dreams (vv. 14–45); and to anticipate the later visions (vv. 31–45). Note how the latter two items are highlighted in Daniel's prayer (vv. 20–23); note further that even though the dream is interpreted, there is no further interest in it at this point, merely intriguing you to read the coming visions. Note finally how verse 49 anticipates the next story, in which Daniel does not appear.

☐ **3:1–30** *Saved from Nebuchadnezzar's Fiery Furnace*

Now the "head of gold" (2:38) makes a monstrous image of gold and commands all provincials to worship it. But just as God watched over them in chapter 1, the three Hebrews are (now miraculously) delivered because of their absolute rejection of idolatry (3:16–18). Part of the power of the narrative lies in its fulsome repetitions. But its greater power lies in its point: The greatest king on earth is no match for the eternal God; not only does God deliver the three Hebrews in grand style from Nebuchadnezzar's arrogance and rage, but the king also promotes them (v. 30) and himself acknowledges the greatness of their God (vv. 28–29), which in turn anticipates the next story.

☐ **4:1–37 *Nebuchadnezzar's Madness***

This ultimate expression of God's sovereignty over earthly kings is magnificently told, highlighted in part by the fact that the whole narrative is a report from the king to the nations (v. 1). It begins with the king's acknowledgment that only God's kingdom is forever (vv. 2–3; cf. 2:44), again anticipating later visions (7:14, 18, 27), and it ends on the same note (4:34–35)—after the arrogant king is humbled by God to the role of an animal. Note that Daniel also reenters as the interpreter of dreams (vv. 8–27).

☐ **5:1–31 *Belshazzar's Feast and the Demise of Babylon***

Picture the drama as you read; also be watching, however, for the ways the story functions—to remind you that the Babylonian Empire came to an end because her king did not honor the true God (v. 23) and to relate this in a context where the king is defying God by using the sacred utensils from the Jerusalem temple (v. 2; cf. 1:2) for idolatrous purposes. Again, Daniel is the central figure, now interpreting the handwriting on the wall.

☐ **6:1–28 *Daniel in the Lions' Den***

This third attack on Jewish faith (see chs. 1; 3) again features Daniel, but now with Babylon under Persian rule. Note how much it corresponds to chapter 3: Daniel knows the decree, as well as its purpose and consequences—being thrown to immediate death—but he refuses to stop praying to his God, he is divinely delivered, and the king does homage to the "living God" (v. 26). And note how Darius echoes Nebuchadnezzar's acknowledgment of God's eternal kingship (vv. 26–27; cf. 4:34–35).

☐ **7:1–28 *The Vision of the Beasts from the Sea***

The four visions of these chapters are all dated—when Daniel is a relatively old man. This first one both echoes items from 2:36–45 and sets up those that follow. Note that in this case the interest centers on the little horn and the coming messianic kingdom. These are highlighted (1) by the way the narrative is set up (the little horn is introduced [v. 8], followed in turn by the divine court scene [vv. 9–10] and then by his ultimate demise [v. 11] and the eternal kingdom of the Most High and his "saints" [v. 18]), (2) by the lack of present interest in the other kingdoms (see ch. 8), and (3) by Daniel's singular interest in the fourth beast and the little horn (vv. 19–20). Note also that the last part of the vision itself, the little horn's oppression of the saints, has been left until verses 21–22 so that the interpretation can focus on this feature, on his ultimate defeat, and on God's everlasting kingdom (vv. 25–27).

□ 8:1–27 *The Vision of the Ram and Goat*

The second and third kingdoms of chapter 7 are now envisioned as a ram and goat and are interpreted as the Medes and Persians, followed by Greece. Pictured are Alexander the Great's victory over Persia (vv. 6–8, 21) and the subsequent fourfold division of his empire among his four generals (vv. 8b, 22), from whom eventually would come the little horn (vv. 9–13, 23–25). Note again the focus of the vision—that he attacks the saints and their worship, and that he himself will be destroyed, but not with human power.

□ 9:1–27 *The Interpretation of Jeremiah's Prophecy*

Daniel's prayer (vv. 4–19) is the theological centerpiece of the book, reflecting Israel's deserved exile for covenant unfaithfulness, but expressing hope in Yahweh's forgiveness and mercy (the only place in Daniel where the name Yahweh appears). This is enclosed by the need for a new application of Jeremiah's seventy years (vv. 1–3, in light of the devastation to be caused by the little horn). The answer (vv. 20–27) is a typical apocalyptic use of numbers, where the original number is multiplied by seven (= at the end of the devastation by the little horn), which, again typically, is portrayed against the backdrop of the final end.

□ 10:1–12:4 *The Angel's Revelation of the Future*

All of the visions have been pointing to this final one. Note the elaborate preparations for it in Daniel's encounter with the angel in 10:1–21. What follows, after an introduction (11:2–4) that picks up from the vision in 8:19–22, is a forecast of the struggle between the Seleucids and Ptolemies over "the Beautiful Land" (11:5–20; cf. Jer 3:19). But, as before, everything leads to the rise and fall of Antiochus IV (Dan 11:21–45), concentrating especially on his devastation of Jerusalem but also again predicting his end. And, as before, his demise is set against the backdrop of the end (12:1–4), which will have the resurrection of the dead and eternal reward of the righteous as its centerpiece.

□ 12:5–13 *Conclusion*

Note that Daniel's concluding questions "How long will it be before these astonishing things are fulfilled?" and "What will the outcome of all this be?" are again given with cryptic number schemes, while Daniel himself will rest until the resurrection.

The book of Daniel, though focusing primarily on one period in Israel's history, looks forward to the great eternal reign of God inaugurated by Jesus Christ; as such it had great influence on the imagery of John's Revelation.

Hosea

ORIENTING DATA FOR HOSEA

- **Content:** Yahweh's compassion for the northern kingdom (Israel), yet his condemnation of them for their unfaithfulness to him
- **Prophet:** Hosea, a northern prophet, probably from Samaria
- **Date of prophetic activity:** ca. 758–722 B.C.
- **Emphasis:** Yahweh's unfailing love for his people, even when he must punish them for unfaithfulness

OVERVIEW OF HOSEA

The structure of this first — and longest — of the Book of the Twelve is less easy to discern than that of most of the prophetic books, due in part to the general lack of introductory or concluding formulas (e.g., "thus says the LORD [Yahweh]"). Two major divisions are clear (chs. 1–3 and 4–14). Part 1 seems intentionally introductory, and its own alternating pattern of judgment (1:2–9; 2:2–13; 3:4) followed by future restoration (1:10–2:1; 2:14–23; 3:5) may serve as a pattern for part 2 as well. The judgments are predicated on Israel's "adultery" (= idolatry, 2:8, 13, 17), and the restoration on Yahweh's unfailing love for his people (2:1, 14, 23; 3:1). Indeed, the tension in the book, as in Micah later, is between Yahweh's love for his people and his justice in carrying out the curses for covenantal unfaithfulness.

So images from Hosea's marriage both mirror Yahweh's long relationship with Israel (marriage, unfaithfulness, "divorce," restoration) and serve as a pattern for the book in its present form. A first cycle of oracles (4:1–10:15) tells the sordid story of Israel's unfaithfulness, both religiously and politically, along with Yahweh's (necessary) coming judgments; while 11:1–11 promises future restoration based on Yahweh's love and compassion. The story of unfaithfulness and judgment is repeated with even greater intensity in a second cycle (11:12–13:16), while 14:1–8 concludes the book with Yahweh's final love song for his people.

SPECIFIC ADVICE FOR READING HOSEA

Along with the close relationship between Hosea's own symbolic marriage actions and Yahweh's relationship with Israel/Ephraim, three other matters are crucial for a discerning reading of Hosea.

First, the *historical context* (see 2 Kgs 14:23–18:16) is influenced in large part by the downs and ups of Assyria. According to 1:1, Hosea began his prophetic calling toward the end of the relatively tranquil and prosperous days of Jeroboam II (see "Specific Advice for Reading Amos," pp. 223–24), but the list of Judean kings, as well as Hosea's own oracles, suggest that most of them were delivered during the years of rapid decline following the death of Jeroboam II (753). Six kings ruled in Samaria in rapid succession—through intrigue, caprice, and assassination (see 8:4)—until the northern kingdom was overthrown by Assyria in 722/1. Part of the intrigue was related to a king's willingness or unwillingness to pay tribute to Assyria, which in turn was related to looking elsewhere (7:8–11) for alliances to protect them against Assyria. In the end, Yahweh will use Assyria as his rod of punishment (10:6–7).

Second, and more important still, is the *religious/theological context*. Although Hosea regularly throws side-glances to Judah (see below), his passion and pathos are for Israel. Picking up where the reforming prophets Elijah and Elisha had left off a century earlier, he is both astounded and incensed at Israel's propensity to abandon Yahweh in favor of Baal—or to mix the two in syncretistic fashion (2:11, 13; see "Specific Advice for Reading Deuteronomy," pp. 57–58). Just as marriage is simultaneously both absolutely exclusive and deeply personal, so is Yahweh's covenant with Israel. Thus Hosea repeatedly reminds his hearers/readers of their beginnings (2:15; 9:10; 11:1–4; 13:4), while he also recalls Israel's history of unfaithfulness (9:10, 15; 10:9). The people's present unfaithfulness, reflected primarily in their idolatry, also finds expression in breaking most of the Ten Commandments, as the preamble in 4:1–3 spells out so forcibly.

At stake in all of this is Yahweh's own character. In turning to Canaanite fertility gods (the Baals and Asherahs), Israel has attributed fruitfulness of both crops and people to them (2:5, 12) and thus has abandoned

Yahweh, the Creator of all, who alone provides the crops and opens the womb (2:8, 18, 21–22; 9:11, 14). At the same time the Israelites have become like the gods they worship — full of lies, deceit, and caprice. Thus the bottom line for Hosea — and the reason for the coming judgment — is that although it should be otherwise, the people simply do not *know* Yahweh (4:1, 6, 14; 8:2–3); they have come to think of Yahweh, not in terms of their own story of redemption, but in terms of Canaanite religion — and the result is deadly.

Third, if at times you find Hosea a difficult read, that, at least in part, may be because he so clearly wears his heart on his sleeve. Here is *passion and pathos* let loose on Israel in oracle after oracle, irony upon irony — and such passion is not always easy to track in terms of where things are going (indeed, hardly any two commentaries agree on the details). At the same time, the oracles themselves do not always fit the ordinary formal patterns, since announcements of judgment and the reasons for it are not neatly packaged, and in many instances they simply blend in the same sentences. Furthermore, his Hebrew text has suffered much in transmission, so there are moments that are very difficult to figure out (observe the many footnotes in the NIV).

But at the same time this very passion is what makes Hosea such a great read. Striking metaphors are his specialty. Watch how Yahweh is lion, leopard, bear, eagle (vulture), trapper (5:14; 11:10; 13:7–8; 8:1; 7:12), as well as husband, lover, parent, green pine tree (2:14–23; 14:3–7; 11:8–9; 14:8). And Israel in her sins is even more vividly described: adulterous wife, stubborn heifer, snare and net, heated oven, half-baked bread, senseless dove, faulty bow, headless stalk, a baby refusing birth (2:2; 4:16; 5:1; 7:4, 8, 11, 16; 8:7; 13:13); she will disappear like mist, dew, chaff, and smoke (13:3); she will float away like a twig on water (10:7); she has sown the wind and will reap the whirlwind (8:7). It is hard not to get the picture. So enjoy, even as you weep with Yahweh and his prophet.

A final word about the book itself, as a book to be read. Although the prophecies are primarily directed toward the northern kingdom (Israel), it is very likely that the book itself was preserved in Judah. Evidence for this is in the heading, which takes the ministry of Hosea down to the reign of Hezekiah in Judah (715, six years after the fall of Samaria). This suggests that, even though Hosea seems to pay only passing attention to Judah in his oracles (see 1:7, 11; 4:15; 5:5, 10, 12–14;

6:4, 11; 8:14; 10:11; 11:12; 12:2), he will not expect his later Judean readers to do the same regarding Judah—nor should we who now read it from the hindsight of the fall of both kingdoms!

A WALK THROUGH HOSEA

☐ **1:1   Heading**

Note that Hosea's book is "the word of the LORD" that came to Hosea over the time span of several Judean kings.

☐ **1:2–2:1   Hosea, Gomer, and Children**

Here Hosea acts symbolically in marrying an "adulterous wife" (lit., "woman of prostitution," perhaps a metaphor for Gomer's disloyalty to Yahweh). His children are given names that speak of God's judgments against his own "faithless wife" (Israel), names they bear to symbolize the stigma of God's judgment and eventual rejection of Israel. But note also that the word of hope (1:10–2:1) reverses the meaning of their names! Note further the different destinies of Israel and Judah in 1:6–7, but their being reunited in God's promised future (v. 11).

☐ **2:2–23   Israel Punished and Restored**

In a poetic oracle, the children of the adulteress are now called on to rebuke their mother (Israel), urging her to give up her idolatry or else Yahweh will show no love for her children (vv. 2–6). Israel feigns return to Yahweh (vv. 7–8), but will pay for her wantonness (vv. 9–13); observe how thoroughgoing her idolatry is. In the word of restoration (vv. 14–23), watch for the various reversals, including promised restoration to the land.

☐ **3:1–5   Judgment and Restoration**

Note how this narrative, symbolizing the coming exile, corresponds to 2:14–23—just as 2:2–13 corresponds to 1:2–8; thus the two narratives (chs. 1 and 3) bookend the oracle in chapter 2. As you read the rest of the book, be looking for the ways the themes of these chapters are picked up.

☐ **4:1–5:7   Yahweh's Charge against Israel for Unfaithfulness**

Much of this material takes the form of a lawsuit against Israel. It begins with an opening charge (4:1–3), where all the major themes of the book are laid out: no faithfulness to the covenant, no knowledge of Yahweh (NIV "acknowledgment"), the land mourns. Then picking up themes from chapters 1–3, charges are leveled against priest, prophet, and people (especially lack of knowledge [4:6–7, 14] that takes the form of idolatry [vv. 10–14, 15, 17–19]). Since they have now gone too far (5:1–4), they will be judged (vv. 5–7). Note that Judah is always in view as well (4:15; 5:5).

□ 5:8–7:16 *Israel's Unfaithfulness through Entangling Alliances*

Yahweh now calls for the watchman (possibly Hosea himself, see 8:1) to sound the trumpet of warning (5:8). Judgment is sure (vv. 9–12, 14–15), and dallying with Assyria is no cure (v. 13), nor is false repentance (6:1–3), since it is like "morning mist" (vv. 4–10); even when Yahweh would restore them (v. 11), their sins continue to be exposed (7:1–7), especially as they continue to trust in other nations for help rather than Yahweh (vv. 8–16). And again watch for the references to Judah (5:10, 12, 13, 14; 6:4, 11).

□ 8:1–9:9 *Once More: Judgment Because of Unfaithfulness*

Another call for the trumpet (8:1) announces again Yahweh's certain judgments, this time in the form of overthrow by the very nations she sold herself to (8:3b, 8–10, 14). Note again the charge of breaking covenant (8:1–3), but added now is the internal decay in the monarchy (8:4), while idolatry continues to be the main issue (8:4–7). The cycle then concludes with yet another announcement of coming judgment and the reasons for it (9:1–9).

□ 9:10–10:15 *Israel Condemned for Not Living Up to Her Calling*

In 9:9 Yahweh reminded them of Gibeah (Judg 19–20); now he picks up a series of such reminders of past covenant disloyalty, which serve as examples for present judgments (Hos 9:10–14, Baal Peor [Num 25:1–9]; Hos 9:15–17, Gilgal [1 Sam 13; 15]; Hos 10:9–10, Gibeah again). Note the role of various kings in the oracles in Hosea 10 (vv. 3, 6–7, 15): Because Israel has rejected Yahweh as King, Israel's own king will be destroyed and her idols taken to the king of Assyria. And note also the invitation in 10:12, which anticipates the word of anguish and compassion that comes next.

☐ **11:1–11** *God's Undying Love for Israel*

In many ways this is the heart of Hosea's message. Yahweh's love for his "son," Israel (vv. 1, 3–4; see Exod 4:22); Israel's unfaithfulness (Hos 11:2, 7); Yahweh's judgment (vv. 5–6); and his promise of restoration (vv. 8–11)—all because he alone is the Holy One, totally other than his human creatures (v. 9). This paves the way for the coming of Jesus Christ.

☐ **11:12–13:16** *One More Time: Israel's Sins and Coming Judgment*

Note how the first of these oracles (11:12–12:14) picks up many of the themes from before—both Israel's (and Judah's) sins (lies, deceit, idolatry [bulls in Gilgal, v. 11]) and God's judgments (12:2, 14) and appeal (v. 6); here alone (vv. 7–8) Hosea explicitly reflects the social injustice found in Amos, Isaiah, and Micah. Observe also, however, that most of the oracle picks up (from 11:1–4) the reminders of their history, especially the roles of Jacob (the good and the bad!) and Moses (12:13).

The second oracle (13:1–16) again repeats the motif of the people's unfaithfulness to Yahweh, especially their ingratitude in turning to idolatry (vv. 1–2, 6, 9–12, 16) after Yahweh has done so much for them (vv. 4–6); therefore, they will come under judgment (vv. 3, 7–8, 15–16). Even so, the word of hope persists (v. 14).

☐ **14:1–9** *Invitation and Restoration*

Note how the book concludes with one more invitation to repent (vv. 1–3) and the promise of restoration and a glorious future (vv. 4–8); could Hosea have done it otherwise? So the book signs off with a word in Wisdom style, calling for discernment (v. 9)—a word that has similarities to Psalm 1.

The book of Hosea, which burns with the fire of God's love for his people, reminds us that the God of the biblical story judges unfaithfulness, even as he lays out hope beyond judgment.

Joel

ORIENTING DATA FOR JOEL

- **Content:** a devastating locust plague sets the stage for a two-fold summons to repentance, to which God responds with a promise of mercy and an outpouring of his Spirit, with a day of judgment on the nations

- **Prophet:** Joel, who is otherwise unknown; his concern for Judah and Jerusalem (2:23, 32; 3:1) suggests that he was from the southern kingdom

- **Date of prophetic activity:** uncertain; perhaps ca. 590 B.C., but possibly after 500 B.C.

- **Emphases:** the impending day of Yahweh—a day of judgment and salvation; Yahweh chastens those he loves, and his chastening calls his people to repentance; Israel's God keeps covenant by showing mercy to his people; Yahweh is sovereign over all the nations and will judge those who have shown no mercy to his people

OVERVIEW OF JOEL

Joel centers much of his message in the concept of "the day of the LORD." Four scenes depict this decisive day, each scene having two parts. Chapter 1 describes the immediate disaster—a devastating locust plague (1:2–12)—which leads to a call for national repentance and prayer because of the severity of the plague (vv. 13–20).

In the second scene (2:1–17), all of this is repeated, but now the plague is likened to—or perhaps implicitly identified as—an army with Yahweh at their head, accompanied by cosmic signs (vv. 10–11), and the summons to repentance is based on Yahweh's character (vv. 12–17). This extended metaphor takes the picture in scene 1 a dimension further and probably refers to God's impending future judgments on Israel and the nations. It may be in fact that "locusts" serves as a kind of code word for the Babylonian armies that invaded Judah in 598 B.C.

The third scene (2:18–32) offers God's response—first to the immediate issue of the locust plague, by restoring "the years the locusts have eaten" (v. 25) through the return of agricultural bounty (vv. 18–27); and second with a special promise of the new age of the Spirit, thus pointing to a glorious future for God's people (vv. 28–32).

The final scene (ch. 3) depicts God's second response by bringing judgment against the nations (vv. 1–16) in the form of a great battle (in the Valley of Jehoshaphat, whose name means "Yahweh judges/has judged"). This scene ends with a picture of God's extraordinary blessings on his forgiven, purified people (vv. 17–21).

SPECIFIC ADVICE FOR READING JOEL

Joel offers us neither date nor specific, identifiable historical markers. This makes the reading of Joel a bit more difficult than in other cases, since understanding a prophet's times is so helpful in understanding his message (see the introduction to the Prophets, pp. 172–73). The "northern army" (2:20, lit., "the northerner") probably refers to the locusts in its first instance, but then metaphorically to the well-known dread of invading armies from the north (Jer 4:6 [referring to Babylon]; cf. Ezek 38:15; 39:2), but nothing more is made of it. Even more striking is the fact that, in a book where calls to repentance hold such a central place (Joel 1:13–14; 2:13–17), there is scarcely a mention of the sins that are responsible for the immediate or coming disasters. To be sure, the nations will be judged for their dividing up Yahweh's land and dealing treacherously with his people (3:2–3, 6), but the sins of Judah and Jerusalem seem primarily to be sins of complacency, and the summons takes the form of a wake-up call to the "drinkers of wine" (1:2, 5). The prophet seems to assume that the people know well where they have broken covenant with their God, but we later readers can only guess.

At the heart of Joel's message is "the day of the LORD," a concept that had been used by the prophets for some time before Joel came on the scene (see Amos 5:18–20; Isa 2:12–18; 3:7, 18; 11:10–11; Jer 30:7–8; Zeph 1:7–2:2). Its earliest mention in Amos indicates that Israel had a sanguine view of this day—that it was a day in their future when God would come to their aid because they were his. But Amos turned that understanding on its head, because Israel's covenant disloyalty has placed them at enmity with Yahweh, and Amos is followed in this by all the other prophets, including especially Zephaniah. Isaiah and Jeremiah further explain it as cutting both ways—a day of judgment on those whose sins deserve such, but followed by a day of salvation for God's gathered remnant. As you read Joel, you will see that he fits into this pattern of describing it. For him, the locust plague has set God's day in motion as judgment on Judah and Jerusalem, but its consummation clearly lies in a great future eschatological event of judgment on the nations and ultimately the restoration of God's people.

You should also note as you read that, even though Joel does not mention it as such, he presupposes Yahweh's covenant relationship with his people at every turn. Locusts and drought are part of the curses for disobedience to the covenant (Deut 28:22, 38–42), as is Israel's being scattered among the nations (Joel 3:2; see Deut 28:64); the call for repentance as the pathway to future restoration is deeply covenantal, as is the idea of God's chastening the people he loves (Deut 30:1–10; cf. Joel's "rend your heart and not your garments" [2:13] with Deut 30:2, 6). Note also that the appeal to God's character in Joel 2:13 is a replay of the language of Exod 34:6, a covenant-renewal moment; God's engagement in the holy war (Joel 2:10–11; 3:9–11) is also part of this motif.

A WALK THROUGH JOEL

☐ 1:1   *Heading*

In contrast to Hosea, Joel's heading is succinct, providing no knowledge of who he is or when he lived.

☐ 1:2–12   *Scene 1A: The Locust Plague*

Note how Joel's words "Hear this" (v. 2) are the beginning of his wake-up call (v. 5) for lamentation and repentance to a nation paying no more attention to her ways than drunkards would (v. 5). It is often pointed out that the description of the plague in verses 6–12 is painfully precise. Watch how the promised blessings in 2:18–27 respond directly to this scene.

☐ 1:13–20   *Scene 1B: A Summons to Repentance*

Not only would such a plague wipe out a people economically for years, but the sacrificial system comes to a grinding halt when there is nothing left to sacrifice; hence the focus on the first call to repentance is on the priests (vv. 13–14). The rest of the summons repeats the cause for mourning (vv. 15–18), followed by Joel's own prayer in the same vein (vv. 19–20).

☐ 2:1–11　Scene 2A: God's Invading Army

Note how this second description of the plague pictures the locusts as something now in the future; it will come against God's people as a vast army led by God himself (the holy war turns against Israel!). There is perhaps a bit of irony here, as Israel expects God to come in their behalf accompanied by winged cherubim (Ps 18:10; Ezek 10:1–20), but instead he comes with winged creatures of destruction.

☐ 2:12–17　Scene 2B: The Summons to Repentance

The second summons to repentance is one of the more memorable moments in the Old Testament. Note especially the echoes of Deuteronomy 30:1–6—that fasting and sackcloth and ashes mean nothing if there is no rending of heart. Here also (Joel 2:13) you find the covenant basis for such repentance: God is gracious and compassionate.

☐ 2:18–27　Scene 3A: God's Response—the Promise of Plenty

Note how much this scene corresponds to the plague as described in 1:2–12 and responds to the assumed repentance in 2:12–17. The "locust" army is pushed into the two seas (v. 20), and abundance is restored. But the ultimate goal is the praise of Yahweh and the removal of the people's shame (vv. 26–27).

☐ 2:28–32　Scene 3B: God's Response—the Promise of the Spirit

A part of the future restoration will be the fulfillment of Moses' yearning that all of God's people will be prophets (Num 11:29). Note how the list of those who will prophesy covers the whole gamut of the social order, including daughters and the lowest on the social ladder—female servants. Note also that this belongs to the eschatological future, accompanied by cosmic signs before the final expression of God's "day," when salvation is for all who call on Yahweh's name.

☐ 3:1–16a　Scene 4A: God's Response—Final Judgment of the Nations

As scene 3A corresponds to 1A, so this scene (4A) corresponds to 2A. Here you find a more typical "woe oracle" (see *How to 1*, p. 195) in which both the nature of God's judgment and the reasons for it are spelled out. Note especially how this fulfills the pledge of the holy war that God will drive out all their enemies.

☐ 3:16b–21 *Scene 4B: God's Response — Future Blessing of God's People*

As with 2:28–32, this final picture is overlaid with images of eschatological abundance: the lavish renewal of the land (v. 18a); a fountain flowing out of Jerusalem (v. 18b; cf. Ezek 47:1–12; Rev 22:1–5); Israel's traditional enemies finished forever (v. 19); an eternal habitation of Judah and Jerusalem (v. 20); and total removal of sin (v. 21). The ultimate basis for this is the return of God's presence to Zion (vv. 17, 21).

Besides prophesying of the great outpouring of God's Spirit, the book of Joel is especially concerned with the great themes of the biblical story: God's judgment on human sin, the need for repentance, and the merciful grace of God, so that all who call on his name will be saved.

Amos

ORIENTING DATA FOR AMOS

- **Content:** in a period of rare economic prosperity and political strength for Israel, Yahweh announces their doom because she has failed to keep covenant with him

- **Prophet:** Amos, a shepherd/farmer from Tekoa, south of Bethlehem in Judah

- **Date of prophetic activity:** ca. 760 B.C., for an apparently brief period (at the peak of the reigns of Jeroboam II in Samaria [793–753] and Uzziah in Jerusalem [792–740])

- **Emphases:** Yahweh is God over all the nations and the whole universe; Yahweh will bring utter ruin to Israel for her covenant disloyalty; syncretistic religion is anathema to Yahweh; Yahweh requires justice for the innocent and mercy for the poor; religious observances are no substitute for doing good and showing mercy

OVERVIEW OF AMOS

This third in the Book of the Twelve is the earliest of the prophetic books. Its basic message is that Yahweh has utterly rejected Israel's present religious and socioeconomic practices, so much so that he is going to bring the northern kingdom to an end and send the people into exile (5:5, 27; 6:7; 7:11, 17). At issue is covenant infidelity in the form of religious syncretism (see "Specific Advice for Reading Deuteronomy," pp. 57–58) and social injustice, carried on especially by the leaders and their indolent wives (4:1; 6:1–6). Indeed, they were glutted on religion, but didn't have a clue about Yahweh and his character (4:5; 5:21–23). So the Lion roars from Zion (1:2), and Amos gives him voice (3:8).

The oracles themselves were probably delivered at the sanctuary—the king's sanctuary—in Bethel (3:14; 7:10–17; cf. 1 Kgs 12:32) and within a brief period of time (Amos 1:1). They come to us carefully arranged.

The first series (1:3–2:16) proceeds from judgment on the surrounding nations for various forms of treachery (1:3–2:3), to Judah for infidelity (2:4–5), to an opening summary judgment against Israel (2:6–16). Then comes a series of three announcement oracles (3:1–5:17; cf. "Hear this word," 3:1; 4:1; 5:1) that spell out both Yahweh's coming judgment and the reasons for it. Next are two woe oracles, which reflect Israel's complacency, based on false security—religion (5:18–27) and material prosperity (6:1–14). Finally, Amos reports five visions, the first two (7:1–6) indicating that the coming judgment will not be like former ones but will involve total destruction, including the king and his sanctuary (7:7–9). This leads to an encounter with the king's priest at Bethel (7:10–17), followed by the final two visions of utter destruction (8:1–9:10).

In all of this there is scarcely a word of comfort and only a few words suggesting that Yahweh might relent (5:5–6, 14–15). But the book itself concludes with an oracle of salvation (9:11–15) that looks beyond the fall of Israel to the fall of Judah as well, promising that "David's fallen tent" (Jerusalem) will be restored in a future age of abundance.

SPECIFIC ADVICE FOR READING AMOS

Amos is the first of our four canonical eighth-century prophets (a contemporary of Hosea, and a bit older than Isaiah and Micah). The historical-political background to Amos can be found in 2 Kings 14:23–15:7 (cf. 2 Chr 26). Jeroboam II (in Israel) and Uzziah (in Judah) came to reign at about the same time, and both had long and prosperous reigns, which included territorial expansion of a kind that together nearly equaled that of David and Solomon. This was made possible mostly because their reigns coincided with a very low period in Assyrian fortunes (782–745), until the rise of Tiglath-Pileser III. And, of course, the royal house and the wealthy considered this period of growth and expansion as evidence of Yahweh's blessing, with a still brighter day of Yahweh awaiting them (Amos 5:18). But instead it turned out to be a brief halcyon period that lasted barely one generation. Thus, even though not mentioned by name in Amos, Assyria is still the ominous power on the political landscape, whose shadow lurks behind several passages (2:13–16; 3:11; 5:3, 27; 6:7, 8–14; 7:9, 17; 9:4). And within less than a generation after the death of Jeroboam the kingdom of Israel ceased to exist altogether (722/1), and Yahweh's voice was no longer heard there (8:11–12)—God having used Assyria as his rod of judgment against his wayward people (see 2 Kgs 17:7–41).

What Amos saw and spoke most clearly at the peak of this period (Amos 1:1) was that everything was in fact the opposite of what it seemed. Their "blessing" had nothing to do with Yahweh, but everything to do with their own corrupt practices; nor did their religion have much to do with Yahweh, even though it was undoubtedly still being carried on in his name. Thus only two broad categories of sin need be denounced: syncretistic religion (2:7–8; 4:4–5; 5:21–23, 25–26; 8:10, 14) and social injustice (2:6–8; 3:9–10; 4:1; 5:7, 10–13, 15, 24; 6:12; 8:4–6), which are clearly spelled out in the opening oracle, where they blend (2:6–8), as they do again in 5:21–24 and 8:4–6. It is this combination of oppression of the poor in a context of distorted religious enthusiasm that leads to Yahweh's judgment in the form of exile.

Crucial to this judgment is Amos's own loyalty to Yahweh and his covenant. At the heart of the covenant, as Jesus himself pointed out, is love for God and love for neighbor (Mark 12:30–31). Thus the Old Testament covenant, along with regulations for proper worship as a way of maintaining love for God, was full of laws that provided a form of equity for all, based primarily on land distribution (and thus creating a mostly rural rather than urban society). And those who were without land (widows, orphans, Levites, foreigners) were to be properly cared for by the others. The reason for this, as the Israelites were constantly reminded in the law (see e.g., Exod 22:21–27; Deut 16:18–20; 24:17–22), was that Yahweh himself had compassion for the poor (including a slave people called Israel, whom he had rescued and made his own).

But during this halcyon period enormous changes had taken place in both Judah and Israel, especially in the latter. An urban mentality developed, with luxurious dwellings and ornate appointments (3:12, 15; 5:11; 6:4–6), which was helped along by a collusion among royalty, priests, prophets, and judges, which became a wealthy aristocracy at the expense of the poor. Yahweh had had enough, so he chose a man of the land from the south, a Yahwist with powerful abilities of speech, to speak his word of judgment on the whole scene. Thus Amos renewed Moses' kind of prophetism among God's people — addressed to leaders and people alike, not just to individuals — announcing that the ultimate curse for not maintaining covenant loyalty, namely, desolation of the land and exile (Lev 26:27–45; Deut 28:25–68), was about to be carried out. And he became the forerunner of many others who were to come, most of whom brought the same message to the southern kingdom.

A WALK THROUGH AMOS

☐ **1:1-2** *Heading*

Note several important features of this heading: (1) Amos is a man of the land from Judah (Tekoa), who carefully dates his "words"; (2) note also that verse 2 is Amos's own words about Yahweh's speech through him, imagery that will be picked up again in 3:8; and (3) don't miss the geography: Yahweh roars in Zion; Carmel withers (NNW of Jerusalem on the Mediterranean, a straight line that would cross Bethel and Samaria!).

☐ **1:3-2:16** *Judgment on the Nations—and Israel*

Watch for three things that give this series its rhetorical power: (1) The patterns repeat ("for three sins ..., even for four"); (2) they are directed against Israel's closest neighbors (beginning with a chiastic NE/SW–NW/SE pattern before going due east and south); (3) all of the sins are forms of treachery until you come to Judah (2:4–5), who has also broken covenant with Yahweh. You can imagine his Israelite hearers cheering Yahweh on—until the shoe drops, on Israel itself (2:6–16). Though patterned after the rest, this final oracle is considerably elaborated, since the main points of Amos's message lie here: first the reasons for judgment (vv. 6–8), then a brief replay of the Israelites' spurning of covenant history (vv. 9–12), concluding with the pronouncement of coming doom (vv. 13–16).

☐ **3:1-15** *First Announcement Oracle: Failure to Keep Covenant*

Watch for the various ways this first "Hear Yahweh's word" oracle sets up the rest of the book. It begins with Israel's covenantal privilege (vv. 1–2), followed by Amos's justification for prophesying (vv. 3–8)—to a people who have commanded him not to (2:12; 7:12–13). Then the Philistines and Egyptians are called on to witness Israel's coming destruction (3:9–10), followed by three announcements of doom (vv. 11, 12, 13–15).

☐ **4:1-13** *Second Announcement Oracle: Rejection of Divine Warnings*

This second "Hear" oracle announces judgment on the indolent wives of the wealthy (vv. 1–3), concluding with an ironic invitation to increase their beloved religious practices (vv. 4–5). This is followed by a series of reminders of past judgments Israel has failed to heed (vv. 6–11), with a call to prepare to "meet your God" in judgment (v. 12); it concludes with a fragment of a hymn (v. 13; cf. 5:8–9; 9:5–6) that describes their God as Creator and Revealer (cf., e.g., Ps 104:2–5).

☐ 5:1–17   *Third Announcement Oracle: False Religion and Injustice*

This third "Hear" oracle in many ways forms the heart of the book. Note its striking chiastic structure. It begins and ends with a lament over Israel's fall (vv. 2–3, 16–17), followed by an invitation to "seek [Yahweh] and live" (vv. 4–6, 14–15), while the inner circle spells out the recipients of this mixture of doom and invitation, namely, those who pervert justice (vv. 7, 10–12). The centerpiece is one more fragment of the hymn, reminding the people that the Creator is also the Judge (vv. 8–9).

☐ 5:18–27   *False Security in Religion*

This first "woe" oracle speaks directly to Israel's false security in multiplied religious exercises (more religion = more favor with God), but the day of the Lord they are looking for will in fact turn out to be a nightmare (vv. 18–20). Indeed, Yahweh hates Israel's religious practices (vv. 21–23), because the people themselves are full of injustice (v. 24). Note especially how the conclusion (vv. 25–26) makes clear the syncretistic nature of their present worship, ending with a final announcement of doom (v. 27).

☐ 6:1–14   *False Security in Material Goods and Military Success*

This second woe is directed at Israel's leaders (v. 1), who will be among the first to go into exile (v. 7). Their security lies in their great wealth and luxury (vv. 3–6 [v. 2 is much debated]) and in some minor military conquests (vv. 12–13; note esp. the pun on the name "Lo Debar" [= "nothing"]); note how both false securities are concluded with announcements of judgment (vv. 8–11, 14).

☐ 7:1–9   *Three Vision Reports: Locusts, Fire, Plumb Line*

With these three visions the final series of judgments begins its move toward Yahweh's determined end. Note how the first two indicate that what is to come will not be like former plagues (locusts/drought; cf. 4:6–9); Israel's future will be full of (lit.) "groaning" (NIV, "plumb line") because their destruction is now inevitable. Note especially that the king is finally specifically named in 7:9, which is what raises the ire of the king's priest, Amaziah.

☐ 7:10–17 *The Encounter with Amaziah*

This little report is full of interest. In turn you learn that (1) Amos is at Bethel, and Amaziah, the king's priest, reports him to the king (vv. 10–11); (2) when Amos is forbidden to prophesy (vv. 12–13), he indicates he is not a prophet by choice, nor does he belong to the prophetic guild (vv. 14–15); and (3) he then uses this encounter to pronounce Yahweh's judgment against Amaziah and his household (vv. 16–17). Thus both the king and the priest are singled out for individual pronouncements of doom.

☐ 8:1–9:10 *Two Vision Reports: The Certainty of Israel's Coming Destruction*

These two visions spell out the final doom of Israel. The first (overripe fruit, 8:1–14) especially recapitulates the issues of the Israelites' false religion mingled with injustice (vv. 4–6), in which their temple songs are turned into wailing (v. 3) and their treatment of the poor turned into the ultimate "famine"—the total loss of Yahweh's word in Israel.

The second (9:1–10) is climactic: Yahweh stands by the altar at Bethel, which crumbles on the heads of the people (vv. 1–4; note the reversal in v. 4 of their failing to seek good and hate evil [5:14–15]); after one more hymnic insertion (9:5–6), it concludes with the announcement of Israel's total annihilation (vv. 8–10). Israel is no better than her pagan neighbors (v. 7).

☐ 9:11–15 *Hope for the Future*

After all that has gone before, this word of hope is welcome relief. It comes in two parts, (1) the promised restoration of Jerusalem (vv. 11–12) and (2) the coming of the great messianic age (vv. 13–15), which have found their beginning fulfillment in Jesus Christ.

The book of Amos declares an important dimension of the biblical story in bold relief: True religion and social justice must go hand in hand, or one is breaking covenant with God.

Obadiah

ORIENTING DATA FOR OBADIAH

- **Content:** a doom oracle against Edom for taking advantage of (probably) the Babylonian conquest of Jerusalem in 588–86 B.C.

- **Prophet:** Obadiah, a prophet from Judah

- **Date of prophetic activity:** probably just after the fall of Jerusalem (586 B.C.?)

- **Emphases:** God's judgment on Edom for her sins against God's people; the defeat of those who think themselves unconquerable; Israel's deliverance and restoration on the day of the Lord

OVERVIEW OF OBADIAH

This fourth of the Book of the Twelve, which is also the shortest book in the Old Testament, is a single, unified prophecy against Edom that was probably spoken to various groups of Judeans to encourage them in the aftermath of their national tragedy. All the parts of a doom oracle are present: the announcement of doom—a prediction of Edom's coming defeat (vv. 1–9); the reasons for doom—a review of Edom's crimes against his "brother" while Judah was helpless (vv. 10–14); and the promised future (for Jacob, not Esau!)—on the day of the Lord Israel's sovereignty will be restored (vv. 15–21).

SPECIFIC ADVICE FOR READING OBADIAH

Edom was Israel's most tenacious foe throughout the history of the two "brother" nations (v. 10; cf. Gen 25:24–34), so it should come as no surprise that Edom is the subject of more foreign-nation oracles than any other people (Isa 21:11–12; 34:5–15; Jer 49:7–22; Ezek 25:12–14; 35:1–15; Amos 1:11–12; cf. Joel 3:19; Mal 1:2–5).

The principles for reading any foreign-nation oracle apply here. Yahweh is God not only of Israel but also of all the nations of the world; it reflects the "curse" side of the Abrahamic covenant ("I will curse those who curse you"); it is the prophet's engagement in the holy war, as a messenger of the Divine Warrior. If Israel's sins are great and deserve punishment, the treachery of Edom will also be punished, since it stands so completely over against God's own character of generosity and kindness. Moreover, if God is to deliver his people completely and permanently, he cannot leave their enemies free to strike again. Here again you find the typical final eschatological backdrop against which temporal judgments are to be understood (see *How to 1*, p. 201).

You may want to read Psalm 137 alongside this oracle to capture the sense of how deeply Israel felt about Edom's treachery. You may also want to read Obadiah 1–6 alongside Jeremiah 49:14–16 (for vv. 1–4) and 49:9–10 (for vv. 5–6); very likely Obadiah is restating and recasting Jeremiah's oracle as his starting point, an oracle that is probably well known to his hearers.

A WALK THROUGH OBADIAH

□ **Verse 1**   *Title and Introduction*

Before Yahweh actually speaks (vv. 2–21), Obadiah presents himself as a messenger from the heavenly court who announces God's judgment on Edom in terms of the holy war.

□ **Verse 2–9**   *Edom's Doom Announced*

At God's command, Edom will be conquered by a coalition of other nations (v. 1), and this in spite of its rocky, mountainous terrain in which it had rested secure for centuries (vv. 2–4); their plunder will far exceed the usual level (vv. 5–6). Note that, treachery for treachery, even Edom's old allies will turn against them and lead to their downfall (v. 7). Finally (vv. 8–9), Yahweh declares the ineffectiveness of two groups in which it took great pride—its famed wise men (Job and his counselors were from a part of Edom) and its warriors.

□ **Verse 10–14**   *The Reasons for Edom's Doom*

The crime is treachery. When the Babylonians invaded Judah (2 Kgs 25), Edom quickly made a separate peace and then took advantage of Judah instead of helping its brother nation (Obad 11–12), seizing Judean towns and farmlands (v. 13) and capturing Judeans fleeing from the Babylonians (v. 14; handing them over probably to be sold as slaves).

☐ Verse 15–21 *The Coming Day of the Lord*

You will note that Edom's judgment is part of the coming day of Yahweh in which all nations will experience his wrath (v. 15). The judgment takes the form of the *lex talionis* ("eye for an eye"), when Esau's and Jacob's fortunes are reversed (vv. 15b–18), as the returning exiles repossess the promised land (vv. 19–21; cf. Deut 30:1–10).

Obadiah reminds us of God's justice in punishing human sinfulness and of God's ultimate victory over earthly powers.

Jonah

ORIENTING DATA FOR JONAH

- **Content:** through a very reluctant prophet, God shows compassion for one of Israel's hated enemies
- **Prophet:** Jonah son of Amittai, who prophesied during the reign of Jeroboam II (see 2 Kgs 14:25)
- **Emphases:** Yahweh as Creator, Sustainer, and Redeemer of all; Yahweh's compassionate concern for the Gentiles (represented by Nineveh); Israel's reluctance (represented by Jonah) to acknowledge Yahweh's compassion for the nations

OVERVIEW OF JONAH

The book of Jonah is unique among the Latter Prophets. Rather than a collection of prophetic oracles, it is instead a narrative about God's compassion for some hated Gentiles by way of a Hebrew prophet who wants nothing to do with it.

The story is in four easily discernible parts (corresponding to our present chapter divisions): (1) Jonah is called to preach judgment against Nineveh—in Nineveh!—to which he responds by fleeing as far in the other direction as he can go. Yahweh sends a storm, and Jonah is thrown overboard and is rescued by God's miraculous provision of a large fish. (2) Jonah responds in prayer, a psalm of thanksgiving for deliverance. (3) Jonah accepts his mission to Nineveh, with these results: Nineveh repents and God relents (in keeping with Jer 18:7–8). (4) Jonah erupts in anger, to which God responds with an object lesson and a final question to Jonah (Jonah 4:9–10)—the point of everything.

SPECIFIC ADVICE FOR READING JONAH

In order to read Jonah well, you need to be watching for two things—the narrator's skill in telling his story and the theological concerns that he brings to it.

First, in order to appreciate the power of this narrative, you might try to put yourself in the sandals of its intended Israelite hearers. The story functions in much the same way as the parables of Jesus (see *How to 1*, pp. 151–56), as the narrator draws his hearers/readers into the story and then catches them off guard with the final question.

The narrator's literary skills are reflected in several ways. For example, the basic story is framed by Jonah's flight from God (1:3) and his reason for it (4:2). Note also how the sailors' response to God's rescue of them anticipates God's compassion on Nineveh. Irony is used throughout to secure theological points: The pagan sailors end up sacrificing to Yahweh, after Yahweh's defiant prophet is thrown into the sea. At the end of his psalm Jonah exclaims (of his own deliverance): "Salvation comes from the LORD"—which is then played out by Nineveh's repentance and God's withholding of judgment. Jonah in his anger with Yahweh nonetheless speaks the truth about Yahweh's character (4:2), which turns out to be the very reason for his anger. And Jonah, rescued from death by Yahweh, in the ends wishes to die rather than to live—because the Ninevites get to live rather than die.

Second, this story is primarily about Yahweh and only secondarily about Jonah. Yahweh is the protagonist throughout: He calls Jonah; he sends a storm when Jonah disobeys—and intensifies it to keep the sailors from rescuing him; he provides a great fish to rescue Jonah; he is the object of praise and thanksgiving in Jonah's psalm; he sends Jonah a second time and then stays his hand when Jonah's preaching is successful; and in the end he provides both the plant and the worm and the scorching east wind to instruct Jonah in Yahweh's ways. Jonah, on the other hand, serves as the foil so that Yahweh's story can be told with power and punch.

At issue in all of this is the Abrahamic covenant (Gen 12:3)—that Yahweh is full of compassion and mercy for all that he has made (Ps 145:8–9, 13, 17) and that he intended all along to bless the nations through his election of Israel. But God's election, always an act of mercy, sometimes becomes the basis for pride and prejudice. And in this case remember that Assyria was the most cruel empire in ancient history (see the book of Nahum), yet God was giving such people a chance to repent—not conversion to Yahweh, but nonetheless a response sufficient for Yahweh to withhold his punishments. It is this "injustice" of God's mercy that is so offensive to Jonah.

A WALK THROUGH JONAH

☐ **1:1–17** *Jonah Runs from the Lord*

This opening narrative sets you up for the rest. Besides the basic story about Jonah, don't miss the two main elements: (1) Yahweh is in control of everything (note especially his role as Lord of land and sea, which the sailors come to recognize and Jonah does not understand), and (2) the deliberate contrasts between Yahweh's close-minded prophet and the increasingly open-minded pagan sailors.

☐ **2:1–10** *Jonah's Prayer of Thanksgiving*

Note that this "prayer" takes the form of an individual psalm of thanksgiving (see *How to 1*, pp. 218–19) and is thus expressed in terms of Yahweh's deliverance even while Jonah is still engulfed by the sea. The psalm is in three parts (vv. 2–4, 5–7, 8–9), the first two of which are parallel, as they interweave distress, rescue, and testimony, and conclude on a similar note—that of looking toward the temple. The final, testimonial, stanza (vv. 8–9) then anticipates the rest of the narrative, expressing Jonah's trust in Yahweh—from whom salvation comes—but doing so in contrast to those who "cling to worthless idols" (e.g., the Ninevites).

☐ **3:1–10** *Jonah's Preaching and Nineveh's Repentance*

Jonah is given a second chance, to which he responds with obedience (vv. 1–3). Note that the repentance of the city focuses on the king, who both sets the example (v. 6) and issues a decree that calls not only for fasting and sackcloth—even by the animals!—but a turning away from their evil ways and violence (vv. 7–8), hoping that such a display of repentance may cause God to relent (v. 9), which in fact he does (v. 10).

☐ **4:1–11** *Jonah's Anger at Yahweh's Compassion*

Here you come to the point of it all. Jonah does not want God to relent and is angry with Yahweh for being true to himself (see Exod 34:4–6)! The rest is dominated by Yahweh's twice-asked question, "Have you any right to be angry?/Do you have a right to be angry?" and Jonah's conviction that he does (vv. 4, 9). Using language from 1:17, the narrator three times points out that Yahweh "provides"—first the vine to give shade, then the worm, and finally the scorching wind. And then the second shoe drops. Jonah's selfish "compassion" over the *plant* more than justifies God's compassion for Nineveh's *people* — and *animals*. And we the readers are implicitly invited to answer Yahweh's question for ourselves — with regard to *our* enemies.

The book of Jonah continues the biblical story of the Creator and Redeemer God who shows compassion not only for his own but also for all whom he has created; the God of Scripture loves his enemies — and ours.

Micah

ORIENTING DATA FOR MICAH

- **Content:** alternating oracles of doom on Israel and Judah for their idolatry and social injustices and of future hope because of Yahweh's mercies

- **Prophet:** Micah, a Judean prophet from Moresheth, a town about twenty-five miles southwest of Jerusalem

- **Date of prophetic activity:** some length of time between the accession of Jotham (740 B.C.) and the death of Hezekiah (686)

- **Emphases:** the threat of divine judgment for breaking covenant with Yahweh; Yahweh as a God of justice and mercy who pleads the cause of the poor and requires his people to do the same; after judgment Yahweh will restore Jerusalem through the promised Davidic king; Yahweh as God of all the nations

OVERVIEW OF MICAH

The book of Micah, sixth in the Book of the Twelve, is a careful—and unique—collection and arrangement of oracles delivered by Micah over an apparently long period (1:6–7 was given well before the fall of Samaria in 722 B.C., while 1:10–16 traces the march of Sennacherib, which took place in 701; see 2 Kgs 18:13–19:37; Isa 36–37). Its uniqueness lies in its (not necessarily chronological) arrangement, which alternates between oracles of judgment and of future hope (basically Mic 1–2; 3–5; 6–7, which are marked off by the call to "hear/listen" 1:2; 3:1; 6:1).

The oracles in 1:2–2:11 are primarily pronouncements of divine judgment on Samaria and (especially) Jerusalem (the capitals representing the two kingdoms); they conclude with a brief promise of future restoration (2:12–13). The second set is introduced by a brief collection of three doom oracles (3:1–4, 5–8, 9–12); it concludes with a longer collection of oracles of hope (4:1–5:15) that focus on the promised (messianic) Davidic king. The third set is more evenly divided between threat (6:1–16) and hope (7:8–20), which are held together by Micah's lament over Israel's decadence (7:1–7).

SPECIFIC ADVICE FOR READING MICAH

Four matters are crucial for a good reading of Micah. First, the arrangement itself not only offers you a handle for reading the text but at the same time says something about Micah's own theology, which mirrors Deuteronomy 28–30. At the heart of things, as in Hosea, is the dynamic tension between the necessity of divine judgment (curses) because of Israel's breaking covenant with Yahweh and Yahweh's own longing to bless his people because they are his and because of his own character (compassion, mercy, forgiveness; see Mic 7:18–20). Micah himself is, as it were, both torn apart and held together by this twofold reality; the final composition of his book presents this tension in bold relief but concludes on the bright note of future hope.

Second, as is true for most of the prophets of Israel, the political history of the period plays an especially important role in understanding the oracles themselves. Micah is the fourth of the eighth-century prophets, a generation after Hosea and Amos, and a younger contemporary of Isaiah. Gone now are the halcyon days that characterized the reigns of Jeroboam II and Uzziah, and all of the seeds of decay and eventual destruction are settling in as the idolatry and social injustice condemned by Hosea, Amos, and Isaiah continued apace. At the same time Assyria is a constant threat on the international scene as she begins reasserting her power in the Near Eastern world (see "Specific Advice for Reading Isaiah," p. 176). Thus Assyria looms large in Micah, but her role is ambivalent: Although she is God's agent of judgment on Samaria (1:6–7, 10–16), she will fail against Judah (5:5–6) and will eventually experience God's judgment (5:15; 7:10). At the same time, as with Isaiah, the anticipation of Babylonian power is also prophesied (4:10).

Third, note especially the reasons for judgment on Judah. As it is with Isaiah and Amos, the issues are two: idolatry (1:7; 5:12–14) and social injustice (2:1–2, 8–11; 3:1–3, 8–11; 6:10–12; 7:2–3). Especially important for Micah is the role of the promised land as inheritance, which here goes in two directions—(1) exile from the land as part of the curse for unfaithfulness to Yahweh (1:16; 2:10; 4:9–10; cf. Deut 28:25–42) and (2) the unfaithfulness itself as the leaders and land barons deprive the rural poor of their traditional inheritance (Mic 2:2, 9; 3:2–3, 9–11; 6:10–12, 16; 7:2).

Fourth, Micah takes Israel's promised role in blessing the nations (Gen 12:3) with full seriousness (Mic 4:1–4; 7:11–13). This is the oath made to Abraham (7:20; the final word in the book), and this is the ultimate role of the messianic king, who will be God's agent for the peace of the nations (5:5). Note, therefore, that chapters 4–5, which express future hope in messianic terms, lie at the very center of the present arrangement. Thus, both the first and second oracles of hope center specifically on the coming messianic king (2:13; 5:1–6), and Micah 5:2 is cited in Matthew 2:6, in a Gospel that is particularly concerned about the Messiah's role in behalf of the nations (Matt 28:19–20).

Finally, you should also note that one hundred years later the oracle in Micah 3:12 is cited by some elders against King Jehoiakim, who wanted to take Jeremiah's life (Jer 26:17–19), a passage which also implies that Micah's preaching was in part responsible for Hezekiah's reforms (2 Kgs 18:1–8).

A WALK THROUGH MICAH

☐ **1:1** *Heading*

Note here (1) the emphasis on this being Yahweh's word, through the agency of Micah (from rural Moresheth, not Jerusalem), (2) its time, and (3) its subject matter.

☐ **1:2–16** *First Series of Threats (against Samaria and Jerusalem)*

Note how the first word (v. 2) sets the pace for the whole, by calling the whole earth to listen to Yahweh. This is followed by an oracle that begins with Yahweh as the Divine Warrior (vv. 3–4)—but now against his own people, whose sins center in the capital cities of Samaria and Jerusalem (v. 5). The threat of doom in this case is especially directed against Samaria for her idolatry (vv. 6–7).

The second threat (vv. 10–16), which begins with Micah's own response to it (vv. 8–9), is against Jerusalem, expressed in marvelous wordplays (see the NIV text notes) on the cities that Sennacherib had destroyed in his coming "even to the gate of Jerusalem" (v. 12). Although not as the result of Sennacherib's invasion, nonetheless the final word of threat is exile (v. 16).

☐ 2:1–11   *The Reasons for Judgment*

Watch carefully for the change of speakers: Micah (vv. 1–2), Yahweh (vv. 3–4), Micah (v. 5), false prophets (v. 6), Micah (v. 7a), Yahweh (vv. 7b–13). Note how the word of doom and its reasons (social injustice on the part of the land barons) come first (vv. 1–2), followed by Yahweh's threat, expressed in terms of the land being taken from them (vv. 3–5). The next oracle is God's judgment against the false theology of the prophets who have sided with the land barons (vv. 6–11).

☐ 2:12–13   *The First Word of Hope*

In direct response to verses 3–5 this first word of hope for the future is expressed in terms of regathering the people, with the messianic king in the lead.

☐ 3:1–12   *Second Series of Threats and Reasons*

With this collection of three oracles (vv. 1–4, 5–7, 9–12), Micah now focuses on the role of the leaders and prophets, who promote social injustice by their policies and prophecies. Note that Micah's own prophetic role is Spirit-inspired (v. 8; cf. 2:7) and that the final word (3:12) is judgment against Zion (Jerusalem and its temple).

☐ 4:1–5:15   *The Second Word of Hope: God's Messianic Kingdom and King*

As the centerpiece of the book, and now in direct response to 3:12, this series of oracles begins with the promised messianic restoration of Zion, where God's word will go forth and the nations gather to hear it (4:1–5; cf. Isa 2:1–4). This is followed in turn by (1) a long oracle promising return after exile, with the crushing of nations who oppose them (Mic 4:6–13), (2) the central role of the messianic king in the restoration (5:1–6), (3) the rest of the exiles triumphing over their enemies by bringing life and death (vv. 7–9), and (4) a final oracle in which Yahweh purges Judah (vv. 10–14) and punishes her enemies (v. 15).

☐ 6:1–16   *God's Case against Jerusalem (the Third Word of Threat)*

Here Yahweh takes Israel to court. He is the plaintiff—but also the judge! The mountains serve as jury (vv. 1–3). The plaintiff's case is made by rehearsing the essential moments in Israel's redemption—all

Yahweh's doing (vv. 4–5). Using the language of temple liturgy (Pss 15:1; 24:3), the defense responds with promises of increasingly more religion (Mic 6:6–7, note the gradual intensification of their offer), to which Yahweh responds by reminding them of what they already know about his character that they are to follow (v. 8). The judgment itself (v. 16) is based on Israel's failure precisely at this point (vv. 9–15).

☐ 7:1–7 *Micah's Lament*

Once again (cf. 1:8) Micah himself laments over Jerusalem's inevitable fall, but his final word is one of hope (v. 7) and serves as a transition to the conclusion of the book.

☐ 7:8–20 *The Third Word of Hope*

Hope for the future is Micah's last word; it begins with an expression of Israel's returning from exile and now fulfilling her role for the nations (vv. 8–13) and concludes with Micah's prayer (v. 14) and Yahweh's response (vv. 15–20). Note especially how the conclusion (vv. 18–20) is expressed in terms of Yahweh's character and prior promises to Abraham and Jacob: There is no God like Yahweh, who pardons sin and forgives transgression.

The book of Micah is a marvelous prophetic representation of the essentials of the biblical story, both in its Old Testament expression and in its anticipation of the New, with the promised Messiah and the restoration of his people.

Nahum

ORIENTING DATA FOR NAHUM

- **Content:** a prophecy of God's judgment against Nineveh (Assyria) for her oppression, cruelty, and idolatry, concluding with the announced destruction of the city

- **Prophet:** Nahum, from Judah, otherwise unknown (even his hometown is uncertain)

- **Date of prophetic activity:** sometime before the fall of Nineveh in 612 B.C., during the period of Judah's being a vassal to Assyria

- **Emphases:** Yahweh's sovereignty over all the nations; Yahweh's execution of justice against cruelty; Yahweh's overthrow of the arrogant who think of themselves as eternal

OVERVIEW OF NAHUM

This seventh in the Book of the Twelve is an unrelenting denunciation of, and pronouncement of God's judgment against, Assyria for her own unrelenting cruelty as master of the nations. As such, Nahum stands in contrast to the book of Jonah, which depicts at an earlier point in time Yahweh's concern for even his bitterest enemies (Assyria). But now Assyria's sin has "reached its full measure" (Gen 15:16), and Yahweh's famous patience is necessarily at an end. The key to Nahum's message is 1:7–8, which simultaneously expresses comfort to Judah and destruction for Nineveh.

The overall progression of the prophecy can be fairly easily seen. It begins with a Divine Warrior victory hymn (1:2–8), the last lines of which (vv. 7–8) serve also to introduce the first major oracle (1:9–2:2). This is followed by a vision of Nineveh's ruin (2:3–10), plus a taunt (vv. 11–13). Next come a series of oracles and taunts that declare the absolute certainty of Nineveh's demise (3:1–17), concluding with a satirical dirge over the fallen empire (vv. 18–19).

☐ **3:8–19** *Concluding Taunts and Dirge over Assyria's Fall*

After a satirical taunt over Nineveh (vv. 8–11; in light of her destruction of Thebes in Egypt), Nahum presents a series of insults (vv. 12–17) and concludes with a satirical dirge (vv. 18–19) that ends with a question. The only other prophetic book to end this way is Jonah, also regarding Nineveh, whose question stands in instructive contrast to this one.

Nahum reminds us of the essential character of the God whose story is told in the Bible, a God of goodness and salvation as well as of justice and judgment standing side by side in a way that is finally exhibited in the same way in the death of Jesus Christ on a cross.

Habakkuk

ORIENTING DATA FOR HABAKKUK

- **Content:** Habakkuk enters into dialogue with God over the question of injustice (How do people get away with evil and God seems to do nothing?) and receives grounds for trust

- **Prophet:** Habakkuk, a prophet of Judah, is unknown apart from this book

- **Date of prophetic activity:** sometime between 612 and 599 B.C., when Babylon had begun to dominate the international scene, but before she had attacked Jerusalem

- **Emphases:** prophetic indignation over God's apparent toleration of injustice; prophetic confidence in the justice and power of God; the stance of the righteous is faithfulness and trust in God; God's assurance that the wicked will be punished

OVERVIEW OF HABAKKUK

You may find this eighth in the Book of the Twelve to be among the easier of the prophetic books to read, because the structure is clear and the train of thought easy to follow. The first two chapters take the form of a dialogue between the prophet and Yahweh over injustice. Chapter 3 is the prophet's final response to God in the form of prayer in which he longs for the new exodus, yet affirms his trust in God no matter what.

In his complaint Habakkuk wrestles with what he knows to be true about God's character alongside God's apparent tolerance of the violence and injustice that abound in Judah (1:2–4). God's response—that he is raising up the Babylonians to handle this matter (1:5–11)—is small comfort to the prophet (1:12–17), since the Babylonians are more violent yet! So he takes his stand like the watchman of the night to see what answer will come in the morning (2:1). God's second response is two-fold: (1) The prophet must wait and continue to trust in God (2:2–4), and (2) the arrogant will surely meet their doom in kind (plunder for plunder, 2:4–20). Habakkuk's prayer is a dramatic metaphorical remembrance of the exodus from Egypt, which inspires hope, trust, and rejoicing in God in the face of all difficulties.

SPECIFIC ADVICE FOR READING HABAKKUK

In many ways reading Habakkuk is like reading an extended lament such as one finds, for example, in Psalm 10 or 13. Everything is predicated on God's character—and the prophet's/psalmist's confidence that God will indeed eventually judge the actions of the wicked. In each case it is precisely because of who God is that the prophet or psalmist cries out, "How long?" at what seems to be divine tolerance of evil.

It is this relationship to the laments in the Psalter that best explains the most unusual feature of Habakkuk, namely, that there is no oracle directed toward God's people as such. Rather the prophet has himself taken on the role of the people in his dialogue with God over present injustice. And the liturgical notations at the beginning and the end of chapter 3 make it clear that Habakkuk intended his prayer/psalm to be sung in the community of the righteous.

For the biblical background to Habakkuk you will want to read 2 Kings 22–23 and 2 Chronicles 34:1–36:4. The way he mentions the raising up of Babylon in Habakkuk 1:6 suggests that she had not yet achieved full international ascendancy (after 605 B.C.), which also means that Habakkuk was a contemporary of Zephaniah, Nahum, and Jeremiah. The descriptions of Judah's sins in these four books confirm the Kings–Chronicles testimony that Josiah's reform was only short-lived and skin-deep, and that Judah was a society of continuing injustice, violence, and rejection of the law. Yet, like his contemporaries, Habakkuk saw the future with clarity—that God's justice would prevail.

You will recognize that the oracles against Babylon are quite in keeping with the whole prophetic tradition, which clearly understood Yahweh to be the sovereign God of all the nations. God is the one who raised up Babylon to execute judgment against Judah.

A WALK THROUGH HABAKKUK

☐ 1:1–4 *Habakkuk's First Complaint*

Note how much the complaint (vv. 2–4) is like the lament psalms—a cry for God to act in light of the present situation, plus a catalogue of reasons for the lament.

☐ 1:5–11 *Yahweh's Answer*

Yahweh's response is scarcely what the prophet is looking for! God is raising up Babylon to mete out his judgment against Judah. You might want to compare the relentless, unstoppable nature of the coming Babylonian attack with either Nahum's vision (Nah 2:3–4, 9–10; 3:1–3) or with Joel's (Joel 2:1–11).

☐ 1:12–2:1 *Habakkuk's Second Complaint*

Try to put yourself in Habakkuk's sandals in order to see how thoroughly unsatisfactory God's answer is. How can this be justice, when the God whose eyes are too pure to look on evil summons the treacherous to "swallow up those more righteous than themselves" (1:13)? So Habakkuk takes the place of the watchman to see how God will respond this time (2:1).

☐ 2:2–5 *Yahweh's Answer*

The answer is threefold: (1) Habakkuk must wait, for the answer ("the revelation") will come at its appointed time, (2) the Babylonians' present stance of arrogance is doomed, and (3) the righteous will live by their faithful trust in Yahweh (v. 4, the passage that became crucial in Paul's theology).

☐ 2:6–20 *Woe Oracles against the Oppressor*

Here watch for the *lex talionis* ("eye for eye") nature of God's justice as his judgment is meted out on Babylon. Picking up a different image in each oracle, God strikes his gavel five times: The plunderer is plundered (vv. 6–8), the haughty conqueror is shamed (vv. 9–11), the builder's building becomes fuel for the fire (vv. 12–14), the one who forces the other to get drunk will drink shame from the cup of God's wrath (vv. 15–17), and the silent idol is silenced before Yahweh, who is present in his holy temple (vv. 18–20).

☐ 3:1 – 19 *Habakkuk's Prayer and Confession*

This marvelous psalm comes in three basic parts: verse 2, a prayer that God would renew his deeds of old; verses 3 – 15, a celebration of God's past victories as the Divine Warrior; and verses 16 – 19, Habakkuk's two-fold commitment to "wait patiently for the day of calamity" and to put his trust and hope in God under any circumstances (cf. 2:2 – 4).

As with many readers, you may find the central section to be hard going. What is crucial to note here is that in three stanzas (3:3 – 7, 8 – 10, and 11 – 15) Habakkuk weaves together (1) God's dominion over the chaotic waters in creation, (2) his causing the sun to stand still for Joshua, (3) the theophany at Sinai, and (4) poetic descriptions of the exodus (cf. Exod 15:6 – 8; Ps 114) into a brilliant, breathtaking reminder of God's triumph over Pharaoh in delivering his people — a picture that makes Habakkuk's hair stand on end, as it were (Hab 3:16). All of this serves to assure God's people that he will act once more on their behalf.

Habakkuk carries on the biblical story in grand fashion — that the Creator, Redeemer God *will* do something about human iniquity, while his people live in hope and with faithful trust in him.

Zephaniah

ORIENTING DATA FOR ZEPHANIAH

- **Content:** oracles of coming catastrophic judgments against Jerusalem (thus Judah) and surrounding nations, plus an oracle of restoration for a remnant of Judah

- **Prophet:** Zephaniah of Jerusalem, possibly of the royal lineage of Hezekiah

- **Date of prophetic activity:** sometime during the reign of Josiah of Judah (640–609 B.C.)

- **Emphases:** the coming day of Yahweh; judgment against Judah for her sins; Yahweh as God of all the nations; judgments against the nations; eventual salvation of a remnant of Judah

OVERVIEW OF ZEPHANIAH

During the reign of Josiah (Judah's last good king), Zephaniah, who was possibly a member of the royal court, received a word from Yahweh, announcing that "the day of the LORD [Yahweh] is near" (1:7, 14, 18; 2:3). The burden of his prophecy is God's judgment on Judah for her idolatry and complacent wickedness (1:3b–18a; 3:1–5). But also included are a call to repentance (2:1–3), judgments against other nations (2:4–15), and the promise of restoration for a faithful remnant (3:9–20). Thus, as you will quickly recognize, Zephaniah—the ninth of the book of the Twelve—carries through with all of the significant concerns found in the Israelite prophetic tradition.

SPECIFIC ADVICE FOR READING ZEPHANIAH

The historical context of Zephaniah is in some ways similar to that of Habakkuk (2 Kgs 22–23; 2 Chr 34–35). In this case, however, since his prophecies are directed primarily against Jerusalem, you may also wish to read the relevant sections about syncretism in the "Specific Advice" for reading Deuteronomy and Kings. Although it is not possible to determine exactly when this marvelous set of oracles was proclaimed—though they would seem to precede rather than follow Josiah's reforms—you will not be able to miss seeing that God's judgment is being pronounced primarily because Jerusalem continues to be a city of religion, but not of pure Yahwism, while at the same time—also over against pure Yahwism—there is little concern for social justice.

Since most people do not find Zephaniah easy reading, it may help you in this regard to see his careful literary structure, which takes the form of a series of concentric patterns (chiasms). First there is the larger frame itself:

A God's Judgment of Judah, with Consequent Wailing (1:2–18)
  B God's Judgment of the Nations (2:1–3:8)
A* God's Redemption of the Remnant, with Consequent Rejoicing (3:9–21)

Within each of these, and sometimes interlocking between them, there are further concentric patterns. Note, for example, how 1:2–18 is framed by announcements of judgment against the whole earth (1:2–3//18b–c echoing the Flood [b–c = poetic lines in the verse]); in the same manner 1:2–3 and 3:8d frame the entire set of judgment oracles. Thus:

1:2–18		3:9–21
1:2–3		3:8d
1:2–3	1:18b–c	

Similarly, the oracles against the nations are framed by a call to repentance on the part of Judah (2:1–3) and judgment because of her refusal to do so (3:6–8; see "A Walk through Zephaniah").

Second, all of this is expressed in brilliant and powerful images. Note, for example, his deliberate placing of God's judgment on Judah and Jerusalem in images and language that echo the Flood account in Genesis 6. This is related to Zephaniah's frequent use of hyperbole (purposeful exaggeration for effect). Thus, for example, he predicts at several points that God will destroy the whole earth and all its inhabitants (1:2–3, 18b–c; 3:8), yet also predicts a great future both for the peoples (3:9) and for Israel (3:10–19). Such overstatement is not to be taken literally (cf. a sports fan's understanding of the headline "Vancouver buries Boston" to indicate a lopsided victory, not the death and burial of a city);

its effectiveness lies in the people's taking seriously the extent of the tragedy that awaits them.

On the matter of the day of Yahewh, refer to "Specific Advice for Reading Joel," pp. 218–19. In Zephaniah "the day" (used 17*x* between 1:7 and 2:3!) refers to a time of decisive change on behalf of the righteous and against the wicked—and Judah is among the wicked.

A WALK THROUGH ZEPHANIAH

☐ 1:1   *The Prophet's Identity*

It is important not to go too fast here; note how the prophet is placed both in his lineage (possibly a descendant of the previous reforming king, Hezekiah) and in his own time (advancing the cause of the king who became the greatest reformer, Josiah).

☐ 1:2–18   *The Day of Yahweh Is Coming (against Judah)*

Don't forget as you read that this is a prophetic oracle, not a narrative, and thus written as poetry intended for oral presentation. Notice the outer frame (1:2–3b, 18b–c), where the judgment against Judah is set against the backdrop of a coming floodlike catastrophe. You will see that the judgment against Judah is in three parts: (1) Verses 3c–9 voice God's coming judgment expressly against Judah and Jerusalem because of their idolatries (note that the judgment is pictured in terms of God's preparing a sacrifice); (2) verses 10–13 describe the response to the day of Yahweh when it comes: the city wailing over its economic ruin and the laying waste of homes and estates; and (3) verses 14–18a describe the inevitable and inescapable nature of the day when it comes.

☐ 2:1–3:8   *Judgment on the Nations Detailed*

Observe the careful structuring of this section down to the smallest detail. It begins with a summons to Judah to repent and become like the humble righteous (2:1–3) and ends on the sad note of Jerusalem's refusal to do so (3:6–8). In between are five oracles, four against five other nations and one against Jerusalem herself, which are expressed in a perfectly balanced construction:

2:1–3	Summons to repent
2:4–7	Philistia (nine lines)—a neighbor's land will belong to Judah's remnant

2:8–11	Moab/Ammon (nine lines)—same as with Philistia
2:12	Cush (one line)
2:13–15	Assyria (nine lines)—a dreaded enemy will be destroyed
3:1–5	Jerusalem (nine lines)—Judah will be like her dreaded enemy
3:6–8	Refusal to repent

There are several other important matters to note as you read—that the reasons for judgment are barely given in the actual series against the other nations (Moab/Ammon for insulting God's people; Assyria for arrogance) but that reasons are amply given for Jerusalem's downfall (treachery by political and religious leaders); that 2:7 and 9 anticipate the remnant in the final oracle of the book (3:9–20); that the express reason for these oracles is to call Jerusalem to repentance (see esp. 3:6–7), although these kinds of oracles always exist in the prophets as reminders that Yahweh is also God over all the nations.

☐ 3:9–20 *Restoration of the Remnant*

As with the opening oracle of judgment, you will observe that this concluding oracle of hope is also in three parts: (1) Verses 9–13 express in Deuteronomic terms the purifying of the gathered remnant, who will rest secure in Jerusalem and live humbly and righteously; (2) verses 14–17, in contrast to the wailing in the opening oracle, describe the rejoicing (both the people's and Yahweh's) that now rings throughout the restored city; and (3) verses 18–20, again in Deuteronomic terms, describe the gathering of the people and their receiving praise and honor in exchange for shame.

The small book of Zephaniah speaks in powerful ways of both God's judgment on sin and his gracious act of salvation for the humble and undeserving, thus anticipating the gospel as expressed in the New Testament.

Haggai

ORIENTING DATA FOR HAGGAI

- **Content:** four oracles encouraging God's people to rebuild the temple in Jerusalem

- **Prophet:** Haggai, a postexilic prophet in Jerusalem and contemporary of Zechariah (see Ezra 5:1; 6:14)

- **Date of prophetic activity:** a four-month period during the second year of the reign of Darius of Persia (520 B.C.)

- **Emphases:** God's people need to rebuild the temple as the place of God's presence and of their worship; current hardships stem from failure in this matter; a glorious future awaits the people of God and Zerubbabel (thus David's kingly line)

OVERVIEW OF HAGGAI

Haggai, the tenth of the Book of the Twelve, consists of reports of four "words" addressed to Zerubbabel the governor, Joshua the priest, and the people in Jerusalem. His main concern is to encourage the people to get on with rebuilding the temple in Jerusalem.

Haggai's first "word" (1:1–11) announces that recent droughts and poor harvests (part of the curses for covenant disobedience; see Deut 28:20–48) are connected to the returned exiles' failure to build God's house (though they had already built their own houses), to which the people respond favorably (Hag 1:12–15). A month and a half later, the second "word" encourages them to continue the work, promising that the glory of the new temple would surpass that of the first (2:1–9). Priestly rulings on defilement serve as the basis for the third "word" (vv. 10–19), where God promises to bless them "from this day on." The final "word" (vv. 20–23) is addressed to Zerubbabel, assuring him that God will be with him.

SPECIFIC ADVICE FOR READING HAGGAI

It will help you in reading Haggai to also read Ezra 1 – 6, which serves as background for the words of Haggai recorded here. After a large group of exiles returned in 539 B.C. under the edict of Cyrus, they immediately rebuilt the altar and laid the foundations of the temple (Ezra 3). Then the work stopped as the people built their homes and worked their farms. Now, some nineteen years later, the work on the temple has gone no further; meanwhile they have regularly experienced drought and poor harvests. Through Haggai, Yahweh calls attention to the connection between these two realities and encourages them to return to the task of rebuilding the temple.

As you read, watch for several features that distinguish Haggai: (1) His oracles are not given in poetic form, but a kind of rhythmic prose; (2) they are most often carried on by way of questions (cf. Malachi), which lead to God's word to the people (Hag 1:4, 9; 2:3, 12 – 13, 19); (3) he also makes effective use of repetitions — "Give careful thought" occurs twice in the first and third oracles (1:5, 7; 2:15, 18); "I am with you" occurs in the first and second (1:13; 2:4); that God will "shake the heavens and the earth" occurs in the second and fourth (2:6, 21); and in language echoing Joshua 1:6 – 7, 9, 19, leaders and people are three times exhorted to "be strong" (2:4). Note also that while there is obvious progression in the four "words," there is also a clear correspondence between the first and third (the covenant curse is now to be overturned by covenant blessing) and between the second and fourth (encouraging Zerubbabel as leader).

Since the central issue of Haggai is the rebuilding of the temple, you will do well to recall the significant role the temple played in the life of Israel, which served as both the place of God's special presence (marking off Israel from all other peoples) and the place of proper worship. See "Specific Advice for Reading Exodus" (pp. 35 – 37) and the notes on Exod 25 – 40 (pp. 40 – 42), and recall that God's Spirit is the way God is present among them (hence Hag 2:5).

The specific days and dates given for these oracles are worth noting. The first (29 August 520) is given on the first day of the (lunar) month, thus in the setting of a New Moon festival (Num 10:10; 28:11) and at the time of the full maturing of the grain; the second (17 October 520) comes at the end of the Feast of Tabernacles (Israel's harvest festival);

and the third and fourth (18 December 520) during the growing season for spring harvest. All these were periods when people had no excuse that they were too busy to pay attention to the temple.

Here you also feel the frequent tension found in the prophetic tradition between present realities and the glorious future of God. As usual, the one (present hope) is spoken in light of the other (future glory). Note how this occurs regarding both the temple (2:1–5, 6–9) and Zerubbabel (2:20–22, 23), both being marked by God's eschatological shaking of the heavens and the earth.

A WALK THROUGH HAGGAI

☐ 1:1–15   *The Call to Rebuild the Temple*

Trace the unfolding of this "word." It begins with the setting (v. 1), God's complaint with his people (v. 2), and the primary question (v. 3)—failure to build God's house, even though the returned exiles have built their own. At the peak of the growing season, God calls them to start building his house! This is followed by two "Give careful thought to your ways" oracles about the present drought and the reasons for it (vv. 5–6, 7–11; drought is one of the curses for breaking covenant, Deut 28:38–40). Note how unlike the earlier prophets the third part is (Hag 1:12–15); the people's response is actually recorded—and it is positive!

☐ 2:1–9   *The Glory of the Second Temple*

You might try to imagine how someone seventy years old or older might have felt when they saw that the partly built temple was obviously not going to be like Solomon's—and far short of Ezekiel's grand vision (Ezek 40–43). Thus the people are encouraged to "be strong," because in time the second temple will exceed the glory of the first (fulfilled finally when Jesus assumes the role of the temple while standing in the courts of this temple; John 2:13–22).

☐ 2:10–19   *A Defiled People Purified and Blessed*

Note that two questions about defilement/undefilement (vv. 10–13) are used by way of analogy (vv. 14–19b) to repeat the essence of 1:8–11 (their land is "defiled" because the people are "defiled"), while verse 2:19c reverses the curse—from this day on God will bless them.

□ 2:20–23   *A Message to Zerubbabel*

Zerubbabel, heir of David's throne but a vassal governor of Judea under Persian rule, is promised a future overthrow of the worldly powers and that he will become God's "signet ring" ("official seal"; cf. Jer 22:24–25, where the last king of Judah was a "signet ring" to be discarded!)—a word also pointing forward to the time of David's greater Son.

Haggai reminds us that God's people are to be identified as a people of God's presence (the role of the temple), finally fulfilled in the coming of Jesus Christ and the Spirit.

Zechariah

ORIENTING DATA FOR ZECHARIAH

- **Content:** visions aimed at encouraging the postexilic community, especially the leadership, to rebuild the temple, plus oracles about the future coming King who would be slain and eventually triumph

- **Prophet:** Zechariah of Jerusalem, a contemporary of Haggai, but with a longer known ministry (cf. Zech 1:1 and 7:1 with Hag 1:1; see also Ezra 5:1; 6:14)

- **Date of prophetic activity:** 520 B.C. until sometime in the early 400s

- **Emphases:** God is with the remnant community of people who have returned from exile; God will prosper her leaders; the future of Jerusalem and Judah is bright and full of peace and glory; Israel's King will come back to Jerusalem in triumph, yet he will be slain for the sins of the people; God will punish his people's enemies, yet many of the nations will come to know the Lord

OVERVIEW OF ZECHARIAH

This eleventh of the Book of the Twelve has two such distinct parts (chs. 1–8; 9–14) that many scholars believe chapters 9–14 to be from someone else. But the Bible presents both parts together, with the second to be understood in light of the first. Here is a case where the near future and the great future of God exist in tension by the very structure of the book.

Both sections have recognizable parts. After an introductory call to repentance (1:2–6), you encounter a series of eight night visions (1:7–6:15), which are interpreted by an "angel who was talking with [Zechariah]" (1:9). These center in visions 4–5, which focus on the leadership of Joshua and Zerubbabel and the building of the temple. The rest of this section (chs. 7–8) uses a question posed about certain fasts to preach about the true nature of fasting and to announce God's future blessing of Jerusalem.

Chapters 9–14 contain two "oracles" (chs. 9–11 and 12–14) having to do with God's glorious future for his people and judgment on his/their enemies. The first contains a judgment against the nations (9:1–8) set in the context of the coming and subsequent rejection of God's kingly Messiah (9:9–17; 11:4–17) and the great regathering of his scattered people (10:1–11:3). The second oracle picks up all of these themes but sets them into an even more obviously eschatological context, as they focus on "that day," climaxing in chapter 14 with the final defeat of God's enemies and the establishment of his universal kingdom, when all the nations come to worship him.

SPECIFIC ADVICE FOR READING ZECHARIAH

Most people find Zechariah an especially difficult read, even for a prophetic book. This is undoubtedly due to the highly symbolic nature of the night visions plus the normally complex character of prophetic eschatological oracles — and these are what make up most of Zechariah. But with a bit of help you should be able to negotiate your way through the book and appreciate some of its grandeur.

For the history of the period and the basic concerns of the prophet, see "Specific Advice for Reading Haggai," p. 253. What is important to note here is that all of the primary concerns of Israel's prophetic tradition occur in Zechariah — judgments of God's people for their own sins; judgments against surrounding nations because of their sins against God's people and because Yahweh is sovereign over all the nations; a glorious future for the redeemed and purified people of God — and all of this set in tension between soon-to-be temporal realities and the final glorious future of God. What is also a pronounced feature of Zechariah is his expectation of God's future messianic king, which is why he is quoted so often by the New Testament writers (especially with regard to Christ and the final expression of the kingdom of God).

A couple of observations may help your reading of the night visions. First, they are arranged in a concentric (chiastic) pattern. Note that visions 1 and 8 (1:7–17; 6:1–8) both envision four groups of colored horses, whose purpose is to go throughout the whole earth, as the backdrop for the building of the temple. Visions 2 and 3 (1:18–21; 2:1–13) and 6 and 7 (5:1–4; 5:5–11) have to do with obstacles facing the restoration community and its building of the temple (in 2 and 3 the obstacles come from without and in 6 and 7 from within). Visions 4 and 5 (3:1–10; 4:1–14) are the centerpiece, dealing especially with Joshua's and Zerubbabel's leadership, both for the building of the temple and for leading the community.

Second, you will note a similar pattern to most of these visions: Zechariah describes what he sees, he asks about its meaning, and an interpreting angel gives the explanation. Four of the visions ([1] 1:14–17; [3] 2:6–13; [5] 4:6–10a; [8] 6:9–15) also contain one or more oracles, which make specific the message of the visions. The heart of all of this is a word of encouragement, declaring to the people that the time is ripe—the conditions are now in place for them to rebuild—while at the same time it is, as with Haggai, a word of encouragement to those in leadership.

The two oracles in chapters 9–14 are especially difficult to follow, but in the main they follow a pattern as well. Both have to do with the triumphal intervention of the Lord in the affairs of Judah and the nations. The first looks toward the more immediate future, the second toward the final coming of God's universal rule. Common to both is the central place of God's kingly Messiah, and the fact that he is rejected by the people.

One final note. Later prophets sometimes make use of the language and images of earlier ones. This is especially true of Zechariah, who not only mentions the "earlier prophets" (1:4, 6; 7:7, 12), but deliberately echoes their language in a number of places (e.g., cf. 1:4 with Jer 35:15). This may be the best explanation for the intriguing piercing and suffering of God's kingly Messiah in Zechariah 11–13, which sounds like further reflection on Isaiah's suffering servant (Isa 52:13–53:12). This also helps to explain why the New Testament writers refer to these two passages so often as the way to explain the Messiah's crucifixion.

A WALK THROUGH ZECHARIAH

☐ **1:1–6** *Introduction*

Both the heading, which dates about two months after Haggai's initial word, and the words that follow serve as a validation of the prophet: This is what God has told Zechariah to tell the people, which affirms that the covenant is still in effect and calls for their obedience (in contrast to the way their ancestors behaved).

☐ 1:7–17   *Vision 1: The Horsemen: God's Return to Jerusalem*

Note the parts as you read: (1) the vision itself (v. 8); (2) Zechariah's question about meaning (vv. 9–10); (3) the interpreting angel's response: They are the patrol who has gone throughout the whole earth and find it at rest; (4) the oracle(s)—Yahweh is returning to Jerusalem, so the people must not rest but must rebuild the temple.

☐ 1:18–21   *Vision 2: Four Horns Destroyed*

Note how this vision is in two parts with explanations. The days of the nations responsible for the exile (of both Judah and Israel) are over.

☐ 2:1–13   *Vision 3: Jerusalem Cannot Be Measured— The Return of Prosperity*

Note how the explanation (vv. 4–13) takes the form of a series of oracles—the coming greatness of Jerusalem with Yahweh as her protector (vv. 4–5); a call to the exiles in Babylon to return (vv. 6–9; thus picking up from vision 2); Yahweh's dwelling in Zion as universal sovereign (vv. 10–13; thus filling out the present vision). Note also how verse 13 echoes Habakkuk 2:20.

☐ 3:1–10   *Vision 4: The Reinstatement of the High Priest*

Remember that this is the first of the two central visions. Since at stake is the rebuilding of the temple, the place of God's presence, this vision has to do with cleansing the high priest, who is to function in the temple once it is rebuilt. Note the progression from clean garments and turban (vv. 3–5) to recommissioning (vv. 6–7) to the promised Branch (v. 8, referring ultimately to the coming Davidic king; cf. Isa 11:1; 53:2; Jer 23:5); the vision concludes by anticipating the oracle in Zechariah 8:1–8.

☐ 4:1–14   *Vision 5: The Lampstand and the Olive Trees— God's Renewing Spirit/Presence*

Note the slightly different structure: the vision (vv. 1–3), now with two sets of questions (vv. 4–5, 11–13) and explanations (vv. 6–10, 14)—to encourage Zerubbabel that God's Spirit will bring about what human power cannot—plus an affirmation of his and Joshua's leadership.

☐ 5:1–4   *Vision 6: The Flying Scroll—Banishment of Evil from Judah*

Now you are back to a brief vision and explanation: The evil that persists in Judah will be banished from the land.

☐ 5:5–11   *Vision 7: The Woman in a Basket—Wickedness Exiled to Babylon*

Watch for the irony in this vision, as well as its relationship to previous visions: The people will return from exile (vision 3), Babylon has been overthrown (vision 2), the temple will be rebuilt (visions 4–5); so what happens to wickedness? It will be exiled to Babylon!

☐ 6:1–15   *Vision 8: The Four Chariots—God at Rest and a Crown for Joshua*

Note how this vision wraps up the series. This new patrol of four horsemen again goes throughout the earth and finds it at rest (especially Babylon, the "north country," v. 6)—all of this to say that the time for rebuilding is now.

The "word" that came to Zechariah that concludes the visions (vv. 9–15) both supplements and reinforces the concerns that have preceded (Joshua, the Branch, the rebuilding of the temple).

☐ 7:1–8:23   *In Response to a Question about Fasting*

A question related to special fasts in connection with the fall of Jerusalem becomes the catalyst for a series of oracles that take a concentric (chiastic) pattern similar to the visions.

    7:1–3   The question: Do we continue to mourn and fast over Jerusalem's fall?

        7:4–14 A judgment against fasting without obedience to the covenant

            8:1–8 A picture of restored Jerusalem, which serves to inspire

            8:9–13 An encouragement to rebuild the temple

        8:14–17 True fasting expresses itself in showing mercy and justice (cf. Isa 58)

    8:18–19 The question answered: Let the fasts be turned into joyful celebrations

Note how the two appended oracles (8:20–23) anticipate the fulfillment of the Abrahamic covenant that includes the Gentiles (Gen 12:3). And finally note how the two sections of the book end on this same note (Zech 8:20–23; 14:16–19).

☐ 9:1–11:17 *Zion's King and the Glorious Future for God's People*

This first oracle resorts to the poetic pattern of the earlier prophets. Look for the following progression: What begins with a judgment on the surrounding nations (9:1–8) turns into the promised restoration of the Davidic king (vv. 9–17) and of a united Israel (10:1, 3b–12). Note that the latter is enclosed by a denunciation of false shepherds (10:2–3a; 11:1–6, 14–17) and that the last of these encloses a picture of God's true shepherd who will be rejected by the people (11:7–13), which in turn anticipates the central section of the next oracle (12:10–13:9).

☐ 12:1–14:21 *The Smiting and Final Triumph of God's King*

Note how this second oracle picks up themes from the first one, especially the rejection of the true shepherd, while setting the whole in a more totally eschatological setting regarding the day of Yahweh ("that day"). This in turn is placed in the setting of the final eschatological expression of the holy war, where the enemy surrounds and ransacks Jerusalem (12:1–3a; 14:1–2) and the King is killed (12:10–13:7)—but in the end God's glorious final kingdom emerges (12:3b–9; 14:3–21).

The book of Zechariah advances the biblical story by reminding us that God's presence by his Spirit is at the heart of a restored Israel, while at the same time anticipating the sacrificial death of the Messiah who is to come.

Malachi

ORIENTING DATA FOR MALACHI

- **Content:** in six disputes with his people, Yahweh warns them of future judgments and promises redemption to the faithful

- **Prophet:** Malachi ("my messenger"), otherwise unknown

- **Date of prophetic activity:** unknown; perhaps ca. 460 B.C., just before the reforms of Ezra and Nehemiah

- **Emphases:** Yahweh is a covenant-keeping God and requires the same of his people; God's people show disdain for God by their apathy and moral and religious decline; God will judge his people in justice for their halfhearted obedience

OVERVIEW OF MALACHI

Malachi's oracle comes by way of six disputes between Yahweh and his people, all having the same root cause: In a time of spiritual disillusionment, Israel has grown weary of Yahweh and of keeping his covenant. The disputes come in two sets of three. The first set takes up the basic issue—their complaint that Yahweh does not love them (1:2–5), and Yahweh's "complaint" that they have shown contempt for him (1:6–2:9; 2:10–16). In the second set, Yahweh twice takes up their complaint that he has done nothing about evil and injustice (2:17–3:5; 3:13–4:3); these two bracket Yahweh's exposing their own form of injustice (3:6–12). At the same time they affirm that the great day of Yahweh will come indeed (3:1–4; 3:17–4:3). The book concludes (4:4–6) with words about the law (Moses) and the prophets (Elijah).

SPECIFIC ADVICE FOR READING MALACHI

Although one cannot be sure when Malachi prophesied, if it was just before the time of Ezra and Nehemiah, as seems likely, you would do well to review briefly what is said about these times in the "Specific Advice" for reading 1 and 2 Chronicles and Ezra-Nehemiah. Malachi's book is a graphic indicator of the moral and spiritual apathy of the time, which expressed itself in various forms of contempt for Yahweh and the covenant. In fact, most of the sins mentioned in Malachi are also mentioned in Ezra and Nehemiah — mixed marriages (Mal 2:11 – 15/ Ezra 9 – 10/Neh 13:23 – 27); failure to tithe (Mal 3:8 – 10/Neh 13:10 – 14); corrupt priests (Mal 1:6 – 2:9/Neh 13:1 – 9); and social injustice (Mal 3:5/Neh 5:1 – 13).

This general malaise and contempt for the covenant probably account in part for the unique form and structure of Malachi. You will see that each of the disputes tends to follow the same pattern:

- Declaration: the issue announced by Yahweh
- The people's question: basically taking the form of "How so?"
- Yahweh's response: reminding them of his past or coming actions, or revealing their actions that show contempt

These disputes function as a wake-up call in a time of disillusionment (see 3:14) when the returnees from Babylon felt generally abandoned by Yahweh. So rather than a court setting (as in Hosea and Micah, for example), Yahweh challenges them by means of declaration, question, and explanation.

There is a kind of progression to the disputes. They begin with Israel's questioning Yahweh's love (= compassion for and loyalty to them). To this, Yahweh responds that not only does he indeed love them (look what I did to Edom) but that there is plenty of evidence that they do not love Yahweh, in the form of contempt for the covenant by priests and people alike (offering blemished animals in sacrifice, and divorce and intermarriage with pagans). The final three disputes start the cycle again. Feeling abandoned by Yahweh, the people speak cynically about the prosperity of those who practice injustice. But, Yahweh responds, they themselves practice injustice by withholding tithes, the means of livelihood for the Levites and of provision for the poor (Num 18:21 – 32; Deut 14:28 – 29). In the final set, there are also assurances of God's coming justice — both judgment of the wicked and salvation of the (new) righteous remnant.

Thus, at the end of the Christian Old Testament (by way of the Septuagint) are prophetic words that Jesus and the New Testament writers see as speaking about his coming. Not only will God send "[his] messenger, who will prepare the way before [him]" so that "the Lord you are seeking will come to his temple" (Mal 3:1), but the final two words speak of Moses and Elijah, who make their appearance with Jesus on the Mount of Transfiguration.

A WALK THROUGH MALACHI

☐ **1:1 Heading**

As with Joel, Malachi's heading does not help us identify either the prophet or his times.

☐ **1:2–5 First Dispute: On Yahweh's Love**

Note how this first dispute sets both the tone and the structure for the rest. Yahweh does love them. How so? By his hating (= rejecting; allying himself against) their "brother"—but ancient foe—Edom, thus fulfilling Obadiah's prophecy.

☐ **1:6–2:9 Second Dispute: On Offering Unacceptable Sacrifices**

Now it's Yahweh's turn. The basic issue is set forth in 1:6—the priests do not love (= they show contempt for) Yahweh. How so? By offering Yahweh blemished animals (see Lev 22:17–25) that they would not dare offer even to a governor. Better to close down the temple altogether than to show such disloyalty (1:10–14), which also dishonors Yahweh's name among the nations. Thus this dispute concludes with strong admonitions for the priests to change their ways (2:1–9).

☐ **2:10–16 Third Dispute: On Intermarriage and Divorce**

Note that the form changes slightly here: Malachi now speaks for God (v. 10) as the dispute turns to the people themselves—over intermarriage with pagans (vv. 11–12), thus breaking covenant with Yahweh (= capitulation to idolatry). The issue of divorce (vv. 13–16) is related (= breaking covenant with a Jewish wife to marry a local woman).

☐ **2:17–3:5 Fourth Dispute: On Wearying Yahweh with Words**

Back to the people's complaint. In their present malaise, they (cynically) call evil people good and ask about justice. Yahweh's answer is twofold: (1) The Lord whom they seek will come suddenly to his temple—as a refining fire (3:1–3a), and (2) his coming will result in both acceptable sacrifices at the temple (thus back to 1:6 – 2:9) and judgment against all forms of injustice (3:3b – 5).

☐ 3:6 – 12   *Fifth Dispute: On Returning to Yahweh*

Notice how this dispute follows closely on what is said at the end of the previous one by putting the ball back in their court: They themselves must return to Yahweh (vv. 6 – 7). To their "How so?" the answer is to stop their own form of injustice — withholding the tithe (food, which is used for the Levites and the poor). Only then can the curse for covenant disloyalty be removed, so that the nations will see again God's blessing on his people (cf. Gen 12:3).

☐ 3:13 – 4:3   *Sixth Dispute: On Speaking Harshly about Yahweh*

This final dispute both wraps up the second set of three and brings the whole series full circle. It indicates why the first dispute was necessary: The people have been saying harsh things about Yahweh — that it is futile to serve him, and that in any case the arrogant prosper, while those who consider themselves as righteous do not (3:13 – 15; cf. dispute 4). Thus the final answer indicates that God will indeed divide the house — the arrogant will be judged (4:1) — and the "sun of righteousness will rise" for the righteous (4:2 – 3).

☐ 4:4 – 6   *Two Appended Words: the Law and the Prophets (Moses and Elijah)*

Malachi concludes by bringing Moses (the Law) and Elijah (the Prophets) into the picture. The people are urged to keep the covenant of law; they can anticipate the coming of a second Elijah who will precede the coming great day of Yahweh.

Malachi reminds God's people that they must take their covenant relationship with him seriously and that a great new day will dawn for them with the coming of Elijah (John the Baptist) to precede the Lord (Jesus Christ).

Glossary of Terms

The following terms are used on a regular basis in this book. Because some of them reflect technical language (allowing us the economy of one word rather than many), we have tried to isolate most of this vocabulary (plus some other technical language referring to pagan deities) and explain it here.

acrostic: Poetry in which each new section or verse begins with a succeeding letter of the alphabet.

agonist(s): In literature the major character(s) in the plot who are involved in a contest or struggle.

anathema: Something or someone placed under God's curse — or the curse itself. Thus, *anathema* can refer to something that is to be avoided as especially ungodly or repugnant.

Asherah: A Canaanite mother-fertility goddess often worshiped by the Israelites when they fell into idolatry. She was regarded as the sex partner of Baal and was worshiped for her supposed power to make animals and crops fertile. Most references to her in the OT are to her idol, a large pole presumably bearing her likeness. Asherah and Ashtoreth (see below) were so similar in the belief system of Canaanite polytheism that they are sometimes referred to interchangeably (Judg 2:13, "served Baal and the Ashtoreths"; Judg 3:7, "served the Baals and the Asherahs").

Ashtoreth: A Canaanite mother-fertility goddess similar to and sometimes considered the same as Asherah (above). Because her name in Greek was *Astarte,* it is usually assumed that the Hebrew form of the name may be the result of scribes' using the vowels (o and e) from the Hebrew word for "shame" to give her name a distorted sound in the biblical text. In some localities, distinctions between Ashtoreth and Asherah were made; in others they apparently were not, since it was the habit of polytheistic syncretism often to blur or interchange the distinctions between gods, with every location free to do its own thing with regard to worship and theology.

Baal: The chief male Canaanite fertility god—or the idol that represented him. Baal was sometimes called "the cloud rider" by the Canaanites because they thought that he controlled the weather, especially the rain, which was the key to agricultural productivity.

canon (canonical): The official collection of books that make up the Bible (or one of its Testaments). A canonical writing is one that is part of the Bible. Works judged not canonical were those that were considered not to "fit" within Scripture. "Canonical" is sometimes used to refer to the *order* of the books within the canon.

chiasm (chiastic): A literary device that follows an AB BA pattern (e.g., "food for the stomach; the stomach for food") of any length (e.g., ABCDCBA), which served the purposes of memory in an oral culture (where most people could not read but had sharp memories for what they heard read to them). This may happen in sentences, paragraphs, or large sections of books. We sometimes use the language of "framing device" or "bookending" or "concentric pattern" to refer to this phenomenon when we are dealing with larger sections of text.

concentric: See chiastic

conflict stories: Stories in the Gospels in which someone presents a challenge to or a criticism of Jesus, and he uses the occasion to provide a moment of instruction.

covenant: A formal legal-contractual arrangement in which both parties have obligations and responsibilities to one another. In the great biblical covenants, God's obligation is blessing and mercy to those who keep covenant with him; the obligation of his people is obedience, especially the obedience as expressed in loving God and neighbor.

cycle: A story pattern or theme that is repeated for emphasis or effect.

Deuteronomic: Notably consistent with and/or actually based on the theology or vocabulary contained in the book of Deuteronomy.

Diaspora: A NT Greek term used to describe believing Jews living outside Palestine in ancient times—especially NT times, although its beginnings go back to the Babylonian exile (when the majority of exiles did not return to Judah) and the self-imposed exile in Egypt recorded in Jeremiah 41:16–45:5. Also called *the dispersion*. In Acts 15:21, James refers to the importance of the Diaspora for the spread of the gospel when he says, "For the law of Moses has been preached in every city from the earliest times...."

discourse: A relatively lengthy and formal speech or written communication on a subject or a group of related subjects.

disfellowship: To remove someone from membership, attendance, and social contact with other believers in a church in order to correct a serious sin and restore the sinner. Such a severe action was undertaken because the sin endangered the church's own life and witness in the community.

Divine Warrior: A description of God in his role as the leader of the holy war (see below), a great fighter on behalf of his people (see, e.g., Exod 15:3; Isa 42:13; Jer 20:11).

doxology: A statement of praise to or about God, usually near or at the end of a biblical book or major portion thereof.

eschatological: Of or about the end times or last days, derived from the Greek word *eschaton,* which means "end."

exilic: Referring to the time during the Babylonian exile, which began in 586 B.C. and was officially over with the decree of Cyrus in 539 B.C.

fertility god: Any of the many Canaanite gods and goddesses, all of whom were seen as having the power to help people's crops and cattle be more fertile in exchange for being given food offerings. (Ancient pagan belief held that the one thing the gods couldn't do was to feed themselves!) See also *Baal* and *Asherah/Ashtoreth.*

Greeks: At a few points in the NT this term is used to refer to non-Hebrew (or Aramaic)-speaking Jews. Sometimes in Paul it also becomes a "stand-in" word for Gentiles.

Hellenists (Hellenistic): People who spoke Greek or followed Greek ways to some degree, even though they might otherwise be Jewish.

hermeneutics: Principles of interpretation, often used with reference to how biblical passages function for a later time and in new circumstances.

holy war: God's special battle against evil and those who manifest evil (very often in the form of idolatry)—a battle God fights on behalf of the righteous but allows his people to participate in. Because of God's omnipotence, there is no question who will ultimately win the war, but because of his great patience in waiting for evil people to turn to him, the war is not yet concluded.

horizontal: In OT law, describing the relationships and obligations of humans to each other; see *vertical.*

idolatry (idolatrous): A system that was inherently polytheistic, syncretistic, and (usually) pantheistic and that was present in virtually all ancient nonbiblical religions. Idolatrous practice relied on the belief that the gods could be influenced by offerings made in the presence of their idols, since the idols "manifested" the gods, including their nature and power; the idol was sometimes understood in both OT and NT to be the locus of demons or demonic power.

Incarnation (incarnate): God's becoming human in the person of Jesus of Nazareth.

messiahship: The position and/or action of fulfilling the OT expectations for God's special anointed servant-leader of Israel.

metanarrative: The great overall, overarching story of the Bible as a whole; the grand narrative of God's redemption of a people for himself, told progressively throughout the Bible.

monarchy: The period of time when Israel and/or Judah had a king, i.e., ca. 1050 B.C. – 586 B.C.

motif: An important idea or theme that constitutes one of the concerns of a book or passage.

oracle: A particular revelation from God; often used synonymously with "prophecy" or "revelation," when these refer to a *specific* message from God to a prophet.

panel: A distinct subsection of a narrative, containing a group of stories sharing a theme or topic.

passion: When used about Jesus, this refers specifically to his suffering and death.

Pharisaism (Pharisaic): The attitude that righteousness before God was related to obeying every OT law to the letter, including the Pharisees' own (often legalistic) extensions and extrapolations of those laws; and the attitude that only people who did so could be accepted as good Jews.

Pentateuch: The first five books of the Old Testament; also known as the "(Five) Books of Moses."

polytheism (polytheistic): The belief that there are many gods and goddesses, each with his or her own specialties and each potentially worthy of worship for what he or she could do better than any of the others. The whole ancient world was polytheistic except for those who kept covenant with Israel's God.

postexilic: The time after 539 B.C., i.e., after the Babylonian exile, which began in 586 B.C. and was officially over with the decree of Cyrus in 539.

preexilic: Before the Babylonian exile began, i.e., before 586 B.C.

Presence: God's special empowering manifestation of himself among humans whereby he gives a discernible sense of his greatness, holiness, support, approachability, etc. In OT times first the tabernacle and then the Jerusalem temple was especially often the locus of his Presence; in NT times it is primarily the Spirit in the church, but also in the individual.

proselyte: A Gentile who converted to Judaism and therefore practiced Jewish law, including especially circumcision, and was accepted into the Jewish community.

protagonist: The main character, main mover, or hero in a story or event.

restoration: The reestablishment of Israel as a people under God after the Babylonian exile.

refrain: A wording, topic, or idea that an author uses repeatedly for clarity or effect.

revelation: God's "unveiling" of himself so as to be "seen"/understood by people; sometimes used to refer to his imparting his truth to people.

sanctions: The part of the covenant that provided incentives to keep it, in the form of blessings (benefits from God) and curses (miseries of various sorts as punishments for disobedience).

sanctuary: A place where God specially manifests his Presence and where God is appropriately worshiped by his people.

Septuagint (septuagintal): The ancient Greek translation of the Old Testament, produced in the third and second centuries B.C. in Alexandria, Egypt. It was the Bible of most New Testament Christians, and it has had enormous influence, including on the order of the books in our English Bibles and in the NT sometimes on the wording itself.

Speculative Wisdom: The process of trying to think through what life and its choices really are all about. Asking and answering questions and responding to assertions—whether in dialogue or monologue format—are common in Speculative Wisdom literature.

syncretism (syncretistic): The sharing and blending of religious beliefs. When the Israelites continued to worship Yahweh as their national god but also worshiped Baal as a fertility God, or when they worshiped Yahweh via golden calf-idols, they were practicing syncretism.

theological (theology): Describing God, his truth, and his relationship to his world; also describing the particular way a given Bible writer conveys his part of the whole of God's truth.

theophany (theophanic): An appearance of God in some form. Although "no one has ever seen God" (1 John 4:12), God has "appeared" in the sense of specially manifesting his presence through angels (Judg 13:22), the incarnate Christ (John 1:18), storms (Ezek 1), etc.

tradition: Shared beliefs and/or practices passed on from one generation to another.

vertical: In OT law, describing the relationships and obligations of people to God; see *horizontal*.

vision: In prophetic literature, a special type of revelation in which what is seen helps orient the prophet to what will be said. What is described as "seen" in a vision is almost always simple, and normally it does not convey a message in itself, apart from the words of explanation that follow.

Appendix:
A Chronological Listing
of the Biblical Books

This appendix is for those who might wish to read the biblical books in a chronological order. Some of this is guesswork, of course, especially in the case of the Old Testament works, since some books (e.g., Joel) are not easily dated. Our list is related primarily to their *content*, not to *date of composition*—although even in this case some exceptions are made: We have put 1–2 Chronicles before Malachi and Ezra-Nehemiah, and the Gospel of John with 1–3 John and the Revelation. Moreover, bear in mind that some books overlap each other in ways that a simple chronological listing cannot fully represent (e.g., Daniel and Ezekiel). The OT books that cover various times or contain few specific chronological clues have been grouped separately at the end of the OT list.

- ☐ Genesis
- ☐ Exodus
- ☐ Leviticus
- ☐ Numbers
- ☐ Deuteronomy
- ☐ Joshua
- ☐ Judges
- ☐ Ruth
- ☐ 1–2 Samuel
- ☐ 1–2 Kings
- ☐ Jonah
- ☐ Amos
- ☐ Hosea
- ☐ Isaiah
- ☐ Micah
- ☐ Zephaniah
- ☐ Nahum

- ☐ Habakkuk
- ☐ Joel
- ☐ Jeremiah
- ☐ Ezekiel
- ☐ Obadiah
- ☐ Lamentations
- ☐ Daniel
- ☐ Haggai
- ☐ Zechariah
- ☐ Esther
- ☐ 1–2 Chronicles
- ☐ Malachi
- ☐ Ezra- Nehemiah

- ☐ Job
- ☐ Proverbs
- ☐ Ecclesiastes

☐ Song of Songs
☐ Psalms

☐ Mark
☐ Matthew
☐ Luke
☐ Acts
☐ 1 Thessalonians
☐ 2 Thessalonians
☐ James
☐ 1 Corinthians
☐ 2 Corinthians
☐ Galatians
☐ Romans
☐ Colossians

☐ Philemon
☐ Ephesians
☐ Philippians
☐ 1 Timothy
☐ Titus
☐ 2 Timothy
☐ 1 Peter
☐ 2 Peter
☐ Jude
☐ Hebrews
☐ 1 John
☐ 2 John
☐ Gospel of John
☐ 3 John
☐ The Revelation